D1490675

Charles Hodge

THE WAY OF LIFE

Edited by Mark A. Noll

PAULIST PRESS
New York ♦ Mahwah

Copyright ©1987
by Mark Noll

Library of Congress Cataloging-in-Publication Data

Hodge, Charles, 1797-1878
    Charles Hodge : selected writings

    (Sources of American spirituality)
    Bibliography: p.
    Includes index.
    Contents: The way of life (1841) — From Commentary on the book of Romans (1836) — From Conference papers (1850-1878) — [etc.]
        1. Reformed Church—Doctrines.   2. Presbyterian Church—Doctrines.   3. Princeton Theology.
4. Spirituality—Reformed Church.   5. Spirituality—Presbyterian Church.   I. Noll, Mark A., 1946-
II. Title.   III. Series.
BS9422.H58   1987   230'.51   87-7029
ISBN 0-8091-0392-3

Published by Paulist Press
997 Macarthur Boulevard
Mahwah, N.J. 07430

Printed and bound in the United States of America

CONTENTS

to
Ruth J. Packer
and the Memory of Robert E. Packer

PREFACE

The works of Charles Hodge in this book are presented, without alteration or deletion, as they appeared in their nineteenth-century editions. Specific bibliographical detail is provided for each selection below, but in every case the readings are unabridged. *The Way of Life* is present in its entirety. The pages from Hodge's commentary on the Book of Romans, his *Conference Papers,* and his *Systematic Theology* represent complete sections from these books.

I would like to thank John Farina of the Paulist Press for the invitation to prepare this volume. In addition I am grateful to David Wells, Darryl Hart, George Marsden, Bruce Kuklick, Nathan Hatch, Andrew Hoffecker, and John Woodbridge for stimulating conversations over the years on the theologians from Princeton Seminary, including Charles Hodge. Although the introduction to this book was written from scratch, as it were, its section on the Princeton Theology does bear some resemblance to things I have written before, and so I am glad to acknowledge Baker Book House and the William B. Eerdmans Company as the publishers of that other material: *The Princeton Theology 1812–1921: Scripture, Science and Theological Method from Archibald Alexander to Benjamin Warfield* (Grand Rapids: Baker, 1983); and "The Princeton Theology," in *Reformed Theology in America: A History of Its Modern Development,* ed. David F. Wells (Grand Rapids: Eerdmans, 1985). Finally, the introduction has benefitted from the kindness of individuals who shared with me their unpublished theses or dissertations on matters relating to Charles Hodge. These include John Auxier, Randall Balmer, Steven Martin, Stephen Spencer, and Timothy Phillips.

Abbreviations in the Notes

Life = A. A. Hodge, *The Life of Charles Hodge, D.D., LL.D., Professor in the Theological Seminary, Princeton* (New York: Scribner's, 1880)
BRPR = *Biblical Repertory and Princeton Review*

GENERAL INTRODUCTION

The first time I heard of Charles Hodge he was the brunt of the wry humor of one of the great historians of our time, Sydney Ahlstrom. Leaning over the podium, his outlandish tie dangling down below his waist, he recounted with an impish grin on his face the boast of Charles Hodge that "a new idea never originated in the (Princeton) Seminary." In that Yale lecture hall that was all that had to be said to stir up great waves of laughter.

But as funny as that statement sounds to our ears and as playful as Ahlstrom was in opening his lecture on the Princeton Theology with it, it should not blind us to the importance of its author Charles Hodge.

In every age religion responds to the cultural environment in which it exists. As Michael de Certeau has reminded us, the language of a spirituality is, by necessity, the language of culture, since the experience of God can only be expressed using the tools of language, myth, and symbol that are products of human social life. The nineteenth century in America was a time when the ways in which people earned a living, obtained their food, sheltered themselves and grouped themselves in corporate states were changing rapidly and significantly. What is more, those changes were of such a magnitude as to be very much a part of the consciousness of the times. Movement away from the ways of the past toward a better future was not only a reality of American life but a pervasive myth that motivated poor and rich alike and gave them a way of understanding the chaotic activity with which the continent teemed.

Although the myth of progress had its eloquent voices like

Emerson and Walt Whitman, it carried with it a more somber side, a half-hidden, more timid misgiving that embodied the obvious caveat to the argument of the providential men of the age. Was continuous progress really possible, or was the age confusing technological advance with moral improvement and facilely assuming that the latter would follow the former? This contrarian voice could be heard in the masterful fiction of a Melville or detected in the blast of a social reformer like William Lloyd Garrison, but in the world of American religion it had no more eloquent and vigorous proponent than Charles Hodge. He gave theological structure to the claims of reality that reminded their hearers of the limitations of human achievement and the fragility of true virtue.

He did this by appealing to classical Calvinism. Yet it would be a mistake to view his traditionalism as an attempt to pretend that the contemporary culture did not exist. Hodge rejected the sectarian response; Princeton was not merely an embattled remnant of true believers. Rather he held that the tradition itself had in it a vitality, an essential truthfulness that made it relevant for the present and made it an accurate interpreter of God's work in history. Hence Hodge in the pages of his *Princeton Review* looked out on the culture and engaged it thoughtfully, energetically, *and* critically.

It is that connection of the past to the present, the tradition to the contemporary culture, that gives a clue to the dynamic relationship between the theoretical and experiential, the notional and the vital aspects of Hodge's religious life. Behind his scathing critiques of the New England Theology of Nathaniel William Taylor, or the New Measures of Charles Finney, or the romantic theology of Horace Bushnell or Friedrich Schleiermacher was an equally persistent attempt to live out his Christian convictions, to make the real the ideal, to put into practice the theoretical. It is that effort that is so well captured by Mark Noll in an extensive and finely textured introduction and in the choice of highlighting Hodge's most popular work, *The Way of Life*. This book, then, represents a challenge both to those who would limit "spirituality" to warm-hearted affective piety and to those that would fail to see in Hodge or in the classical Reformed tradition that he represented the basic dynamics of intense religious experience that engages the full range of human capacities.

John Farina

INTRODUCTION

Charles Hodge (1797–1878) was the first American to serve a full half century as a professor of theology. By the time of his jubilee at Princeton Theological Seminary in 1872, Hodge had personally instructed more theological students than had attended any other seminary in the country. The journal which he edited, and which was a redoubtable engine of his convictions, had become the second oldest quarterly review of any kind in the United States and had outlived all of the religious journals in existence when the *Biblical Repertory and Princeton Review* was first published in 1825.[1] For length of days and long life, if for nothing else, Charles Hodge was a religious force to be reckoned with in nineteenth-century America.[2]

There was, however, a great deal else, for Hodge was also a man whose convictions carried weight, whose point of view was noticed, respected, and sometimes followed in America and selected locations overseas. Blessed with a quick but thorough mind, persevering intellectual energy, congenial colleagues and a loyal family, manifold connections with the elite society of the Atlantic seaboard, and a tirelessly facile pen, Hodge possessed the gifts and the circum-

---

1. *BRPR. Index Volume from 1825 to 1868* (Philadelphia: Peter Walker, 1870–1871), vol. I, inside back cover.

2. The principal source for Hodge's life remains the biography by his son published in 1880. The "Select Bibliography" lists other, more recent accounts of his life and thought. Material about Hodge's life in this introduction comes from A. A. Hodge's *Life*, unless otherwise indicated.

1

stances necessary for an influential career with words. Add to this
his determined theological convictions and his cultivated religious
sensibility, and it becomes clear why a large circle of friends, a
greater number of admirers, and a considerable group of theological
opponents carefully heeded what he wrote. And over the course of
his long career he wrote and wrote—more than 5,000 pages of
closely printed text in the *Princeton Review* as well as a comparable
amount elsewhere, including a systematic theology more than 2,000
pages long, several extensive commentaries on books of the New
Testament, and a small shelf of sermons, ecclesiastical treatises, his-
tories, and devotional works. The breadth of Hodge's concerns is
disconcerting for our age, accustomed as we are to specialists who
mark out carefully defined fields for ever more minute examination.
It was not so a century ago. Like several of his contemporaries
Hodge considered the world fair game for commentary. So while he
concentrated on questions of moment for his Presbyterian denomination, on issues of theological controversy at home and abroad, and
on trends in American religious life, he also wrote with authority on
the great events of American politics, on new proposals in philosophy, on a wide range of historical subjects, and on the religious implications of scientific questions.

In this book we are more narrowly concerned to display
Hodge's convictions about the religious life. That subject—whether
trucked out in formal learning for his academic peers or stripped to
its essentials for the consumption of a broader public—was always
near the heart of his concern. The pages which follow contain four
examples of Hodge's writing on Christian spirituality—the entire
text of a work, *The Way of Life,* published in 1841 "for the use of
educated youth" by the American Sunday School Union;[3] an extract
from an 1836 commentary on the Book of Romans; a selection from
the sermon outlines that Hodge prepared for Sunday afternoon "conferences" with students at Princeton Seminary; and a brief extract
from his *Systematic Theology* (1872) on the relation between the
Scriptures and the work of the Holy Spirit.

To introduce these works we look first at Hodge's life, then con-

---

3. Hodge, *The Way of Life* (Philadelphia: American Sunday School Union,
1841), p. 341.

sider the "Princeton Theology" which he helped to forge, and finally discuss the relation between mind and heart in Hodge's picture of the holy life.

Charles Hodge was born in Philadelphia on December 27, 1797. His paternal grandfather, Andrew, was a transplanted Scotsman who emigrated from Northern Ireland early in the eighteenth century to Philadelphia where he established a prosperous business on Water Street. Hodge's father, Hugh (1755–1798), graduated from Princeton College in 1773, at a time when patriotic sentiments were rising steadily at that institution.[4] With most of his family Hugh Hodge eagerly joined the struggle for American independence. After pursuing medical studies, he served as a military surgeon with Pennsylvania units during the Revolutionary War until he was captured in November 1776 at Fort Washington, New York, with a large body of American troops. He was held prisoner of war under difficult conditions for several months and released only upon giving his oath not to re-enter the struggle. When Charles Hodge came to write his memoirs, he wanted his own children to know that "their ancestors and kindred were Presbyterian and patriots."[5]

After his release by the British, Hugh Hodge practiced medicine in Philadelphia and also joined his brothers in the family business. In 1790 he married Mary Blanchard (1765–1832), an orphaned Bostonian who had came to Philadelphia to live with her brother five years before. She was from a well-born family which included as collateral relatives Major-General Joseph Warren, who fell at Bunker Hill, and Timothy Pickering, a member of the cabinet under Presidents Washington and Adams. Hugh Hodge and Mary Blanchard were married in Philadelphia's Second Presbyterian Church by the family pastor, the Reverend Ashbel Green, whose career would

---

4. Richard A. Harrison, "Hugh Hodge," in *Princetonians 1769–1776: A Biographical Dictionary* (Princeton: Princeton University Press, 1980), pp. 295–97.

5. *Life*, p. 5.

be interwoven with the fortunes of the Hodges for several decades to come.

The first three children of Hugh and Mary Hodge died during Philadelphia's great Yellow Fever epidemics of 1793 and 1795. Charles Hodge was the second of two surviving sons born in 1796 and 1797. His older brother, Hugh Lenox Hodge, became a physician in Philadelphia, a noted authority on obstetrics, and an elder in the Second Presbyterian Church. The Hodge brothers were exceptionally close throughout their lives, Charles writing almost weekly to his brother for over fifty years and Hugh Lenox regularly supplying his brother's financial necessities when his salary from the seminary was delayed or failed to meet the needs of a growing family.

Less than seven months after Charles Hodge's birth his father died from complications of a chronic infection contracted during the 1795 outbreak of Yellow Fever. The father's death left the small family of mother and two infant sons in straitened circumstances. Relatives, including several surviving siblings of Hugh Hodge, provided some material assistance as well as standards to be upheld. This extended family became Charles Hodge's entree into a world of well-connected merchants, lawyers, politicians, and ministers. Two of Hodge's aunts married twins, John Rubenheim and James Asheton Bayard, who became prominent in Pennsylvania and New Jersey politics. Through such connections Hodge enjoyed the company of considerable wealth and influence. Among his Bayard cousins, for example, were the wife of New Jersey's chief justice, the president of Philadelphia's Commercial Bank, miscellaneous physicians and merchants, a clerk of the United States Supreme Court, and a United States Senator.

Primarily, however, it was Mary Blanchard Hodge who kept the little family going. She had a small income from commercial interests left by her husband. But this resource eventually withered away about the time her sons set off for college because of the Non-Intercourse Act and the Embargo which preceded the War of 1812. To augment her income Mary Hodge also took in boarders at her Philadelphia home. She made sacrifices in sending her boys to the primary schools where they studied reading and writing, arithmetic, geography, and drawing. Their religious training she carried on herself with the assistance of Ashbel Green, to whom the boys recited the Westminster Catechism. In 1810 Mrs. Hodge arranged for

Charles and Hugh Lenox to attend a classical academy in Somerville, New Jersey, close to the home of a Bayard cousin. There study began in Latin, and Charles cemented friendships with several wealthy Dutch families whose members once again included merchants, physicians, lawyers, and members of Congress.

In further pursuit of her sons' education, Mary Hodge moved the entire family to Princeton in the summer of 1812 at a crucial juncture in the intellectual history of that village.[6] As the Hodges took possession of a house on Witherspoon Street, directly north of the college which the boys proposed to enter, Princeton College itself was undergoing a change of direction. Since 1795 the college had been led by Samuel Stanhope Smith, the son-in-law of John Witherspoon, Princeton president from 1768 to 1794 and one of the great men of the age. Witherspoon had been a leader among the Presbyterians (primary organizer of the General Assembly), in the nation (the only clergyman to sign the Declaration of Independence), and in education (tireless in promoting "The College of New Jersey at Princeton"). Stanhope Smith, though delicate in health, was a worthy successor who established his reputation by defending the harmony between modern science and the inherited truths of Scripture. Yet Smith increasingly had become estranged from the influential Presbyterians who constituted his board of trustees. The proportion of Princeton students entering the ministry had declined dramatically since the end of the War. Student unrest, climaxing in major riots in 1800 and 1807, called into question Smith's ability to discipline his charges. And his fondness for abstract reasoning on moral questions seemed to some trustees, especially Ashbel Green, to border on the heretical. The result was an alienated board which at specially called meetings in June and August, 1812, maneuvered Smith into retirement and called as his replacement the pastor of Charles Hodge's Philadelphia church, Ashbel Green.

A change at Princeton College was, however, only part of the excitement at Princeton that summer. For over a decade a feeling had been growing among leading Presbyterian ministers, including Ashbel Green, that a special school was needed to train ministers for the

---

6. The following paragraphs draw upon Mark A. Noll, "The Founding of Princeton Seminary," *Westminster Theological Journal* 42 (Fall 1979): 72–110.

church. Not only were the colleges failing to produce the ever larger
number of ministers necessary for the pulpits of a rapidly expanding
country, but training at colleges like Princeton seemed suspiciously
influenced by modern speculation, unnecessarily reserved in the pro-
motion of traditional biblical faith. Ashbel Green and a rising young
minister in New York City, the Reverend Samuel Miller, had been
campaigning for several years to see the Presbyterians establish a
centrally located theological seminary for the training of the denomination's ministers. To this partnership Green contributed a dogged
concern for orthodoxy and a talent for organization while Miller contributed an intellectual flare, for which he was already distinguished,
and a concern for preserving the respectability of the ministerial
profession.[7] Their efforts finally succeeded in 1811 when the Presbyterian General Assembly agreed to open such a school. The next
year's Assembly, taking advantage of assistance offered by the trustees of the College of New Jersey, resolved to locate the school in
Princeton. The new seminary would be run by the General Assembly
with no formal ties to the college, but the central locale of Princeton,
as well as Princeton College's staunchly Presbyterian history and its
overwhelmingly Presbyterian board, made the selection of that village a logical one for the seminary. Even as the Hodge family took
up its residence in Princeton and the college board replaced Stanhope
Smith with Ashbel Green, the seminary directors, whose chairman
was also Ashbel Green, were making final preparations for opening
the new school. One teacher had been named, Archibald Alexander
of Virginia. Instruction was due to commence in the fall.

Alexander, who came to play a large part in the intellectual and
spiritual development of Charles Hodge, had enjoyed a full career
before arriving at the seminary in 1812.[8] He was born in 1772 to

---

7. See Ashbel Green, *The Life of Ashbel Green, V.D.M.,* ed. Joseph H.
Jones (New York: Robert Carter, 1849). Miller was known as author of a long book
of nearly universal scope, *A Brief Retrospect of the Eighteenth Century . . . con-
taining a sketch of the Revolution and Improvements in Science, Arts, and Literature, during that period* (New York: T. & J. Swords, 1803). A good overview of
Miller's career is found in Belden C. Lane, "Democracy and the Ruling Eldership:
Samuel Miller's Response to Tension Between Clerical and Lay Authority in Early
Nineteenth-Century America" (Th.D. dissertation, Princeton Theological Seminary, 1976).

8. See James W. Alexander, *The Life of Archibald Alexander* (Philadelphia:

Scotch-Irish parents in Virginia, educated privately by the Rev. William Graham (a student of John Witherspoon), and ordained as a minister in 1790. After four years of private study and evangelistic itineration, he became the pastor of two Presbyterian churches in Charlotte County, Virginia. In 1797 he added responsibilities as president of Hampden-Sydney College before moving a decade later to the Third Presbyterian Church of Philadelphia, whence he was called to Princeton. Alexander was a winsome person. Testimonies concerning the moving power of his preaching, the effectiveness of his spiritual counsel, the relaxed atmosphere of his family circle, and the relative latitude of his ecclesiastical views mark him as a forceful and engaging presence of larger-than-life proportions.

Charles Hodge, therefore, arrived in Princeton at a crucial turning point in Presbyterian history. For over 60 years the village remained the center of his world, his life dominated by the affairs of the seminary, the denomination, and the college.

It did not take Hodge long to be caught up in the larger events occurring in his new village. While his brother entered the college itself, Charles began to remedy deficiencies in Greek at the school's classical academy. On August 12, he attended Alexander's inauguration. Writing over sixty years later, Hodge reported that he could "well remember, then a boy of fourteen, lying at length on the rail of the gallery listening to the doctor's inaugural address and watching the ceremony of investiture."[9]

The activities of the day in Princeton's Presbyterian church were indeed impressive. Samuel Miller delivered the principal address, on II Timothy 2:2. In it he described "a faithful ministry" as one characterized by "Piety, Talents, Learning, and Diligence," and he expounded at length on how the church should provide for such a ministry. Alexander took John 5:39 ("Search the Scriptures") as the text for his inaugural address and spoke learnedly on what he perceived to be the two main tasks in studying the Bible: "to ascertain that the scriptures contain the truths of God: and to . . . ascertain

---

Presbyterian Board of Publication, 1855); and Lefferts A. Loetscher, *Facing the Enlightenment and Pietism: Archibald Alexander and the Founding of Princeton Theological Seminary* (Westport, CT: Greenwood, 1983).

9. *Life,* p. 18.

what these truths are.'' The ceremonies concluded with a charge to professor and students by the Rev. Phillip Millerdoler of New York City who reiterated the General Assembly's desire for ''a learned, orthodox, pious, and evangelical Ministry.''[10]

Even more impressive, however, was the personal interest which the new seminary's professor took in the young Philadelphian. During that same summer Alexander strolled into the academy where he found Hodge ''stammering over a verse in the Greek Testament.'' Alexander stayed to help with instruction, and this, as Hodge reported, ''was the first thread of the cord which bound me to Dr. Alexander—a cord never broken.''[11] Soon Alexander was taking young Hodge along on preaching excursions, and a relationship with great importance for Hodge, and significant implications for the history of theology in America, was firmly established. Not too many years later Hodge was writing to Alexander as ''my dear father'' and affirming that ''there is no person beyond my own family of whom I think as frequently, or with as much affection . . . as yourself; and there is no person excepting my mother to whom I feel more obligated.''[12] Hodge would name his own first son Archibald Alexander.

In the fall of 1812 Charles Hodge entered Princeton College as a sophomore and graduated three years later. His college experiences left indelible impressions. They provided habits of careful study and warm personal friendships that lasted a lifetime. Princeton's fortunes had declined somewhat since Witherspoon's days, but still it remained a trusted place for elite families in the Atlantic states and the Upper South to send their sons. As an undergraduate Hodge rubbed shoulders with men who later became judges, congressmen and senators, governors, influential ministers, pioneering missionaries, and more.[13] He grew especially close to John Johns and Charles P. M'Ilvaine, who became Episcopalian bishops, and to John Maclean,

---

10. *The Sermon, Delivered at the Inauguration of the Rev. Archibald Alexander . . . To Which are Added, The Professor's Inaugural Address and the Charge to the Professor and Students* (New York: J. Seymour, 1812), pp. 12, 62, 108.

11. *Life,* p. 18.

12. Hodge to Alexander, Nov. 2, 1826, in *Life,* pp. 105–09. For similar remarks even later, see *Life,* pp. 275, 276.

13. A list of Hodge's college classmates is provided in *Life,* pp. 34–36.

later the president of Princeton College and a contributor to Hodge's *Princeton Review.*

Important as these friendships were, Hodge considered his religious growth in these years even more significant. Ashbel Green had ushered in his new regime at the college with a steely determination to return piety to its hereditary supremacy on the campus. While Green did not repudiate Witherspoon's emphasis on public affairs or Stanhope Smith's devotion to science, he turned his energies first to promoting revival. Princeton's early days under Samuel Davies, the awakener of Virginia, and Jonathan Edwards, the leading theologian of colonial New England, once again loomed large at the college. On coming to Princeton, Green determined, "I would either work a reformation or sink under the attempt."[14] To that end he set aside Sunday afternoons for the formal study of the Scriptures and required students to recite a catechism. And he took all possible steps to promote revival.

The turn to piety for which Green longed finally occurred in the winter of 1814–1815. One of its earliest manifestations was the decision by Hodge and a young friend publicly to profess their Christian faith and to join the Presbyterian Church in Princeton, an event that occurred on January 13, 1815. This action ushered in a period of unusual spiritual concentration among the undergraduates. More than a third of Princeton's 105 students were converted, or as Green put it with the reserve that would also come to characterize Hodge, "in regard to whom, so far as the time will permit us to judge, favorable hopes may be entertained that they are the subjects of renewing grace."[15] During the revival Green often called upon Alexander to address the students, for Alexander had a rare ability to encourage the piety which Green prized without the loss of control

---

14. Green to William Sprague, Apr. 10, 1832, Letter XVIII in Appendix to Sprague's *Lectures on Revivals of Religion* (London: Banner of Truth, 1959 [orig. 1832]), p. 132. See also Thomas Jefferson Wertenbaker, *Princeton 1746–1896* (Princeton: Princeton University Press, 1946), p. 154.

15. Sprague, *Lectures on Revivals,* p. 134. On this revival, see also *Life,* pp. 34–36; and Ashbel Green, *Report to the Trustees of the College of New Jersey, relative to a revival of religion among the students of said college, in the winter and spring of the year 1815* (Philadelphia: W. Fry, 1815).

he feared. The 1815 Princeton revival turned the thoughts of many young men, including Charles Hodge, to lives of religious service. Under the strong influence of Alexander and Green, as well as his own mother, Hodge determined to study for the ministry.

After a year of rest to alleviate mysterious and troubling pains in his chest, Hodge entered Princeton Seminary in November 1816. In October of the same year he had accompanied Alexander on a preaching tour of Virginia, an experience which allowed him to observe Alexander's piety firsthand while strengthening bonds of affection to the seminary's senior professor. By that time, the institution had added a second teacher, Samuel Miller, who in his turn made a significant contribution to Hodge's spiritual formation. Miller had nearly completed a personal metamorphosis from cosmopolitan intellectual to Presbyterian polemicist by the time he came to Princeton. To Hodge he offered a picture of dignity and self-composure combined with unfeigned devotion and academic precision.

Under Miller and Alexander, Hodge throve as a student and an aspiring Christian. Seminary instruction was rigorous, with frequent recitations based on the Scriptures in their original languages and on sturdy Reformed theologies like that of Geneva's Francis Turretin. Even more influential were the lessons in piety offered by daily contact with the professors, by Alexander at the mid-weekly prayer meeting, and by both professors at the Sunday afternoon "conferences" where the faculty led the seminarians in a consideration of practical religion. Hodge's own son has left this picture of Alexander at a prayer meeting in the mid-1840s:

> The instant the students were in their seats he came in rapidly, his cloak hanging often diagonally from his bent shoulders, his head inclined as in revery, yet flashing sudden glances on either side with piercing eyes, which seemed to penetrate all the secrets of those upon whom they fell. He sat down with his back to the windows, and his right side to the students, sitting low—almost hidden by the desk. Drawing the large Bible down before him, he seemed to lose at once all sense of human audience, and to pass alone into the presence of God. As he read, and mused and ejaculated the utterances of all the holy exercises of his soul upon the Divine Word, a solemn hush fell

upon us, and we felt not as those who listened to a teacher, but as those who are admitted to approach, with the shoes from off their feet, to gaze in and listen through an opened window to the mysterious workings of a sanctified soul under the immediate revelations of the Holy Ghost.[16]

The hagiographical tone of such an account should not obscure the profound lessons in piety which students at Princeton learned by pretext and example from their mentors.

By the time Hodge finished his seminary course in 1819, the seminary had grown too large for its two professors. Hodge's own class numbered 26 members, while an additional 58 were also attending in 1819.[17] The need for another instructor, especially someone to teach the biblical languages and the literature of the Bible, was acute. Yet the General Assembly's purse was nearly bare; it was doubtful if even enough money could be found to hire a junior instructor for such tasks. Nonetheless, Alexander took the initiative to secure the needed assistance. He first approached Hodge's closest friend, John Johns, who was also finishing his seminary course in 1819, but Johns had determined to seek Episcopal ordination. And so on the morning of May 6, 1819, when Hodge payed a visit to Alexander on some minor matter, the professor surprised Hodge by asking, "How would you like to be a professor in the Seminary?" Hodge was flabbergasted, but also deeply touched by this show of confidence.[18]

Three eventful, yet uncertain, years followed that conversation in Alexander's study. Hodge finished his seminary program in September 1819. He then repaired to his native city for private instruction in Hebrew from the Rev. Joseph Banks, a minister of the Scottish Associated Presbyterian Church and one of the few Protestants of the day versed in the writing of Hebrew with vowel points. In October he was licensed to preach by the Presbytery of Philadelphia. From that time through May 1820 Hodge kept a week-by-week

---

16. *Life*, pp. 456–57.

17. Edward Howell Roberts, *Biographical Catalogue of the Princeton Theological Seminary 1815–1932* (Princeton: Princeton Theological Seminary, 1933), pp. 7–15.

18. *Life*, p. 65.

journal reporting on his preaching assignments, his pursuit of piety, and the turmoils of his soul. Hodge experienced a normal degree of uneasiness at finding himself an appropriate vocation. And he was laboring to internalize the standards of godliness which Alexander had exhibited. A typical entry (November 21, 1819) begins, "This day I entered on my duties as Missionary [for the Philadelphia Presbytery to supply vacant pulpits in the surrounding vicinity]. Oh thou source of all good grant me the continued aid of thy grace that with purity of motive & singleness of object I may zealous & faithfully discharge my responsible duties. Do, Bless me o my God."[19] He then wrote of preaching in the morning at East Falls and in the afternoon at the United States Arsenal in Frankfort and about religious conversations and prayer in the evening with a younger seminarian.

The journal ended the same week in May 1820 that the General Assembly offered Hodge a one-year appointment as assistant teacher of the biblical languages at Princeton for a salary of $400. Hodge immediately moved into quarters at Princeton and almost as soon began to suffer pain and weakness in his right thigh (he called it rheumatism) which would trouble him intermittently for the next twenty years. In October of the same year Hodge traveled to New England to consult with ministers and theological professors on the teaching of Hebrew, Greek, biblical interpretation, and theology. In the course of the journey he reported stimulating conversations with many of the rising figures of New England religion, including Moses Stuart of Andover Seminary (a later opponent on the interpretation of the book of Romans) and Nathaniel W. Taylor of the Yale Divinity School (whom Hodge would one day attack in the *Princeton Review* as the source of most of what was wrong with religion in New England).

In his early teaching, Hodge, as so many before and since, strained every nerve to remain a few steps ahead of his classes. On more than one occasion Hodge's mother had written to his brother about Charles's dilatory habits which would prevent him from doing "himself justice."[20] But knowledge of the boy was not the best prep-

---

19. From Charles D. Cashdollar, "The Pursuit of Piety: Charles Hodge's Diary, 1819–1820," *Journal of Presbyterian History* 55 (Fall 1977): 271–72. Cashdollar provides a good introduction to this diary.

20. *Life*, p. 33n.

aration for measuring the man. Diligence was now his trademark, and soon he was reveling in the teaching, more because of the difficulties than in spite of them.

At the same time other dimensions of his life were also coming into focus. He was ordained as a full minister by the Presbytery of New Brunswick in November 1821. Early the next year at the urging of Alexander, who wanted him to display his skills as an advertisement to the denomination at large, Hodge published his first work, a pamphlet *On the Importance of Biblical Literature*. With this public notice and a record of successful teaching, Alexander convinced the General Assembly in May 1822 to name Hodge to a regular post as Professor of Oriental and Biblical Literature. With the salary of $1,000 per annum which his professorship entailed Hodge was then married the next month. His bride was Sarah Bache, a great-granddaughter of Benjamin Franklin, who as a fourteen-year-old had come to Princeton in 1813 from Philadelphia with her widowed mother and taken lodgings with Mary Hodge. The wedding itself was conducted by the Episcopal Bishop, William White, pastor of the Bache family for many years. In September 1822 Hodge delivered his inaugural address which began with a theme to which he would often return: "The moral qualifications of an Interpreter of Scripture may all be included in Piety: which embraces humility, candor, and those views and feelings which can only result from the inward operation of the Holy Spirit."[21]

With the exception of one future expedition away from Princeton, the course of Hodge's life was now set. He entered into his fuller duties with enthusiasm and applied himself to master the tools of learning and the habits of mind required of a professional student of the Scriptures. To further these aims he founded in 1825 the *Biblical Repertory*, a journal designed to reprint and translate the most recent literature from Europe on the Scriptures.

Hodge's concern for the best modern learning soon led him to question the adequacy of his own training. When Hodge read the fruits of European scholarship, he was struck by how limited his own intellectual attainments had been. As he expressed it in a letter to his brother in 1826, his education had been "by the force of circum-

21. Quoted in *Life*, p. 94.

stances, very defective. . . . I feel constantly the most painful sense of unfitness for my work, and the conviction that with nothing more than fragments of time at my command, I can make little progress.''[22] The solution was to go to Europe. Already the practice of rounding out a theological education on the Continent was well established among aspiring American theologians. The seminary overseers agreed to continue Hodge's salary for a two-year period of study. Hodge moved his family, which now included two small children, to live with his mother and brother in Philadelphia. From the rental of his Princeton house he supplied a substitute teacher for his own responsibilities. And then he embarked for the Continent. Hodge's substitute at Princeton was a highly regarded young graduate, John W. Nevin, who later moved to the German Reformed church and helped formulate the so-called Mercersburg Theology about which Hodge had many doubts.

Hodge was gone from Princeton from October 1826 through September 1828. The full letters which he wrote back to his wife, mother, brother, and colleagues provide an intriguing picture of the questing American scholar abroad. Hodge studied French, Arabic, and Syriac in Paris into early 1827. He then resettled at the University of Halle where he applied himself with customary energy to his tasks. He worked hard on his German with a tutor, George Müller, who would later be well-known for his orphanage in Bristol, England. Hodge soon made the acquaintance of distinguished scholars and struck up an especially warm friendship with the accomplished young theologian Augustus Tholuck. As he would later also in Berlin, Hodge seems to have moved easily in his new circles, eagerly learning all he could, but also retaining a sharp critical faculty. Hodge was immediately impressed with the depth of German scholarship. He also admired the sincere Christian faith of Tholuck and a few other ''pious'' leaders. And he could express an unparochial appreciation for the elaborate music and more formal liturgies of the European churches. At the same time, he found the ''speculative spirit'' of the German theologians most uncongenial. The philosophy of the post-Kantians (which exalted the creative power of the human spirit), the vogue for Hegel (who claimed to see the World Spirit

---

22. *Life*, p. 100.

coming to its fullest expression in nineteenth-century Prussia), and the theology of F. D. E. Schleiermacher (which based religion on a feeling of utter dependence) struck Hodge as a debasement of sound thinking no less than of sound theology.

From home Hodge received a steady stream of encouragement, affection, and admonition. Alexander, for instance, warned Hodge in a letter of March 1827: "Remember that you breathe a poisoned atmosphere. If you lose the lively and deep impressions of divine truth—if you fall into skepticism or even into coldness, you will lose more than you gain from all the German professors and libraries. May the Lord preserve you from error and from all evil."[23] Alexander need not have feared, for Hodge did not depart from the foundation which his mentors had laid.

Late in 1827 Hodge transferred his base of operations to the University of Berlin where he was much impressed with the results of a recent revival among the "evangelical" party and where he benefitted especially from instruction and friendship with Ernst Wilhelm Hengstenberg and Johann August Wilhelm Neander, leaders of the conservative wing of the German Protestants. The move to Berlin also brought Hodge into closer contact with the philosophy of Hegel and the theology of Schleiermacher, a circumstance which only confirmed judgments made at Halle: "The universal attention to philosophy required of the students in Germany" led to "acute and discriminating" learning, but a scholarship "amazingly deficient in plain, healthy good sense."[24] More than the technical training with which he busied himself faithfully, these more general impressions of the state of Christianity where a vague religious experience or a speculative philosophy prevailed were the most enduring legacies of his study in Europe.

Hodge returned to his duties at Princeton broadened culturally and enriched intellectually. In Germany he had rubbed shoulders with the Protestant world's best-known theologians. He had heard Schleiermacher preach and Neander lecture. On his way home he had attended a sermon in Cambridge by Charles Simeon, leader of the evangelical party in the Church of England. He had been awe-

---

23. *Life*, p. 160.
24. *Life*, p. 172.

struck by the glories of the Alps. He had heard a Roman Catholic speak on prayer and concluded that his remarks were "very excellent." In Berlin on a spring event he had joined friends in singing around a piano, an occasion which included "also one piece from an old German composer, Bach, whose works have long been neglected, but which they say are equal to almost any of the best German compositions."[25]

Unlike other American theologians who made the trek to the continent, however, this broadening of mind did not affect theological allegiance. Hodge returned to Princeton even more dedicated to the formal principles he had learned from Ashbel Green and Archibald Alexander, even more convinced of the necessity for time-tested, clearly stated theological propositions, even more convinced that piety rested on a foundation of truth. In Europe his critical faculties had been sharpened and he had come to appreciate several styles of European religious life, but these experiences did not alter the foundations of his faith and practice.

The external character of Hodge's life after his return to Princeton in 1828 was largely uneventful. During the 1830s the pain in his leg returned, and he was immobilized for several years. For four years (1833–1836) he met his classes in his studies, and he endured "heroic" treatment on his leg, including the application of galvanism from his friend Joseph Henry, who later established the Smithsonian Institution. Yet his pen did not flag. During the years he was confined to bed Hodge published twenty-eight articles in the *Princeton Review,* which he had reorganized upon his return from Europe, a major commentary on the book of Romans, and a lengthy history on the Presbyterian Church in America. He also lent his support to the Old School, or conservative, party in a dispute that split his Presbyterian denomination in 1837. While Hodge was not as rabidly opposed to the New England influence and the social activism of the New School party as Ashbel Green and some other Old Schoolers, he nonetheless defended the need for the Presbyterians to define their doctrine carefully and to advance in society more cautiously.

Hodge regained the use of his leg in the late 1830s, though he continued to require a cane for the rest of his days. In 1840 he re-

---

25. *Life,* pp. 167, 183.

lieved Alexander of some of his duties and broadened his own activities by becoming Professor of Exegetical and Didactic Theology. Hodge enjoyed the society of a growing family which included two sons who eventually joined him on the seminary faculty. When his wife died on Christmas Day in 1849, Hodge was smitten, as he was also in 1845 on the passing of his faithful co-worker on the *Princeton Review,* Albert Dod, and by the deaths in rapid succession of Samuel Miller (1850) and Archibald Alexander (1851). Now of a sudden he was a widower and the senior professor in one of America's most influential seminaries.[26]

As he had been in his early days, Hodge remained a successful teacher, but now the number of his students was growing steadily. By 1850 he was widely recognized as the leading spokesman for confessional Calvinist theology in America. Through a wide network of friends, which extended into Germany and Scotland, no less than through his many essays in the *Princeton Review* and the books which also flowed from his pen, Hodge had become a figure of considerable importance. Friends and foes alike knew that this reputation rested on his ability to defend a particular style of Old School Calvinism, the Princeton Theology, against other varieties of religious faith in America and abroad. This theology, in turn, defined the character of his piety.

CHARLES HODGE AND THE PRINCETON THEOLOGY

Charles Hodge became, in Sydney Ahlstrom's phrase, "the great theological arbiter of mid-century Presbyterianism"[27] because of his forthright defense of traditional Calvinism. When he died in 1878, the press—both religious and general—was filled with encomiums. Eulogy from Hodge's fellow-Presbyterians and from his own

---

26. The untimely deaths of Alexander's sons, James Waddel in 1859, and especially Joseph Addison in 1860, were likewise difficult burdens for Hodge to bear. On July 8, 1852, Hodge married Mary Hunter Stockton, the widow of a naval lieutenant and scion of an influential Princeton family, who survived him by two years.

27. Ahlstrom, "The Scottish Philosophy and American Theology," *Church History* 24 (Sept. 1955): 265.

students could only be expected. But it was a Methodist journal, the *National Repository,* which offered the most sweeping assessment. The editor acknowledged differences with Hodge "in many things," yet called him "not only *par excellence* the Calvinistic theologian of America, but the Nestor of all American theology . . . the grandest result of our Christian intellectual development." Another non-Presbyterian admirer, Charles Porterfield Krauth of the Lutheran Theological Seminary in Philadelphia, said much the same thing when reflecting specifically on Hodge's polemical career: "Mistakes he has made, and very important ones; but designed misrepresentations he has never made. Next to having Dr. Hodge on one's side is the pleasure of having him as an antagonist."[28]

Recent assessment of Hodge and the Princeton Theology he embodied is more varied. At the start of the twentieth century the historian of New England Theology, Frank Hugh Foster, casually dismissed Hodge for a fusty lack of originality.[29] But more generally, even those without a personal stake in Hodge's theology have given him credit for unusual achievement. Ahlstrom, for example, held that Hodge's acquaintance with German theology "gave an authority to his pronouncements that was scarcely equalled in America."[30] At the same time, Ahlstrom felt that Hodge made erratic concessions to philosophical conventions and Victorian morality which undercut the force of his work. A similar assessment appears in a recent work by Bruce Kuklick who sees Hodge as "one of the leading churchmen-theologians of his day," who nonetheless made "unimaginative" use of traditional theology to "block theological innovation."[31] Modern admirers of Hodge speak more unreservedly about his sterling efforts to counter the mixing of Christian faith and American ideology in the nineteenth century and about what David Wells has called "the great integrity" with which Hodge "followed single-mindedly his calling to obey the teaching of the biblical Word,

28. Quoted in *Life,* pp. 585, 616.
29. Foster, *A Genetic History of the New England Theology* (Chicago: University of Chicago Press, 1907), p. 432.
30. Ahlstrom, "The Scottish Philosophy," p. 266.
31. Kuklick, *Churchmen and Philosophers from Jonathan Edwards to John Dewey* (New Haven: Yale University Press, 1985), p. 75.

and through this to live his life to God's glory.[32] The common historical note in modern judgments, quite apart from questions of evaluation, is that Princeton Seminary enjoyed a "learned and mighty faculty" and that Charles Hodge was "the most brilliant and resolute voice of Princeton Calvinism and leading spokesman for the Old School."[33]

The achievement of Charles Hodge was to develop and invigorate the general theological positions which Archibald Alexander brought to Princeton Seminary, and to do this at an institution which exerted a significant influence on nineteenth-century American culture. The achievement is all the more remarkable in light of the fact that American culture was moving in directions largely opposed to the Princeton emphases. Hodge and Princeton stood for divine sovereignty in salvation where American religion was more and more emphasizing the ability of individuals to control the time, means, and place of their redemption. Hodge affirmed the intractable character of human evil while all around Americans took aim squarely at perfection. Hodge propounded confessional interpretations of the Bible and forthrightly upheld the value of theological tradition in an America with little time for history. And although Hodge too shared something of the American fascination with the individual, he nonetheless defended the concept of corporate solidarity: because Adam sinned, we are all sinners; because Christ took our punishment, we may be saved. Hodge's term for the dynamic of these corporate relationships was "imputation," the crediting to an entire group of the results of the actions of a single person. His defense of the term was the source of unending controversy in an America where it had become the received wisdom that every man must stand on his own two feet.

The pioneering work of Professor Timothy L. Smith has shown that an ever smaller proportion of American Christians were affirming these traditional Calivnistic conceptions in the years before the

---

32. David F. Wells, "Charles Hodge," in *Reformed Theology in America: A History of Its Modern Development*, ed. Wells (Grand Rapids: Eerdmans, 1985), p. 75.

33. Perry Miller, *The Life of the Mind in America from the Revolution to the Civil War* (New York: Harcourt, Brace & World, 1965), p. 17; J. David Hoeveler, Jr., *James McCosh and the Scottish Intellectual Tradition: From Glasgow to Princeton* (Princeton: Princeton University Press, 1981), p. 227.

Civil War.[34] The explosive growth of Methodists, Disciples, and Congregational defenders of an autonomous human will, as well as of many non-Calvinist groups, meant that while Princeton retained its reputation for intellectual gravity and theological rigor, its specific point of view had a precarious existence in nineteenth-century America.[35] Since Princeton Seminary rested securely in the bosom of the Presbyterian church, where more traditional ideas in theology still prevailed, Hodge may not have seen as clearly as modern historians that the tide was sweeping away from the Calvinist shore. Yet he still could realize that most of the forceful theological reasoning of his own age had passed beyond the bounds of traditional Calvinistic understanding.

These were the circumstances in which Alexander introduced and Hodge fleshed out the Princeton Theology. It was a theological position defined by a belief in biblical authority, committed to confessions of historic Reformed faith, allied with the modern philosophy of Scottish Common Sense, and encouraging a vibrant style of religious experience. Each of these aspects of the theology deserves further consideration.

Scripture   In the context of the nineteenth century, the Princeton allegience to the Bible as its theological norm was neither unusual nor remarkable. Expressed confidence in the truth-telling character of Scripture was a regular feature of public life as well as life in the churches during the first two-thirds of the nineteenth century.[36] Moreover, the American confidence in Scripture was widely diffused and culturally powerful. Everywhere Bible societies distributed the sacred text and everywhere individuals took it upon themselves to become expert in its pages.

---

34. Smith, *Revivalism and Social Reform: American Protestantism on the Eve of the Civil War* (Nashville: Abingdon, 1957), pp. 15–33.

35. See Donald Meyer, "The Dissolution of Calvinism," in *Paths of American Thought*, eds. A. M. Schlesinger, Jr., and Morton White (Boston: Houghton Mifflin, 1963), pp. 71–85.

36. See Nathan O. Hatch, *"Sola Scriptura and Novus Ordo Secolorum"* and Mark A. Noll, "The Image of the United States as a Biblical Nation, 1776–1865," in *The Bible in America*, eds. Hatch and Noll (New York: Oxford University Press, 1982), pp. 59–78, 39–40; and for the theological world, Randall H. Balmer, "The Princetonians and Scripture: A Reconsideration," *Westminster Theological Journal* 44 (1982): 352–65.

Princeton was distinguished not so much by its mere allegiance to the Bible as by its insistence that the Bible be studied academically as well as devotionally, that it be treated as a norm for corporate action as well as a fount of personal inspiration. In a sermon before the Presbyterian General Assembly in 1808 that fueled the drive for a seminary, Alexander called for a learned defense of "the doctrines which relate to Christ the Redeemer" as a means to stem the "infidelity" that "has come in like a flood, and threatened to inundate the church with a horrible species of philosophical atheism."[37] Later as the seminary's first professor, Alexander set out on the path of dilligent application to the study of the Bible which Hodge and Alexander's own sons, James Waddel and Joseph Addison would also follow. To Alexander the Bible was the foundation of Christian truth and the norm for Christian life in several particulars. The Bible would stiffen the resolve of the church, it would lay bare the inadequacies of Roman Catholic conceptions of Christianity, and it would provide the boundaries for a legitimate science.[38]

This confidence in Scripture which Hodge received from Alexander only built upon the training he had received from Ashbel Green both as a youngster in Philadelphia and an undergraduate at the College of New Jersey. Green's attachment to the Bible was less academic than Alexander's, but when he encouraged his Philadelphia congregation in domestic reading of Scripture and when he assembled his undergraduates on Sunday afternoons to recite on assigned passages of Scripture, he was laying the foundations for a lifetime of serious devotion to Scripture in Charles Hodge and many of his peers.

For his part, Hodge took for his own the beliefs of Alexander and Green in the full truthfulness of the Bible and in its supreme authority, especially in all matters specifically religious. Hodge considered faithfulness to the message of Scripture as the appropriate defense against what he called "rationalism" (e.g., the higher crit-

---

37. Alexander, *A Sermon Delivered at the Opening of the General Assembly* (Philadelphia: Hopkins & Earle, 1808), pp. 10–11.

38. For a sampling of these views, see the selections by Alexander in Mark A. Noll, ed., *The Princeton Theology 1812–1921: Scripture, Science, and Theological Method from Archibald Alexander to Benjamin Warfield* (Grand Rapids: Baker, 1983), pp. 51–54, 61–104.

icism of the Scripture) or "mysticism" (e.g., the concentration on religious experience exemplified by Schleiermacher). As modern views of the Bible came to exert a greater influence on the Continent, Hodge began more carefully to refine Alexander's general conception of biblical authority, a process which his successors in Princeton's chair of theology, A. A. Hodge and B. B. Warfield carried further in their own way.[39]

Still, this general confidence in the Bible, for which Hodge argued in considerable detail at the start of *The Way of Life,* was commonplace in the nineteenth century. More unusual was the Calvinistic interpretation which Hodge and the Princeton theologians gave to Scripture.

Reformed Confessionalism When Alexander stepped aside from Princeton's chair of theology in 1840 out of deference to Hodge, little change occurred in the actual teaching of that subject. Hodge continued to quiz the students on their reading, to assign theological questions for their homework, and to use as textbook the seventeenth-century dogmatics (in Latin) of the Swiss Reformed theologian Francis Turretin.[40] Successive generations of seminary students grumbled about the effort to plow through Turretin (at least until sufficient English cribs could be copied for those whose Latinity was rusty), but none doubted Hodge's persistent loyalty to the Reformed theological tradition as defined by classic statements of the sixteenth and seventeen centuries. For Alexander and Hodge, John Calvin, the great lights of English Puritanism, the Westminster Confession of Faith, and the influential Calvinistic dogmaticians of seventeenth-century Europe were all reliable guides for understanding the Bible.

The theology which Hodge took from these sources was, in his opinion, simply the distillation of biblical teaching. The Fall of Adam and Eve perverted a perfect creation, led to divine condem-

---

39. See A. A. Hodge and B. B. Warfield, "Inspiration," *Presbyterian Review* 2 (Apr. 1881): 225–60.

40. The discussion of Turretin's influence on the Princeton Theology will be affected by Timothy Ross Phillips, "Francis Turretin's Idea of Theology and its Impact Upon His Doctrine of Scripture" (Ph.D. dissertaion, Vanderbilt University, 1986), a work which shows that Turretin's views were less mechanical and less scientific than is sometimes asserted.

nation, and established human guilt before God. Adam's sin was imputed to all humans who properly deserved the condemnation which sinfulness entails. The same process of imputation that rendered humanity doomed in Adam justified the elect through faith in Jesus Christ. God expressed his saving purposes by covenanting to offer salvation through Christ. Sinners, turned from God by rebellious natures, were "bound" to their own sinful desires until God changed their hearts through the "means" of Scripture, Christian nurture, preaching, and the sacraments of baptism and the Lord's Supper. Redeemed sinners must continue to struggle with the lingering effects of the Fall, but were also fitted by the Holy Spirit for fruitful service in the Kingdom of God. Hodge himself summed up the gist of these convictions in 1850 at the close of a sharp polemical exchange with Edwards Amasa Park of Andover Seminary, to which we will return, as the "representations of the Bible": "That a sentence of condemnation passed on all men for the sin of one man; that men are by nature the children of wrath; that without Christ we can do nothing; that he hath redeemed us from the curse of the law by being made a curse for us; that men are not merely pardoned but justified."[41]

To Hodge the various testimonies in the broadly Reformed tradition were all harmonious voices in one chorus. At various places in his *Systematic Theology,* for example, he interwove citations from Calvin, the Second Helvitic Confession of 1566, the English Westminster Confession and Catechism of the mid-seventeenth century, and the works of seventeenth-century theologians like Turretin. The purpose was not simply to pile up earthly authorities but to suggest that a common, well-attested tradition existed for understanding the meaning of the Bible.

Hodge's commitment to the older Reformed theology was part of a more general conservatism. Unlike most of his fellow Americans, for whom the more recent was intuitively the superior, Hodge went out of his way to deny the novelty of work at Princeton. In 1870 he reviewed the course of the *Princeton Review* with these words: "Whether it be a ground of reproach or of approbation, it is believed to be true, that an original idea in theology is not to be found on the

---

41. Hodge, "The Theology of the Intellect and That of the Feelings," *BRPR* 22 (Oct. 1850): 674.

pages of the *Biblical Repertory and Princeton Review* from the beginning until now. The phrase 'Princeton Theology,' therefore, is without distinctive meaning.'' In 1872 at the semicentennial observance of his election as professor, he said much the same thing: ''I am not afraid to say that a new idea never originated in the Seminary.''[42]

This stance grew from his love of traditional Reformed theologies, but also expressed a preference for an older style of argumentation in which clarifying distinctions counted for more than heeding one's own individual spirit. In 1844 he closed a review of a new book from Germany with a fulsome word on the virtues of the older theologians:

> After all the alleged improvements in theological research, we never feel so much disposed to take down one of the old Latin dogmatic writers of the seventeenth century, as immediately on closing a fresh work from Germany. These antiquated writers have a thousand faults, it may be; they are stiff, they are prolix, they are technical, they are intolerant and austere, they are scholastic in their distinctions, but they have one great merit—they always let us know what they mean. Their atmosphere, if wintry and biting, is clear. . . . Especially [do they] beget a repugnance to dreamy contemplation and the use of vague diction for concealment.[43]

To put it simply, Hodge was comfortable with the theologically tried and true. Yet the hyperbole with which he repudiated innovation at Princeton has led to an underestimation of his achievement in *restating* Reformed theology for an America very different from Calvin's Geneva or the England of the Westminster Confession. Hodge himself probably did not grasp how unusual it was in forward-looking America for someone to take a stand on old Protestant confessions of the sixteenth and seventeenth centuries.

Scottish Common Sense Philosophy   The Scottish Philosophy

---

42. *BRPR Index Volume* (1870–1871), vol. I, p. 11; *Life*, p. 521.
43. Hodge, ''Neander's History,'' *BRPR* 16 (Apr. 1844): 182.

of Common Sense was the intellectual coin of the realm in the United States throughout the first two-thirds of the nineteenth century. With most other American thinkers of the period, theologians at Princeton adapted this philosophical orientation to their own purposes. In its turn, this philosophy left its mark on Charles Hodge's conception of religious truth and experience.[44]

Scottish Common Sense Realism was a philosophy designed to save the benefits of England's "moderate" Scientific Revolution from radicals, to preserve the benefits of the work of Sir Isaac Newton and John Locke. It was a point of view developed by professors in Glasgow and Edinburgh like Francis Hutcheson (1694–1746) and Thomas Reid (1710–1796) who sought a philosophy to serve both narrow intellectual purposes and broad social concerns. Eventually it would be used to counter the skepticism of Scotland's David Hume, the idealism of Bishop George Berkeley, and the revolutionary social theory of the French Enlightenment. The Scottish philosophers stressed the "common sense" of humankind. They argued that normal people, using responsibly the information provided by their senses, could actually grasp directly the character of the real world. Furthermore, humans possessed a "moral sense," analogous to the physical senses, which grasped directly basic principles of ethics. Because all humans *in common* could perceive basic truths about the physical world and the human mind in this way, such a common sense provided the basis for a full-scale philosophy.

With these moves the Scottish philosophers defended the great traditions of modern English thought. They affirmed Francis Ba-

---

44. Good discussions of the Scottish Philosophy of Common Sense and its importance in America are found in Ahlstrom, "The Scottish Philosophy"; Theodore Dwight Bozeman, *Protestants in an Age of Science: The Baconian Ideal and Antebellum American Religious Thought* (Chapel Hill: University of North Carolina Press, 1977); E. Brooks Holifield, *The Gentlemen Theologians: American Theology in Southern Culture, 1795–1860* (Durham, NC: Duke University Press, 1978), pp. 72–154; George M. Marsden, *The Evangelical Mind and the New School Presbyterian Experience* (New Haven: Yale University Press, 1970), pp. 47–52; Henry F. May, *The Enlightenment in America* (New York: Oxford University Press, 1976), pp. 307–62; Elizabeth Flower and Murray G. Murphey, *A History of Philosophy in America*, 2 vols. (New York: G. P. Putnam's Sons, 1977), I, 203–393; and D. H. Meyer, *The Instructed Conscience: The Shaping of the American National Ethic* (Philadelphia: University of Pennsylvania Press, 1972).

con's insistence that truth arises from empirical and inductive methods. They confirmed John Locke's trust in sense information while eliminating his confusing discussion of ideas. And they identified themselves with Isaac Newton by insisting that the highest form of knowledge arises from our empirical study of the outside world and, by analogy, of our own minds. The Scottish philosophers regarded truth as a static entity, open equally to all people. They placed a high premium on scientific investigation. They were deeply committed to an empirical method through which relevant facts could be gathered into coherent generalizations. They abhorred "speculation" and "metaphysics" as flights from the basic realities of the physical world and the human mind. And at least some of them assumed that this approach could be used to convince all rational souls of the truth of Christianity, the necessity of traditional social order, and the capacity of scientific methods to advance our understanding of the world.

The principles of the Scottish Philosophy were first articulated in America by John Witherspoon (1723–1794), who came from Scotland to serve as president of Princeton College in 1768. Under his leadership Scottish Common Sense swiftly replaced the idealistic metaphysics of Jonathan Edwards as the dominant philosophical orientation for American Presbyterians. Among Witherspoon's many students who themselves became teachers was William Graham (1746–1799) of Virginia, who was Archibald Alexander's instructor in both general education and theological subjects.[45] Alexander, who provided introductory lectures on the "Nature and Evidence of Truth" to incoming theological students for most of his tenure at Princeton Seminary, passed on in those lectures the principles of the Scottish Philosophy to Hodge and many other students.[46]

Hodge's pastor and college president, Ashbel Green, was just as strongly committed to these Scottish principles, for he had also been a devoted student of Witherspoon. When Green became pres-

---

45. Wesley Frank Craven, "William Graham," in *Princetonians 1769–1775*, pp. 289–94.

46. See Alexander, "Nature and Evidence of Truth," a lecture transcribed in Noll, ed., *The Princeton Theology*, pp. 62–71, 317–19; and for a fuller statement, Alexander, *Outlines of Moral Science* (New York: Charles Scribner, 1852).

ident of Princeton College in 1812, his major change in the curriculum was to restore Witherspoon's lectures on Moral Philosophy as the text for the senior course in epistemology, ethics, and politics.

From these influences Hodge naturally accepted the basic tenets of the Scottish Philosophy. He put them to use most strikingly in the introduction on theological method to his *Systematic Theology,* but they had informed his entire career. In *The Way of Life,* for instance, Hodge put Common Sense principles to use in combatting "sophistical objections against the doctrine of the Bible." To Hodge it was folly for supposedly intelligent people to deny the evidence supporting the divine character of Scripture, evidence which came from external proofs and internal intuitions. He spelled out the philosophical reasons for such conclusions in phrases which he had learned from Alexander:

By the laws of our being we are imperatively required to confide in the well ascertained testimony of our senses; to rely upon the veracity of our own consciousness; to receive the unimpeachable testimony of our fellow men, and to abide by those truths which are matters of intuitive perception, or the necessary conclusions of reason. These are laws of belief impressed upon our constitution by our creator; and are therefore the authoritative expressions of his will.[47]

Hodge's commitment to the Scottish Philosophy of Common Sense had two contradictory influences on his vision of religious life. In the first instance this philosophy tended toward an overly confident view of the power of induction. Because of what a modern commentator has called "Charles Hodge's ever-simple view of scientific method,"[48] Hodge sometimes failed to register the influence which world views, cultural conventions, and moral tendencies exert upon reasoning, especially reasoning from what Hodge took to be the simple "facts" of Scripture. This aspect of the Scottish Philosophy led to a mechanical, naive belief that a process of brute ratiocination

47. Hodge, *The Way of Life,* pp. 85, 97–98.
48. J. I. Packer, book review, *Crux* 16 (Mar. 1980); 31.

could assemble statements from the Bible into a spiritually compelling religion.

At the same time, however, the place of intuition in the Scottish Philosophy—we know basic things about ourselves and the world directly without the need for inferential reasoning—reinforced Hodge's willingness to ascribe a direct role to the Holy Spirit in convincing people of Christian truth. Reliance upon a "moral sense" opened the door to ways of approaching religion that were not based upon simplistic models of scientific reasoning, but which rather rested on the human ability to grasp important truths about God and the world directly.

Much modern controversy has swirled around the question of Hodge's use of the Common Sense Philosophy.[49] For our purposes it is enough to note the importance of that philosophy in his thought, and also to recognize that it left an ambiguous influence. In some instances it pushed him in the direction of a naive scienticism, in others it moved him in the direction of religious immediacy.

For Charles Hodge, commitments to the Bible as ultimate authority, to Reformed Confessionalism as the best expression of Christian faith, and to Scottish Common Sense Realism as a philosophical guide were always part and parcel of unswerving commitment to lively religious experience. When we come to examine the piety of Charles Hodge below, we will be able to observe how each of these other commitments helped to shape his conception of religious life.

But first it is necessary to comment briefly on the great influence of Hodge and the Princeton Thelogy in the nineteenth century. Even if the Calvinism of Princeton was becoming a minority viewpoint in American religious life, a combination of powerful institutions and personal networks made Hodge's Princeton Theology a significant force throughout his century.

Princeton Seminary has remained a dominant voice in American religion since its founding in 1812, and it was even more powerful in the nineteenth century when theological seminaries were the

---

49. Some of this discussion is canvassed in Mark A. Noll, "Common Sense Traditions in American Evangelical Thought," *American Quarterly* 37 (Summer 1985): 215–38.

largest and best developed schools of graduate education in the country. Princeton Seminary poured out a steady stream of graduates who powerfully influenced the Presbyterian Church and who often found influential places in other denominations as well. More students attended that seminary in the nineteenth century than any other American institution of graduate higher education.[50]

The printed page added to the visibility of the Seminary and its instructors. Books of all sorts—essays, commentaries, treatises, pamphlets—on all manner of topics poured from Princeton throughout the century, making it an acknowledged influence everywhere in the country south of New England. The *Biblical Repertory and Princeton Review* extended Princeton's influence through its regular commentary on the great theological issues of the day as well as on a wide variety of other topics. Theological friends and foes alike recognized how important this journal was—"the most powerful organ in the land" said the editor of Lyman Beecher's autobiography, who was not particularly well-disposed toward Princeton; "beyond all question the greatest purely theological Review that has ever been published in the English tongue," according to an admirer from the *British Quarterly Review* in 1871.[51] These opinions may have overestimated matters, but they also testify to the weight which Hodge and his associates carried on matters of concern to the religious world of the nineteenth century.

The reputation of the *Princeton Review* largely rested on its capacity for controversy. Hodge was a fair combatant, but a determined one. If he felt that a religious opinion undercut the authority of the Bible or misrepresented the reality of Christian life, he was quick to take up arms. The controversies that resulted amounted to some of the most momentous discussions of theological, and more generally intellectual, matters in the history of American civilization. In the pages of the *Princeton Review,* for example, Hodge took E. A. Park and Andover Seminary to task for giving up without cause the most important doctrines of Jonathan Edwards on the human will

---

50. The stories of some influential graduates are found in *Sons of the Prophets: Leaders in Protestantism from Princeton Seminary,* ed. Hugh T. Kerr (Princeton: Princeton University Press, 1963).

51. *Life,* pp. 260, 257.

and the sovereignty of God in salvation, he scored John W. Nevin and Philip Schaff for using uncritically the resources of German idealism, he criticized the revivalism of Charles G. Finney for importing an alien concept of self-determination into the heart of Christian faith, he upbraided leaders of the Oxford Movement in the Church of England for blindly ignoring the errors of Roman Catholicism, and he scolded Horace Bushnell for destroying the meaning of language with respect to religious truths.[52] Within his own house, as it were, he was a moderate critic of New School Presbyterians in 1837 and a firm opponent of Presbyterian reunion after the Civil War.[53] And on matters of interest to the country, he held to positions that upset even many of his fellow Presbyterians: slavery was not an evil as such, but the American system of slavery was; allegiance to the Union should not be a test of denominational loyalty; once begun, the Civil War deserved to be fought vigorously and the President supported in the extreme measures necessary for its completion.[54]

No one, not even his closest friends, believed that Hodge emerged the victor in all of these controversies. But by the same token, no religious leader during Hodge's active years with the *Princeton Review* could merely ignore the polemics that poured forth quarter by quarter in the pages of that formidable journal.

The circle of Hodge's influence extended far beyond what seems logical from a modern viewpoint. We think of him today as the doughty defender of Old School Presbyterian Calvinism. Yet he sustained long and fruitful friendships with Episcopalians, including two bishops who were his classmates under Alexander at Princeton

---

52. See Hodge, "Professor Park and the Princeton Review," *BRPR* 23 (Oct. 1851): 674–95; a review of Nevin's *The Mystical Presence, BRPR* 20 (Apr. 1846): 227–78; "The New Divinity Tried" [vs. Finney], *BRPR* 4 (Apr. 1832): 278–304; "Oxford Tracts," *BRPR* 10 (Jan. 1838): 84–119; and a review of Bushnell's *God in Christ, BRPR* 21 (Apr. 1849): 259–98.

53. See Hodge, "Voluntary Societies and Ecclesiastical Organization," *BRPR* 9 (Jan. 1837): 101–52; and "Principles of Church Union, and the Re-union of Old and New School Presbyterians," *BRPR* 37 (Apr. 1865): 271–313.

54. See Hodge, "Slavery," *BRPR* 8 (1836); reprinted in *Essays and Reviews: Selected from The Princeton Review* (New York: Robert Carter, 1857), pp. 473–511.

Seminary. He expressed a consistent appreciation for Lutheran dogmatics and dogmaticians, even when compelled to differ with their interpretations of Scripture. He read German theology with appreciation, as well as with polemical intent, throughout his life. And at a time of intense anti-Catholic feeling in America, he even defended the validity of Roman Catholic baptism, and recognized the Catholic church as a legitimate, if decrepit, manifestation of historic Christianity.[55] Through students his influence reached into unexpected corners of the American landscape. During the bleak days of the Civil War the layman whom Reinhold Neibuhr once called America's greatest theologian, Abraham Lincoln, regularly attended the services of the New York Avenue Presbyterian Church in Washington whose minister Phineas D. Gurley had graduated from Princeton Seminary in 1840.[56] E. Y. Mullins, the leading Southern Baptist theologian at the turn of the century, told the centennial celebration at Princeton Seminary in 1912 that he honored Princeton for its instruction of his own theological mentor, James P. Boyce, who had graduated from Princeton as a student of Charles Hodge in 1852.[57]

In the end, however, when all has been said that can be said about Charles Hodge's breadth of influence and his considerable ecumenicity, he remains the great representative of conservative Calvinism in the nation's last two hundred years. It is as such that his vision of the religious life must be assessed. The polemical career of Charles Hodge, no less than his many efforts in constructive theology, biblical commentary, and simple Christian proclamation, embodied his commitment to traditional Calvinism. A question most appropriate for a series on American spirituality is whether Hodge defended Calvinism because he saw it as the best form of Christian

---

55. Hodge, "Is the Church of Rome a Part of the Visible Church?" *BRPR* 18 (Apr. 1846); reprinted in *Essays and Reviews*, pp. 220–44. See also *Life*, pp. 340–43.

56. William J. Wolf, *The Almost Chosen People: A Study of the Religion of Abraham Lincoln* (Garden City, NY: Doubleday, 1959), p. 126; Roberts, *Biographical Catalogue of Princeton Seminary*, p. 103.

57. Edgar Young Mullins, "From the Seminaries of Other Churches," *The Centennial Celebration of the Theological Seminary of the Presbyterian Church in the United States of America at Princeton, New Jersey* (Princeton: At the Seminary, 1912), p. 557.

proposition, or because he felt it expressed the experie.itial faith of Christianity in its fullest form. Such issues call for a direct examination of Hodge's vision of the religious life.

THE PIETY OF CHARLES HODGE

To Charles Hodge and the Princeton theologians two elements were indispensable to genuine religion. One was the objectivity of truth revealed in the Bible. The other was the subjectivity of lived religious experience. In their minds these were but two sides of the same coin, two facets of one great jewel. Opponents in the nineteenth century and some commentators in the twentieth have perceived difficulties in this conception of the spiritual life.[58] The Princeton theologians, it is charged, misconceived both the nature of the truth to be found in the Bible and the quality of life to be desired in faith. In addition, others have charged, Princeton artificially divided questions of intellect and life by putting far too much stress on propositional definitions of Christian faith.

Hodge himself self-consciously framed the discussion of authentic religion in terms of intellect and life. A review in 1860 of three European works provided an occasion for addressing the question "What is Christianity?" Hodge's answer set out the two sides of Princeton's position succinctly:

> Christianity objectively considered, is the testimony of God concerning his Son, it is the whole revelation of truth contained in the Scriptures, concerning the redemption of man through Jesus Christ our Lord. Subjectively considered, it is the life of Christ in the soul, or, that form of spiritual life which has its origin in Christ, is determined by the revelation concerning his person and work, and which is due to the indwelling of his Spirit. In one sense, therefore, we may affirm that Christianity is a doctrine,

---

58. For a summary of this criticism, with references, see Jack B. Rogers and Donald K. McKim, *The Authority and Interpretation of the Bible: An Historical Approach* (San Francisco: Harper & Row, 1979), pp. 274–99.

and in another sense we may with equal truth affirm that Christianity is a life.[59]

In other places, especially *The Way of Life,* Hodge provided a more compact statement of the way these two sides of religion came together: "Truth is in order to holiness," he wrote in that book. "And all truth is known to be truth, by its tendency to promote holiness."[60]

Hodge held to the cohesion of doctrine and life with steely intellectual resolve and with passionate emotion. This conviction spurred him to attack Horace Bushnell's proposal in 1849 that religious language by its nature possessed an imprecision regularly misunderstood by theologians. And it inspired the most extensive polemics of his career, an exchange with Edwards Amasa Park of Andover Seminary in which Hodge hoped to demonstrate the ineluctable bond between formal truth and practical religion.[61] When in 1850 Park published a sermon entitled "The Theology of the Intellect and That of the Feelings," Hodge sprang immediately into action. Park was advancing the suggestion by then common among New England's intellectual elite that language was at best an approximate vehicle for conveying the ultimate realities of life. Although Park was uneasy with the radical implications of such an idea, he saw how it could still be a useful tool for understanding the Scriptures. In particular, theologians might employ some passages—like those speaking of Christ receiving the wrath of God's judgment in place of sinners, or of God's ability to work sovereignly among people without regard to human acts of will—as the proper expressions of the heart in gratitude to God's grace. At the same time they would

---

59. Hodge, "What is Christianity?" *BRPR* 32 (Jan. 1860): 119.

60. Hodge, *The Way of Life,* p. 180.

61. Hodge, review of Bushnell's *God in Christ, BRPR* 21 (Apr. 1849): 259–98. The first two blows in the lengthy exchange were Park, "The Theology of the Intellect and That of the Feelings," *Bibliotheca Sacra* 7 (July 1850): 533–69; and the response by Hodge with the same title in *BRPR* 22 (Oct. 1850): 642–74. For an overview of the controversy over religious language as it involved Bushnell, Park, and Hodge, see Darryl G. Hart, "Divided Between Heart and Mind: The Critical Period for Protestant Thought in America," *Journal of Ecclesiastical History,* in press.

realize that a Christian theology alert to the best wisdom of the nineteenth century would recognize these biblical phrases as figures of speech to be interpreted according to the ethical standards of the modern age.

Such an idea, even in the conservative shape which Park gave it, was an abomination to Charles Hodge. He immediately responded with a blast in the *Princeton Review,* asserting that "a Christian does not understand the Bible in one way when he reads it as a critic, and in another way when he reads for spiritual edification." Moreover, the Christian's "thoughts of God and Christ when endeavoring to discover the truth revealed concerning them are the same as when he is engaged in acts of worship."[62] For Hodge, the words of Scripture both framed doctrine and inspired devotion. The question was not one of literal or figurative usage, for Hodge could recognize a metaphor when he saw one, and unlike modern fundamentalists was willing to concede that entire sections of the Bible like the Book of Revelation were intended to be read as an elaborate figure.[63] The question was rather whether the declarative sentences of the didactic parts of the Bible meant what they seemed on the surface to say. On this matter he never wavered.

Hodge's determination to consider true religion as the marriage of objective truth and subjective experience was complicated by the nature of his larger commitments in faith and intellect. Hodge was a Calvinist, but also an American Calvinist of the nineteenth century. As such, he was both an Augustinian voluntarist and a Baconian intellectualist, terms which require brief explanation. As a classical Calvinist, Hodge held to positions first fully worked out by St. Augustine (354–430) on the basis of his understanding of Scripture, especially the writings of the Apostle Paul. In this view, Adam's fall involved the entire human family in rebellion against God. A state of sinfulness, the inheritance of the first misdeed, was then imputed to all people who, without the redeeming actions of God's grace,

---

62. Hodge, "The Theology of the Intellect and That of the Feelings," *BRPR* 22 (Oct. 1850): 668.

63. I have been helped at this point by John Auxier, "Princetonian Eschatology 1812–1878: The Neglect of *The Apocalypse*" (M.A. thesis, Trinity Evangelical Divinity School, 1986).

were doomed. Moreover, in a state of sin humans are concerned only with self-exaltation and so act only in their own self interest. Their wills are thus "bound" to self and sin, in the sense that they *cannot* turn to God because they *will* not. God's sovereign act of grace, arising from his predestinating will and coming to fruition in the sacrifice of Christ for sinners, is therefore necessary to break the self-seeking bondage of the will and restore the sinner to God. With other Augustinians like Martin Luther, John Calvin, or Blaise Pascal, Hodge held that although God acts to save through visible, physical means, the accomplishment of his saving purposes rests on the supernatural activity of the Holy Spirit. True religion, therefore, arises entirely from God's work in and with an individual (the Augustinian position), and it begins with the supernatural redirection of the will which then enables the redeemed sinner to recognize divine truth and carry out God's will (the voluntarist assertion).

Hodge's first communication to the students at Princeton Seminary after his return from Europe in 1828 gave full expression to this Augustinian voluntarism. Since the "feelings" reflected the character of the soul, "opinions on moral and religious subjects depend mainly on the state of the moral and religious feelings. Mere argument can no more produce the intimate persuasion of moral truth than it can of beauty. As it depends on our refinement of taste, what things to us are beautiful, so it depends upon our religious feelings, what doctrines for us are true."[64] In other words, salvation of the heart is the foundation for light to the mind.

As a nineteenth-century American intellectual, however, Hodge also placed a very high value on the objective deliverances of a value-neutral science. Francis Bacon was a near demi-god in America during the first half of the nineteenth century because, it was thought, Bacon had shown how observant minds could build universally accepted truth by a methodical collection and arrangement of the facts of experience.[65] The rapid development of science

---

64. Hodge, "Lecture, Addressed to the Students of the Theological Seminary," *BRPR* 1 (Jan. 1829): 90.

65. Two good discussions of this phenomenon are George Marsden, "Everyone's Own Interpreter?: The Bible, Science, and Authority in Mid-Nineteenth-Century America," *The Bible in America,* pp. 79–100; and Bozeman, *Protestants in an Age of Science.*

and philosophy in the decades after Newton and Locke (the supreme exemplars of Baconian method) seemed to demonstrate the validity of Bacon's methods and to suggest that they paved the way for every kind of intellectual inquiry. Other considerations—what a scientist might hold about the world more generally, what a Baconian observer might believe about God or the absence of God, what a society might presuppose as matters of cultural convention—were of no account in discerning the truth. It was not characteristic for Hodge to share without adjustment the conventions of this age, but in this particular he seemed to agree wholeheartedly. In famous phrases from his *Systematic Theology* Hodge showed what it meant to do theology by such "scientific" procedures:

> The Bible is to the theologian what nature is to the man of science. It is his store-house of facts; and his method of ascertaining what the Bible teaches, is the same as that which the natural philosopher adopts to ascertain what nature teaches. . . . The duty of the Christian theologian is to ascertain, collect, and combine all the facts which God has revealed concerning himself and our relation to him. These facts are all in the Bible. . . . The theologian must be guided by the same rules in the collection of facts, as govern the man of science. . . . In theology as in natural science, principles are derived from facts, and not impressed upon them.[66]

The result was to suggest that the truths of the Bible lay on the ground for anyone to discover who would approach them with proper methodological rigor.

This Baconian turn in Hodge's thought could lead, on occasion, to intellectualist conclusions, that is, to an equation of religious life with religious belief. "Christianity," he wrote in 1857, "always has had a creed. A man who believes certain doctrines is a Christian. If his faith is mere assent, he is a speculative Christian; if it is cordial

---

66. Hodge, *Systematic Theology,* 3 vols. (New York: Charles Scribner's Sons, 1872–1873), vol. I, 10, 11, 13.

and appreciating, he is a true Christian."[67] The last qualification is important, since it reflects Hodge's voluntarism, but the ease with which he could equate assent to Christian doctrine and possession of Christian faith was still a significant feature of his larger work.

The two sides of Hodge's spirituality tended to come unglued especially because of his labors as an apologist.[68] Because Princeton set itself the task of defending the old faith of inherited Calvinism, its theologians devoted most of their energies not to innovative re-creations of theology but to sniffing out detractions, subtractions, weaknesses, undercuttings of the inherited faith. For most of his life Hodge was content to write polemical rebuttals for the *Princeton Review* and to use a seventeenth-century theology as the textbook at Princeton since he was comfortable with the inherited faith, but uncomfortable with the innovations of his own day. Only after prodding from his friends did he commit his own theology to print, but even then we have seen his claim that there was no such thing as a "Princeton Theology," only an inherited Calvinism continuing its well-deserved existence in the precincts of his seminary. The ingenuousness of such an attitude arises from the fact that polemical concerns regularly tug and skew, modify and develop an inherited deposit. This is especially the case with Hodge, for he felt constrained to combat error from opposite directions.

Hodge lived in the age of the dividing of the western mind. On the one hand, science (the more objective the better) was responsible for ever increasing triumphs in the physical world. Rationalization, technique, method, precision, and efficiency were more and more the order of the day. At the same time, however, the nineteenth century of scientific objectivity was also the nineteenth century of unmediated human experience. The age of utilitarianism was the age of Romanticism. Ralph Waldo Emerson strove with John Stuart Mill. The heart, said the poet and dreamer, marches to the beat of its own drummer. Efficiency, said the utilitarian, is all. Practical the-

---

67. Hodge, "Inspiration," *BRPR* 29 (Oct. 1857): 693.

68. A fine discussion of just this point is found in W. Andrew Hoffecker, *Piety and the Princeton Theologians: Archibald Alexander, Charles Hodge, Benjamin Warfield* (Grand Rapids: Baker, 1981), pp. 79ff.

ology, religious life, was in the middle. Could it at one and the same time demonstrate its rationality to the scientific minded and its sentimentality to the romantic minded?[69] Hodge thought it could, and so he was active on many fronts.

At the start of his career, after confronting various European "rationalisms" first hand, and at its end, when examining the proposals of Charles Darwin, Hodge devoted considerable effort to defending the deliverances of the heart against the pretentious claims of modern science. He was distressed by the claims of English deists, took note of the "positive philosophy" of Auguste Comte which replaced religion with scientific sociology, and later chastised Darwin for promoting a form of atheism.[70] For these efforts, the principles of Scottish Common Sense Philosophy, no less than the traditions of Augustinian Christianity, were Hodge's main weapons. From the Scots, as mediated through John Witherspoon and Ashbel Green, he knew that the deliverances of the mind concerning basic epistemological and ethical questions raised a great bulwark against any "rationalism" that would deny the reality of the soul or the existence of God. From the Augustinian tradition he knew that the voice of conscience countered the slide toward materialism and its fatal consequences. Most important, as he expressed it in *The Way of Life,* the Holy Spirit impressed upon human hearts the great truth that the Bible was a genuine revelation from God. While this truth could indeed be demonstrated through a parade of evidence such as to satisfy the scientist, it rested first and foremost upon the "internal" evidences which God had designed to communicate to intuition, conscience, and the heart.[71]

Hodge's polemics against deistic rationalism, against Darwin's attack on teleology, and against critical assaults on the Bible drew fully, in other words, on Hodge's own religious experience. He

---

69. For solid reflection on this problem, see James Turner, *Without God, Without Creed: The Origin of Unbelief in America* (Baltimore: Johns Hopkins University Press, 1985).

70. On Comte, see Hodge, *Systematic Theology,* I, 254–61. Hodge's attack on naturalistic evolution as a variety of atheism is found in his last book, *What Is Darwinism?* (New York: Scribners, Armstrong, & Co., 1874), especially pp. 173–77.

71. Hodge, *The Way of Life,* pp. 9–30.

could stand forth confidently against this variety of modern heresy because he knew in his heart—through the common moral sense given to all humans, through conscience, and through the truths of Scripture which the Holy Spirit verified in his own experience—that Christianity was true. If this is the only Hodge we knew, he would have been regarded as a pietist pure and simple.[72]

But in fact the bulk of Hodge's polemical effort was directed toward what he considered errors from the other direction. Not rationalists but the proponents of a self-directed religious experience loomed as the gravest dangers for the faith. This danger, moreover, was as multi-faceted as it was insidious. Hodge had experienced one variety personally during his German sojourn, which coincided with the ascendency of Schleiermacher. Although Hodge admired Schleiermacher's intellectual gifts, he shuddered before what he called "the fundamental principle of Schleiermacher's theory, that religion resides not in the intelligence, or the will or active powers, but in the sensibility." This meant, in turn, that "the Scripture, as a rule of faith, has no authority."[73]

Hodge set himself boldly against teachings which made feelings the source of religious authority, or which even appeared to. From Princeton's vantage point nothing could be clearer than that Horace Bushnell in Hartford, E. A. Park in Andover, and J. W. Nevin in Mercersberg all were rushing headlong after Schleiermacher. And so they must be brought up short.

Closer to home, moreover, was a different form of heresy appearing under the banner of religious experience, a form even more dangerous than the German import because of its hold on American religious practice. This danger was the dynamics of unchecked revivalism.

A certain amount of ambiguity entered Hodge's thinking at this point since he was a loyal student of Archibald Alexander, ever the

---

72. I have been aided in considerations of Hodge's belief in the work of the Holy Spirit by Stephen R. Spencer, "A Comparison and Evaluation of the Old Princeton and Amsterdam Apologetics," (Th.M. thesis, Grand Rapids Baptist Seminary, n.d.); and Steven L. Martin, "The Doctrines of Man, Reason, and the Holy Spirit in the Epistemology of Charles Hodge" (M.A. thesis, Trinity Evangelical Divinity School, 1984).

73. Hodge, *Systematic Theology*, I, 65.

Virginia revivalist while the Princeton professor. In addition, the revival of Hodge's student days remained a life-long inspiration. For
him not all revivals were created equal. It was important to distinguish between the proper sort and the wrong kind. Sadly, as he
viewed the world, the wrong kind had predominated in America. It
could be seen in the enthusiasm of the First Great Awakening which
derailed the largely sound theology of Jonathan Edwards and led
New England into its errors concerning human self-assertion and the
autonomous power of the will.[74] The same problem was present in
the frontier revivals of Hodge's own day when ardent religious sentiment threw over the bonds of order, decency, and the authority of
Scripture. And the error was writ large in the public statements of
leading contemporary revivalists like Charles Finney who simply
took it for granted that humans had the power to control their own
destinies if only they would *exert* themselves.[75]

In a remarkable review from 1847 Hodge actually agreed with
Horace Bushnell that God normally works gradually among people
through what Bushnell called "Christian Nurture," rather than
through the unusual excitements of revival. Bushnell may have ov-
eremphasized religious experience as a source of truth, yet he still
saw clearly that God had fixed ordinary and deliberate means for in-
culcating faith, rather than the disorderly and disruptive. Although
American revivalists often sounded more orthodox than foreign theologians, Hodge still thought they led to the same evil:

> No one can fail to remark that this too exclusive depen-
> dence on revivals tends to produce a false or unscriptural
> form of religion. It makes excitement essential to the peo-
> ple, and leads them to think that piety consists in strong
> exercises of feelings, the nature of which it is difficult to
> determine. The ordinary means of grace become insipid or
> distasteful, and a state of things is easily induced in which

74. Hodge, *The Constitutional History of the Presbyterian Church in the
United States of America* (Philadelphia: Presbyterian Board of Publication, 1851
[orig. 1840]), Part II, pp. 11–101.

75. Hodge, "Finney's Lectures on Theology," *BRPR* 19 (Apr. 1847): 237–
77.

even professors of religion become utterly remiss as to all
social religious duties of an ordinary character.[76]

For Hodge religious experience should lead to steady-state religion. It is a mistake to suppose, as he wrote in *The Way of Life,*
"that religion is a fitful sort of life; an alternation of excitement and
insensibility. Those who labour under this delusion, are religious
only on certain occasions. . . . No form of life is thus intermittent."[77] Genuine religion rather is the result of God working objectively through means rather than subjectively through emotional
excesses. It is a religion which stresses, as he wrote in the review of
Bushnell, "the divinely appointed means of careful Christian nurture" especially "family training of children and pastoral instruction
of the young."[78]

Against the riot of enthusiasm Hodge offered the objective
truths of Scripture and the well-tried traditions of Calvinism. Furthermore, when Christians interpreted the Bible faithfully, in accord
with the Protestant confessions, the way was opened to genuine religious experience. They were allied with the truth, rather than destroying it.

For over thirty years the burden of Hodge's polemical life was
to pose an alternative to unchecked religious experience, whether of
the German philosophical variety or the American revivalistic type.
In other words, Hodge defended a vision of religion that was American in its belief in "the Bible only" and its common sense approach
to truth, but which was also confessional in its deference to the historical Calvinistic confessions. Such a faith, Hodge held, opened the
way to religious life.

Was he correct?

Hodge's own life apparently manifested the burden of his assertions. Contemporaries and historians have both drawn attention to
the way in which personal devotion and love of truth merged har-

---

76. Hodge, "Bushnell on Christian Nurture," *BRPR* 19 (Oct. 1847): 520–
21.

77. Hodge, *The Way of Life,* p. 294.

78. Hodge, "Bushnell on Christian Nurture," *BRPR* 19 (Oct. 1847): 521.

moniously in his life.[79] Hodge's piety made an especially strong impression on his own children. Although he was constantly busy, his study was regularly open to them, and then later to his grandchildren. "If they were sick," wrote A. A. Hodge, "he nursed them. If they were well, he played with them. If he were busy, they played about him." It was the force of Hodge's godliness, however, which created the strongest impression. Again the testimony of his oldest son:

> He prayed for us all at family prayers, and singly, and taught us to pray at his knees with such soul-felt tenderness, that however bad we were our hearts all melted to his touch. During later years he always caused his family to repeat after him at morning worship the Apostles' Creed, and a formula, of his own composition, professing personal consecration to the Father, and to the Son, and to the Holy Ghost. But that which makes those days sacred in the retrospect of his children is the person and character of the father himself as discovered in the privacy of his home, all radiant as that was with love, with unwavering faith, and with unclouded hope.[80]

Hodge's other familiar relations were nearly as intense, and equally suffused with religious feeling. When his wife died in 1845, this was the reaction in his daily record book: "Blesst saint; companion of my boyhood—my first and only love—my most devoted wife—mother of my children—all sacred memories cluster around you; and all who knew you pronounce you blessed. May the God of infinite mercy send the Holy Spirit to take in this family your place, and be the instructor, guide and comforter of your household and bring all your children to a life of devotion to the Lord Jesus.[81] For his older colleague Archibald Alexander and several younger contemporaries, especially Albert Baldwin Dod and Joseph Addison

79. See the repeated testimonies in *Life*, pp. 509–30, 605–11; and the discussion in Hoffecker, *Piety and the Princeton Theologians*, pp. 44–55.
80. *Life*, p. 127.
81. Hoffecker, *Piety and the Princeton Theologians*, p. 53.

Alexander, Hodge displayed a love almost as intense. Something of the same spirit also bound Hodge to many of his Princeton students.

Hodge liked to sing hymns, with others and by himself, and before lameness made it impossible, he would walk up and down in his study singing songs of devotion. These hymns often centered on the person and work of Christ, themes to which Hodge regularly returned when leading his own family in worship. After his death a life-long friend, Henry Boardman of Philadelphia, wrote that "Christ was not only the ground of his hope, but the acknowledged sovereign of his intellect, the soul of his theology, the unfailing spring of his joy, the one all-pervading, all-glorifying theme and end of his life." From Boardman came also a testimony about Hodge's humility, a trait more evident in private life than in his polemical writing. When Boardman once told Hodge he should be a very happy man because of what he had accomplished, Hodge replied: "All that can be said is, that God has been pleased to take up a *poor little stick* and do something with it. What I have done is as nothing compared with what is done by a man who goes to Africa, and labors among a heathen tribe, and reduces their language to writing. I am not worthy to stoop down and *unloose the shoes* of such a man."[82] The personal piety of Charles Hodge, it seems clear, was one of unusual depth.

As an intellectual system, however, it is possible to question whether Hodge's vision was as cohesive as he hoped. W. Andrew Hoffecker, the most thorough student of "Princeton piety," has written of "the hiatus that exists in general between the systematic and devotional writings" of both Alexander and Hodge. Hoffecker's conclusion is that "this disparity . . . is not quite as great as might formerly have been supposed. Nevertheless, one is cognizant of a difference between the formal or didactic way in which theological issues are discussed in the systematic works and some of the passages from the devotional writings which suggest a comparatively greater dependence on the emotive faculty."[83] Hodge's life testifies to the possibility of bringing together intellectualism and voluntarism, Bacon and Augustine. And the substance of his works, if not always

---

82. *Life*, pp. 606, 608n.
83. Hoffecker, *Piety and the Princeton Theologians*, p. 89.

entirely persuasive, at least demonstrates the importance of the effort he made to harmonize a living subjective faith with a stable objective truth.

Whatever we may think about the forcefulness of Hodge's religious vision, it is certain that few Americans have made such a determined effort to combine faithfulness to biblical authority, deference to traditional Protestant conceptions of the faith, and a full commitment to a proper religious experience. The ideal that Hodge proposed remains intriguing, both as a landmark in nineteenth-century religious history and a beacon lighting a path for at least some Christians today.[84]

Hodge presented this ideal in several kinds of work. Several essays in the *Princeton Review* reflected directly on the way a confessional interpretation of the Bible undergirded a lively religious experience. In addition, the same emphasis is found in some of his biblical commentaries, in the sermons presented on Sunday afternoons at Princeton, and even in certain passages from his systematic theology. Selections from the last three kinds of writings are found below. But the fullest and most winsome presentation of Hodge's vision of piety appeared in a separate book, *The Way of Life,* to which we now turn.

---

84. Hodge's effort may also be instructive for traditionalist Jews, Muslims, or members of other faiths who desire to combine vital religion with inherited orthodoxy.

I

THE WAY OF LIFE

Charles Hodge wrote *The Way of Life* as a popular statement of Christian faith for the American Sunday School Union. The Union had been established in 1824 through an amalgamation of local Sunday School societies under the leadership of the Philadelphia Sunday and Adult School Union.[1] Its purposes were to support Sunday instruction of a broadly evangelical type and to distribute literature for Sunday School teachers and the general public. By 1841 the Union had sent out its own missionaries into the countryside to establish centers of Christian instruction, it had held national Sunday School conventions, it had started several periodicals for Sunday School pupils and their teachers, and it had already published thousands of titles, including both inexpensive pamphlets for teachers to distribute to their students and more substantial books of biblical exposition, church history, and devotional writings. Hodge's manuscript was among the weightier Union publications in the 1840s, but it nonetheless was intended as a popular effort to broadcast the Christian message as widely and as simply as possible.

The book's preface set out its aim;

It is one of the clearest principles of divine revelation, that holiness is the fruit of truth; and it is one of the plainest

---

1. On the American Sunday School Union, see *The New Schaff-Herzog Encyclopedia of Religious Knowledge* (reprinted Grand Rapids: Baker, 1950), XI, 157–58.

inferences from that principle, that the exhibition of the truth is the best means of promoting holiness. Christians regard the word of God as the only infallible teacher of those truths which relate to the salvation of men. But are the Scriptures really a revelation from God? If they are, what doctrines do they teach? And what influence should those doctrines exert on our heart and life?[2]

Hodge employed a simple outline to answer these questions. The first chapter examines the authority of the Bible. Both "internal evidence" (i.e., the direct testimony of the Holy Spirit) and "external evidence" (the testimony of Christians through the ages and the record of fulfilled biblical prophecy) show that the Scriptures are an authoritative revelation from God. The heart of the book is Hodge's interpretation of what the Bible teaches about the need for redemption and the means by which God brings it about. This central section presents a Calvinistically shaded, but still generically Protestant understanding of sin, justification, faith, and repentance. The book ends with two matters of practice—a discussion of the "profession of religion" that emphasizes the importance of baptism and the Lord's Supper in nurturing a Christian's faith, and a chapter on "Holy Living" that appeals for Christian growth grounded in "the reading, hearing, and meditating upon the word of God [i.e., Scripture], which is the truth whereby we are sanctified."[3]

The heart of the work was Hodge's presentation of Christian salvation as interpreted from the Scriptures. Preliminary arguments for the authority of the Bible were meant to confirm its message of reconciliation with God. Hodge's own use of scriptural texts illustrates the way he put the Bible to use in explaining the Christian faith. Hodge footnoted 438 separate citations from the Scriptures of which three-fourths were from the New Testament and one-fourth from the Old. In the New Testament Hodge turned first to the book of Romans (sixty-seven citations) and then to the Gospel of John and three other Pauline epistles on which he lectured at the seminary (Galatians, I Corinthians, Ephesians). From the Old Testament he drew most

---

2. Hodge, *The Way of Life*, p. 3.
3. *Ibid.*, p. 336.

from Isaiah and the Psalms. He did not make much use of the historical parts of the Bible (almost no citations from the books of Old Testament history and only a total of fifty-one from the synoptic gospels and Acts). Clearly for Hodge the didactic portions of Scripture marked out "the way of life." This, however, is not the full story of Hodge's use of the Bible, for many of his own phrases are but loose paraphrases of scriptural material for which he offers no citation.

When Hodge showed the manuscript of the book to Archibald Alexander, Alexander expressed heart-felt approval. At the same time he wondered whether the American Sunday School Union, which by its nature had to serve a broad range of denominations, would tolerate Hodge's emphasis on the imputation of Christ's righteousness, a theme about which influential theologians in New England were expressing their doubts. Alexander also offered practical advice: Hodge should break up the book's chapters into shorter sections, since even Alexander found "that in my own reading I am often turning to see how many pages remain before the termination of the chapter."[4] This was a suggestion that Hodge followed in revising the manuscript for the Sunday School Union.

In spite of Alexander's doubts, the publication committee of the Union, meeting on July 5, 1841, heartily approved the book and ordered that it be published.[5] The committee did have one problem, but it concerned only the title. Hodge had proposed, "The Narrow Way," but members of the committee did not think that was adequate. At its August 30 meeting the committee "agreed to submit to the author the following title for the new book—'The Path of Peace,' " and someone else suggested "Scripture Truth Illustrated by Christian Experience" at that same meeting. In September the committee was still worrying the question, but its minutes for October record the assignment of "The Way of Life" to the book, al-

---

4. Alexander to Hodge, May 11, 1841, in *Life*, p. 327.

5. Materials on the deliberations of the committee are from "Publications Committee Records, 1821–1915," entries for July 5, August 9, August 30, September 13, October 11, and November 2, 1841, and January 18, March 8, and June 27, 1842; as provided in Reel 223 of the microfilm edition of the American Sunday School Union's papers on deposit in the Presbyterian Historical Society, Philadelphia.

though it is not clear from these records whether the committee or Hodge came up with this felicitous suggestion.

Hodge was paid $250 for the copyright, a sum augmented by the £50 received from the London Religious Tract Society for the privilege of reprinting the book in England. In a commentary on how rapidly works could move from manuscript to print in the days before "time-saving" mechanization, the committee made its final decisions on the book in October and the book was out before the end of the year.

It was offered for sale in the Sunday School Union's 1842 catalogue along with the twelve other new "Library Books" it published in 1841.[6] The book cost seventy-five cents in a regular edition, or eighty-seven and one-half cents in an edition with extra muslin. It achieved almost immediate popularity, as testified by its rapid reprinting in England, and by favorable reviews at home. The *Boston Recorder* wrote, "We doubt whether any book of our day can be named which promises a greater amount of immediate and even enduring good to Zion than this. . . . It is heart-searching, enlightening, stimulating and strengthening to faith and every other Christian virtue." And other journals praised it as well.[7]

By 1843 the book was being offered in three editions: "cheap" for thirty-five cents, in an edition featuring "large sized type with beautiful engraved vignette and title page . . . muslin" for fifty cents, and the same "in Turkey morocco, extra gift" for $1.50.[8] By the early 1880s the Sunday School Union had sold 35,000 copies, and it had been translated into Hindustani and Spanish.[9]

---

6. *Catalogue of Books and Other Publications of the American Sunday School Union* (22nd ed.; Philadelphia: General Depository, 1842), p. 2 (Reel 233 in microfilm edition).

7. Quotation from the 1843 Catalogue. Favorable reviews from other journals are recorded in *Life,* p. 326. See also the recommendations in *The American Biblical Repository* 8 (1842): 489; and *American Quarterly Register* 14 (May 1842): 419.

8. 1843 Catalogue of the American Sunday School Union (Reel 233). By 1863 the same three editions were selling for $0.60, 0.90, and 2.00.

9. *Life,* p. 325. The book's translation as *El Camino de la Vida* (New York: American Tract Society, 1883) was made by J. Milton Green, Princeton Seminary class of 1868. As late as 1970 a second, revised edition of a Chinese translation was issued in Taipei by the Reformation Translation Fellowship as *Sheng-ming chi tao.*

The Way of Life solidified Hodge's reputation as a practical theologian. His admirers in the twentieth century continue to look upon it as one of his most important works. The Scottish Presbyterian, John Murray, who taught for long years at Westminster Seminary in Philadelphia, called it "from one viewpoint . . . a masterpiece, a work not so well known in many circles but one that, above all else, meets the need of the lay reader."[10] In his own day, Hodge on more than one occasion was reproved for failing in other works to match the irenic simplicity of this work. During his great debate on "The Theology of the Intellect and That of the Feelings," for instance, E. A. Park upbraided Hodge the polemicist for abandoning the consistency and the winsomeness found in *The Way of Life*. When Hodge's *Systematic Theology* appeared, *The Baptist Quarterly* averred that "the 'Way of Life' is better than the 'Systematic Theology' " on the question of baptism.[11]

Since 1841 *The Way of Life* has enjoyed a wide circulation. While never wildly popular, it has been kept in print steadily.[12] The book's straightforward style, its clear form, and its combination of assertion and devotion make it Hodge's most well-rounded depiction of the spiritual life. These same qualities, however, also appeared in other things that Hodge wrote. To illustrate the range of such work, three selections from other works are introduced and presented below, following *The Way of Life*. The text of *The Way of Life* which follows is the complete work published in 1841 by the American Sunday School Union in Philadelphia.

PREFACE

It is one of the clearest principles of divine revelation, that holiness is the fruit of truth; and it is one of the plainest inferences from that principle, that the exhibition of the truth is the best means of

---

10. Murray, "Foreword" to Charles Hodge, *Princeton Sermons* (London: Banner of Truth, 1985), p. v.

11. Park, "New England Theology," *Bibliotheca Sacra* 9 (Jan. 1852): 215n; review of *Systematic Theology* in *The Baptist Quarterly* 7 (1873): 125.

12. Most recently it was published by Baker Book House (Grand Rapids, 1977) and the Banner of Truth Trust (London, 1959).

promoting holiness. Christians regard the word of God as the only infallible teacher of those truths which relate to the salvation of men. But are the Scriptures really a revelation from God? If they are, what doctrines do they teach? And what influence should those doctrines exert on our heart and life?

The publishing committee of the American Sunday-school Union have long felt the want of a book which should give a plain answer to those questions, and be suitable to place in the hands of intelligent and educated young persons, either to arouse their attention, or to guide their steps in the WAY OF LIFE.

The following work has been prepared at the request of the committee, with the hope that it may in some measure answer the purpose just stated. In a Christian country it might seem unneccessary to raise the question whether the Scriptures are the word of God? But those who have had much intercourse with young men, know that even among those who have been religiously educated, there is more or less skepticism upon this point; and where there is no absolute skepticism, there is often an impression that the evidence of the divine origin of the Bible is not so decisive as it might, or even should be. Hence it is that the want of faith is seldom felt to be a great sin. It was therefore deemed important that the question, Why we are bound to believe the Bible to be the word of God? should be distinctly, though briefly, answered.

The still more comprehensive question, What do the Scriptures teach? is of course here considered only in reference to those great practical doctrines which are essential to evangelical religion, viz.: the doctrines of sin, justification, faith, repentance, and holy living.

With regard to the influence which these doctrines should exert upon the heart and life, or, in other words, with regard to religious experience, reference might be made to the numerous records of the exercises of the people of God, or to what we see daily in his church. As, however, the Scriptures themselves not only teach us what the truth is, but also how it operates upon an enlightened conscience and believing heart, our safest appeal is to them. It is there that we can best learn how we ought to feel and act in view of what the Bible teaches us of sin, of justification, faith, and repentance; since genuine religious experience is simply the accordance of our views and feelings with the truth of God.

If this little book should be instrumental, by the simple exhibition of the truth, of pointing out the WAY OF LIFE to those who are anxious to know what they must believe and what they must experience in order to be saved, it will answer the design of its preparation and publication.

CONTENTS

THE WAY OF LIFE.

Chapter I.

The Scriptures are the Word of God.

SECTION I. *The Internal evidence of the divine origin of the
Scriptures.*

It often happens that those who hear the gospel, doubt whether
it is really the word of God. Having been taught from infancy to regard it as a divine revelation, and knowing no sufficient reason for
rejecting it, they yield a general assent to its claims. There are times,
however, when they would gladly be more fully assured that the Bi-

ble is not a cunningly devised fable. They think if that point was absolutely certain, they would at once submit to all the gospel requires.

Such doubts do not arise from any deficiency in the evidence of the divine authority of the Scriptures; nor would they be removed by any increase of that evidence. They have their origin in the state of the heart. The most important of all the evidences of Christianity, can never be properly appreciated unless the heart be right in the sight of God. The same exhibition of truth which produces unwavering conviction in one mind, leaves another in a state of doubt or unbelief. And the same mind often passes rapidly, though rationally, from a state of scepticism to that of faith, without any change in the mere external evidence presented to it.

No amount of mere external evidence can produce genuine faith. The Israelites, who had seen a long succession of wonders in the land of Egypt; who had passed through the divided waters of the Red Sea; who were daily receiving by miracle food from heaven; who had trembled at the manifestations of the divine majesty on Mount Sinai; within sight of that mountain, made a golden calf their God. The men, who saw the miracles of Christ performed almost daily in their presence, cried out, Crucify him, crucify him. Hence our Saviour said, that those who hear not Moses and the prophets would not be persuaded though one rose from the dead. We may confidently conclude, therefore, that those who now believe not the gospel, would not be persuaded had they seen all the miracles which Christ performed.

It is important that the attention of the doubting should be directed to the fact that their want of faith is to be attributed to their own moral state, and not to any deficiency in the evidence of the truth. If our gospel be hid, says the apostle, it is hid to them that are lost; in whom the god of this world hath blinded the minds of them that believe not, lest the light of the glorious gospel of Christ, should shine unto them.

There is nothing in the doctrine here stated, out of analogy with our daily experience. No truth can be properly apprehended unless there is a harmony between it and the mind to which it is presented. Even abstract or speculative truths are not seen to be true, unless the understanding be duly cultivated to apprehend them. With regard to objects of taste, unless there is a power to perceive the correspondence between them and the standard of beauty, there can be no appreciation of their excellence. And still more obviously in regard to moral and religious truth, there must be a state of mind suited to their apprehension. If our moral sense were entirely destroyed by sin, we could have no perception of moral distinctions; if it is vitiated, what is true in itself and true in the view of the pure in heart, will not be true to us. A man, who has no adequate sense of the evil of sin, cannot believe in the justice of God. If you awaken his conscience, he is convinced at once, without the intervention of any process of proof.

No one can fail to remark that the Bible demands immediate and implicit faith from all who read it. It may lie neglected in the study of the philosopher, or in the chest of the outcast sailor; or it may be given by a missionary yet ignorant of the language of the heathen to whom he ministers. The moment, however, it is opened, in these or any other circumstances, it utters the same calm voice, He that believeth on the Son hath everlasting life; he that believeth not the Son shall not see life, but the wrath of God abideth on him. If this demand was confined to the educated, we might suppose it to rest on evidence which the educated only are able to appreciate; or if it was made of those only to whom the scriptures are presented by regularly commissioned ministers, we might suppose it rested on their authority; but it is not thus confined. It is inseparable from the word itself. It is as imperative when the Bible is read by a child to a company of pagans, as when it is proclaimed in a cathedral. But if this demand of faith goes with the word wherever it goes, it must rest upon evidence contained in the word itself. The demand of faith cannot be more extensive, than the exhibition of evidence. Unless, therefore, we restrict the obligation and the benefits of faith to those who are capable of appreciating the external evidence of the Bible, we must admit that it contains its own evidence.

To make the testimony of others to the truth of Christianity, the ground of faith, is inadmissible for two obvious reasons. In the first place, as already intimated, it is not sufficiently extensive. The obligation to believe rests on multitudes to whom that testimony is not addressed. In the second place, it is entirely inadequate. The great mass of men cannot be required to believe on the testimony of the learned few, a religion which is to control their conduct in this world and to decide their destiny in the next. Besides, learned men testify in behalf of the Koran as well as in favour of the Bible. That, therefore, cannot be an adequate ground of faith, which may be urged in support of error as well as of truth. To require the common people to be able to see why the testimony of learned Christians may safely be relied upon, while that of learned Mussulmans should be rejected, is to require of them a task as severe as the examination of the historical evidences of Christianity. There is, therefore, no way of justifying the universal, immediate and authoritative demand, which the Bible makes on our faith, except by admitting that it contains within itself the proofs of its divine origin.

It may not be easy, or perhaps possible, to give any adequate exhibition of the nature of this proof to those who profess not to see it. Enough however may be said to show that it is a rational and adequate ground for implicit confidence. Every work bears the impress of its maker. Even among men it is hard for one man successfully to counterfeit the work of another. Is it wonderful then that the works of God should bear the inimitable impress of their author? Do not the heavens declare his glory? Does not the mechanism of an insect as clearly evince the workmanship of God! Why then should it be deemed incredible that his word should contain inherent evidence of its divine origin? If the Bible be the work of God, it must contain the impress of his character, and thereby evince itself to be divine.

It may be objected that we are not competent to judge of this evidence. If it requires so much cultivation of the intellect to judge of the excellence of human productions, and so accurate an acquaintance with the character of their authors, in order to decide on the genuineness of such productions, who can pretend to a knowledge of God which shall enable him to judge what is, or what is not worthy of his hand? This would be a fatal objection if the internal evidence of the scriptures consisted in their intellectual excellence. It loses its force however when it is remembered that this excellence is, in a great measure, moral, and that goodness carries with it its own evidence. To appreciate evidence of this kind requires no great degree of knowledge or refinement. It requires merely right moral feelings. Where these exist, the evidence that goodness is goodness is immediate and irresistible. It is not because the Bible is written with more than human skill, and that its discrimination of character or its eloquence is beyond the powers of man, that we believe it to be divine. These are matters of which the mass of men are incompetent judges. The evidence in question is suited to the apprehension of the humblest child of God. It is partly negative and partly positive. It consists, in the first place, in the absence of every thing incompatible with a divine origin. There is nothing inconsistent with reason, and there is nothing inconsistent with goodness. Did the scriptures contain any thing contrary to reason or to right moral feeling, belief in its divine origin would be impossible. Such a belief would involve the ascription of folly or sin to its author. There is more in this negative evidence than we are apt to imagine. It can not be urged in behalf of any other book but the Bible, claiming a divine origin. An impassible gulf is thus placed between the scriptures and all apocryphal writings. The claims of the latter are in every instance disproved by the fact that they contain statements which cannot be true.

It is however the positive internal evidence of a divine origin, which gives power and authority to the claims of the Bible. This evidence consists mainly in its perfect holiness, in the correspondence between all its statements respecting God, man, redemption and a future state, and all our own right judgments, reasonable apprehensions and personal experience. When the mind is enlightened to see this holiness; when it perceives how exactly the rule of duty prescribed in the word of God agrees with that enforced by conscience; how the account which it gives of human nature coincides with human experience; how fully it meets our whole case; when it feels how powerfully the truths there presented operate to purify, console and sustain the soul, the belief of the scriptures is a necessary consequence. The idea that such a book is a lie and a forgery involves a contradiction. The human mind is so constituted that it cannot refuse to assent to evidence, when clearly perceived. We cannot withhold our confidence from a man whose moral excellence is plainly, variously and constantly manifested. We cannot see and feel his goodness, and yet believe him to be an imposter or deceiver. In like manner, we cannot see the excellence of the scriptures, and yet believe them to be one enormous falsehood. The Bible claims to be the word of God; it speaks in his name, it assumes his authority. How can these claims be false and yet the Bible be so Holy? How can falsehood be an element of perfect excellence? The only possible way of shaking our confidence in the competent testimony of a man, is to show that he is not a good man. If his goodness is admitted, confidence in his word cannot be withheld, and especially when all he says finds its confirmation in our own experience, and commends itself to our conscience and judgment. Thus also it is impossible that we should discern the excellence of the scriptures and feel their correspondence with our experience and necessities, and yet suppose them to be untrue.

When the woman of Samaria reported to her townsmen that Jesus had told her all that ever she did, many of them believed. But after they had themselves listened to his instructions, they said to the woman, Now we believe, not because of thy saying, for we have heard him ourselves, and know that this is indeed the Christ, the Saviour of the world.[1] No Christian can be surprised at this declaration, or think the faith in Christ founded upon what he said, either irrational or enthusiastic. We can well believe that there was such an ineffable manifestation of goodness in the Redeemer's countenance, manner and doctrines, as to conciliate entire confidence. Those who were rightly affected could not fail to believe all he said; that he was the Christ, that he came to seek and save them that are lost, to lay down his life for his sheep and to give himself a ransom for many. Can we doubt that the goodness of the Saviour, the elevation, holiness and power of his instructions, their correspondence with our own nature, experience and wants, would of themselves constitute an adequate ground of faith? All this we have. This every man has, who reads the Bible. There the Saviour stands in the majesty of unapproachable excellence. He utters in every hearing ear the words of eternal life; declares his origin, his mission, the design of his advent and death; offers pardon and eternal life to those who come unto God through him. There is the most perfect accordance between his claims and his conduct; between his doctrines and what we know and what we need. To disbelieve him, is to believe him to be a deceiver, and to believe this, is to disbelieve our own perceptions; for we know what goodness is, and we know that goodness cannot deceive, that God cannot lie.

It makes very little difference as to the force of this kind of evidence, whether we personally saw and heard the Saviour for ourselves, or whether we read the exhibition of his character and the record of his instructions. For the evidence lies in his goodness and

---

1. John iv: 42.

in the nature of his doctrines. It is the same to us who read the Bible, as it was to those that heard the Saviour. There is therefore the same violence done to reason and duty in our rejecting it, as was offered by those who believed not because they were not of his sheep, that is, because they were insensible to the constraining influence of the grace and truth which were in Him. Does any one ask, how we know that the Bible is not a forgery? Let him consider what such an assumption involves. It supposes either that the authors of the Bible were fools, which we can no more believe than that Newton was an idiot; or that they were wicked, which no man can believe who knows what goodness is. Wherever, therefore, the Bible goes, it carries with it evidence, that is irresistible (when attended to and appreciated,) that its authors were neither dupes nor deceivers.

It may be asked, If the Bible contains such clear evidence of its divine origin, why are there so many unbelievers? To this it may be answered, that there are two things necessary in order that evidence should produce conviction. The first is that it should be attended to; otherwise it might as well not exist. Of the many millions of people in Christendom, comparatively few give the Scriptures any serious attention. That such persons should have no effective faith, is no more a matter of surprise than that they should be ignorant of what they never learned. The second requisite for the reception of evidence, is that it should be understood or really apprehended. If this evidence is addressed to the understanding, there must be strength of mind enough to comprehend its nature and bearing; if addressed to the moral faculty, there must be moral sensibility to appreciate it, or it will be like light shining on the eyes of the blind. The internal evidence of the scriptures is in a great measure of this latter kind. It consists in their perfect holiness. In proportion as men are corrupt, they are blind to this kind of evidence. It may exist in all its force, and men be insensible to it. Another part of this evidence consists in the accordance between the scriptures and the religious experience of men. Those who have not the experience, cannot see this accordance. Still another portion of the evidence is made available by the power of God in subduing sin, in purifying the affections, in diffusing peace and joy through the heart. Those who have never felt this power cannot appreciate this kind of proof. The fact, therefore, that so large a proportion of mankind have no adequate faith in the Scriptures, affords no presumption against the existence of sufficient evidence. This fact is in exact accordance with what the Bible teaches of the moral state of man.

Another objection to the view of the ground of faith given above, is that it leads to enthusiasm, and breaks down the distinction between true and false religion. Every enthusiast, it is said, thinks he sees wonderful excellence in the pretended revelations which he embraces. It is a sufficient answer to this objection to ask, whether the scholar has less faith in the excellence of the great standards of poetry, because the writers of doggrel rhymes have had their admirers? That the sensual, selfish and cruel character of Mohammed appears good in the eyes of a Turk, does not prove him to be an enthusiast who bows with reverence before the supreme excellence of Jesus Christ? That the pagan world saw evidence of the existence of their gods in the heavens and in the course of nature, does not make him an enthusiast, who recognizes in the works of God the manifestations of infinite power, wisdom and goodness. It is most unreasonable to assume that we must not feel the force of truth and excellence, because others have ascribed these attributes to error and vice. It is not according to the constitution of our nature that one man should cease to know a thing to be true or good, because others do not see it. The evidence is complete for him, though all the world reject it.

If it is asked, where the standard is? What criterion of excellence exists by which I am authorized to decide that what I call goodness is really such? The rule is given in the nature of man. We know that benevolence is better than malice, veracity than deceit, humility than pride, and by the same rule we know that Christianity is better than Hindooism, and the blessed Redeemer than the Arabian impostor. No judgment can be more sure than this, no persuasion more intimate, no confidence either more firm or more rational. It is, therefore, no objection against admitting the excellence of the Scriptures to be a proof of their divine origin, that besotted or deluded men have ascribed excellence to folly and wickedness.

SECTION II. *The internal evidence of their divine origin is the proper ground of faith in the Scriptures.*

The Scriptures themselves clearly teach that the faith which they demand is founded upon the authority of God, manifesting itself in them by the excellence and power of the truth which they contain. They everywhere represent faith as the effect and evidence of right moral feeling, and unbelief as the result of moral or spiritual blindness. Our Saviour said to the Jews, If any man will do his will, he shall know of the doctrine whether it be of God.[2] Again, He that is of God, heareth God's words; ye therefore hear them not because ye are not of God.[3] On another occasion he said, Ye believe not, because ye are not of my sheep; my sheep hear my voice.[4] The apostle speaks to the same effect, Hereby know ye the Spirit of God. Every spirit that confesseth that Jesus Christ is come in the flesh, is of God. We are of God. He that knoweth God heareth us; he that is not of God heareth not us. Hereby ye know the spirit of truth and the spirit of error.[5] In like manner Paul says, The natural man receiveth not the things of the Spirit of God; for they are foolishness unto him, neither can he know them because they are spiritually discerned.[6] And again, If our gospel be hid, it is hid to them that are lost; in whom the god of this world hath blinded the eyes of them that believe not, lest the light of the glorious gospel of Christ, who is the image of God, should shine unto them. But God, who commanded the light to shine out of darkness, hath shined in our hearts to give the light of the knowledge of the glory of God in the face of Jesus Christ.[7] The doctrine taught in these and similar passages, is that there is in the word of God and especially in the person and character of Jesus Christ, a clear and wonderful manifestation of the divine glory. To this manifestation the natural man is blind, and therefore does not believe, but those who have the Spirit of God discern this glory and therefore believe.

It is in accordance with this view that unbelief is represented as so grave a moral offence, and faith as so important a duty. Atheism is every where regarded as a crime, because the evidences of the existence of God are everywhere present, above us, around us and within us. They are addressed to the moral constitution, as well as

---

2. John vii. 17.
3. John viii. 47.
4. John x. 26, 27.
5. 1 John iv. 2, 3.
6. 1 Cor. ii. 14.
7. 2 Cor. iv. 3–6.

to the speculative understanding. They cannot be resisted without the same violence to moral obligations or the authority of moral considerations, that is involved in calling virtue vice, and vice virtue. Hence the Scriptures always speak of unbelief as a sin against God, and the special ground of the condemnation of the world. He that believeth on him is not condemned, but he that believeth not is condemned already, because he believeth not on the only begotten Son of God.[8] Who is a liar, but he that denieth that Jesus is the Christ? He is anti-Christ, that denieth the Father and the Son. Whosoever denieth the Son, the same hath not the Father.[9] Disbelief of the Son as revealed in the Scriptures, is an offence of the same nature as the denial of God. In both cases supreme excellence is revealed and disregarded. Much to the same effect the Saviour says, He that hateth me, hateth my Father also.[10] On the other hand, faith is represented as the highest act of obedience, as a moral act of the greatest worth in the sight of God. Whosoever believes that Jesus is the Christ is born of God.[11] As many as received him, to them gave he power to become the sons of God, even to as many as believed on his name.[12] And our Saviour told the enquiring Jews, This is the work of God, that ye believe on him that he hath sent.[13] These representations cannot be reconciled with the assumption that faith is founded on external testimony, which does not address itself to our moral nature, and an assent to which has so little concern with moral character. All is plain, however, if we are required to believe in the Son because his glory as of the only begotten of the Father is presented to us; and to receive the Scriptures because they bear the impress of the divine perfections. If this be the ground of faith, unbelief is indeed a crime. It is a refusal to recognise wisdom and holiness, and to acknowledge the manifested excellence of God.

This view of the ground of faith is confirmed by the effects ascribed to that grace. It works by love, it purifies the heart, it overcomes the world, it produces peace and joy. It is indeed conceivable

---

8. John iii. 18.
9. 1 John ii. 22, 23.
10. John xv. 23.
11. 1 John v. 1.
12. John i. 12.
13. John vi. 29.

that the conviction of truths affecting our interests, however produced, should call forth fear, sorrow or joy according to their nature.
But it is not conceivable that belief of moral or religious truths,
founded upon the testimony of others, should control our affections.
A man may believe on authority, or on merely rational grounds, that
we are under a moral government, and that the law by which we are
bound is holy, just and good, but such a faith will not subdue his
opposition. He may be, by argument or miracle, convinced of the
existence of God, but such a faith will not produce love. Faith therefore cannot have the effects ascribed to it, unless it is founded on a
spiritual apprehension of the truths believed.

Hence it is that faith is represented as the gift of God. The evidence indeed is presented to all, or there would be no obligation to
believe; but men are morally blind, and therefore the eyes of their
understanding must be opened that they may understand the things
which are freely given to them of God. The apostle therefore says to
his believing brethren, Ye have an unction from the Holy One, and
ye know all things, I have not written unto you, because ye know
not the truth, but because ye know it, and that no lie is of the truth.
The anointing which ye have received abideth with you, and ye need
not that any man teach you: but as the same anointing teacheth you
of all things, and is truth, and no lie, and even as it hath taught you,
ye shall abide in him.[14] It is here taught, as in other passages already
quoted, that believers are the recipients of an influence, an unction,
from the Holy One, which convinces them of the truth, makes them
see and know that it is truth. Hence Paul says, his preaching was not
with the enticing words of man's wisdom, but in the demonstration
of the Spirit and of power; that the faith of his hearers might not stand
in the wisdom of men, but in the power of God. That is, that their
faith might not be the effect of skillful reasoning, but of the spiritual
perception and experience of the truth.

All this is confirmed by the constant practice of the inspired
teachers. Though they appealed to all kinds of evidence in support
of the doctrines which they taught, to signs and wonders, and divers
miracles and gifts of the Holy Ghost, yet they by no means rested
the obligation to believe either exclusively or mainly upon these ex-

---

14. 1 John ii. 20, 21, 27.

ternal signs. In many cases faith was demanded by those inspired men, who never wrought miracles of any kind, as was the fact in the case of some of the prophets; and still more frequently it was required of those among whom no such wonders had been performed. When the Jews demanded a sign and the Greeks wisdom, the apostles preached Christ, and him crucified, as the wisdom of God and the power of God unto salvation. Their constant endeavour was by the manifestation of the truth to commend themselves to every man's conscience in the sight of God. And if their gospel was hid, it was hid to them that are lost.

It is, therefore, plainly the doctrine of the scriptures themselves, that the word of God is to be believed because of the authority or command of God manifesting itself therein, in a manner analogous to the exhibition of his perfections in the works of nature. If, as Paul teaches us, the eternal power and godhead are so clearly manifested by the things that are made, that even the heathen are without excuse; and if their unbelief is ascribed not to the want of evidence, but to their liking to retain God in their knowledge; we need not wonder that the far clearer manifestation of the divine perfections made in the scripture, should be the ground of a more imperative commmand to believe.

It is the experience of true Christians in all ages and nations that their faith is founded on the spiritual apprehension and experience of the power of truth. There are multitudes of such Christians, who, if asked why they believe the scriptures to be the word of God, might find it difficult to give an answer, whose faith is nevertheless both strong and rational. They are conscious of its grounds though they may not be able to state them. They have the witness in themselves, and know that they believe, not because others believe, or because learned men have proved certain facts which establish the truth of Christianity. They believe in Christ for the same reason that they believe in God; and they believe in God because they see his glory and feel his authority and power.

If then the truth of God contains in its own nature a revelation of divine excellence, the sin of unbelief is a very great sin. Not to have faith in God, when clearly revealed, is the highest offence which a creature can commit against its creator. To refuse credence to the testimony of God, when conveyed in the manner best adapted to our nature, is to renounce our allegiance to our creator. To disregard the evidence of truth and excellence in Jesus Christ, is the highest indignity that we can show to truth and excellence. This sin is common, and therefore is commonly disregarded. Men do not easily see the turpitude of evils with which they are themselves chargeable. The faults of those who go beyond them in iniquity they are quick to discern. And therefore the man who feels no compunction at want of faith in the Son of God, will abhor him who pronounces the Redeemer a wicked imposter. He will wait for no explanation and will listen to no excuse. The mere fact that a man, acquainted with the Scriptures, is capable of such a judgment respecting the Son of God, is proof of depravity which nothing can gainsay. Yet how little difference is there between the state of mind which would admit of such a judgment, and the state in which those are who have no faith in the declarations of Christ; who disregard his promises and warnings; who do not feel them to be true, and therefore treat them as fables. The want of faith therefore of which men think so lightly, will be found the most unreasonable and perhaps the most aggravated of all their sins. It implies an insensibility to the highest kind of evidence, and involves the rejection of the greatest gift which God has ever offered to man, pardon, holiness, and eternal life.

SECTION III.   *External evidence of the divine origin of the Scriptures. The Testimony of the Church.*

As God has left the heathen to the unauthenticated revelation of himself in his works, and holds them responsible for their unbelief, so he might have left us to the simple revelation of himself in his word. He has been pleased, however, to confirm that word by external proofs of the most convincing character, so that we are entirely without excuse.

The testimony of the church is of itself an unanswerable argument for the truth of Christianity. The validity of this testimony does not depend upon the assumed infallibility of any class of men. It is merely the testimony of an innumerable body of witnesses, under circumstances which preclude the idea of delusion nor deception. For the sake of illustration take any particular branch of Christ's church, as for example the Lutheran. It now exists in Europe and America. It every where possesses the same version of the Scriptures, and the same confession of faith. Its testimony is, that it owes its existence as an organized body, to Luther; to whom it ascribes the translation of the Bible, and under whose auspices it professes to have received the Augsburg Confession. It is clearly impossible that these documents could, during the present century, have been palmed upon these scattered millions of men. They all bear testimony that they received them as they now are from the hands of their fathers. As to this point, neither delusion or deception is conceivable. In the eighteenth century we find this church scarcely less numerous than it is at present. It bore the same testimony then, that it does now. With one voice it declared that their fathers possessed before them the standards of their faith. This testimony is repeated again in the seventeenth, and again in the sixteenth century, till we come to the age of Luther. This testimony, conclusive in itself, is confirmed by all kinds of collateral evidence. Every thing in the style, doctrines and historical references of the standards of the Lutheran church, agrees with the age to which they are referred. The influence of a society holding those doctrines is traceable through the whole of the intervening period. The wars, the treaties, the literary and religious institutions of the period, to a greater or less degree, received their character from that Society. Much therefore as men may differ as to Luther's character, as to the wisdom of his conduct or the truth of his doctrines, no sane man has ever questioned the fact that he lived, that he translated the Scriptures, that he organized a new church, and gave his followers the Augsburg confession.

The same series of remarks might be made in reference to the church of England. That extended and powerful body has her thirty-nine articles, her liturgy, and her homilies, which she testifies she received from the Reformers. This testimony cannot be doubted. At no period of her history could that church either deceive or have been deceived, as to that point. Her testimony moreover is confirmed by all collateral circumstances. The liturgy, articles and homilies are in every respect consistent with their reputed origin; and the whole history of England during that period is interwoven with the history of that church. The consequence is, no man doubts that the English reformers lived, or that they framed the standards of doctrine and worship universally ascribed to them.

This argument when applied to the whole Christian church is no less conclusive. This church now exists in every quarter of the globe, and embraces many millions of disciples. Every where it has the same records of its faith; it is every where an organized society with religious officers and ordinances. It every where testifies that these records and institutions were received from Christ and his apostles. That this vast society did not begin to exist during the present century, is as evident as that the world was not just made. It is no less plain that it did not begin to exist in the eighteenth, the seventeenth, the sixteenth, nor in any other century subsequent to the first in our era. In each succeeding century, we find millions of men, thousands of churches and ministers uniting their testimony to the fact that they received their sacred writings and institutions from their predecessors, until we come to the age of Christ himself. Did the origin of the church run back beyond the limits of authentic history, so as to leave a gap between its reputed founder and its ascertained existence, this argument would fail; an essential link would be wanting, and the whole extended chain would fall to the ground. But as this is not the case, its testimony as to the historical facts of its origin, is as irresistible as that of the church of England as to the origin of its articles and liturgy. The Christian church is traced up to the time of Christ by a mass of evidence which cannot be resisted; so that to deny that Christ lived, and that the church received from his followers the sacred writings, is not merely to reject the testimony of thousands of competent witnesses, but to deny facts which are essential to account for the subsequent history and the existing state of the world. A man might as well profess to believe in the foliage of a tree, but not in its branches and stem.

This testimony of the church as to the facts on which Christianity is founded, is confirmed by all kinds of collateral evidence. The language in which the New Testament is written is precisely that which belonged to the time and place of its origin. It is the language of Jews speaking Greek, and in its peculiarities belonged to no other age or people. All the historical allusions are consistent with the known state of the world at that time. The history of the world since the advent of Christ pre-supposes the facts recorded in the New Testament. It is beyond a doubt that the religion taught by a few poor men in Judea, has changed the state of a large part of the world. Paganism has disappeared, a new religion been introduced; laws, customs, institutions and manners become prevalent, and they all rest upon the facts to which the church bears her testimony.

Beyond all this, the internal character of the scriptures is worthy of the origin ascribed to them; a character which gives the only adequate solution of the revolution which they have effected. When God said, Let there be light, there was light. And when Jesus Christ said, I am the light of the world, the light shone. We cannot doubt that it is light; neither can we doubt when it arose, for all before was darkness.

This testimony of the church, thus confirmed by all internal and external proofs, establishes the fact that Christ lived and died, that he founded the Christian church, and that the New Testament was received from his immediate followers. But these facts involve the truth of the gospel as a revelation from God, unless we suppose that Christ and his apostles were deceivers. The evidence against this latter assumption is as strong as the evidence of the existence of the sun. The blind, if they please, may deny that the sun exists, and none but the morally blind can resist the evidence which the New Testament affords of the moral excellence and intellectual sobriety of the sacred writers. If they were trustworthy men, men who we are to believe spoke the truth, then they actually possessed and exercised the miraculous power to which they laid claim. To these powers Christ and his apostles appealed as an unanswerable proof of their divine mission; and we cannot reject their testimony without denying their integrity.

SECTION IV. *The argument from Prophecy.*

The same course of argument which proves that the version of the scriptures and the Augsburg confession in the possession of the Lutheran church; that the articles, liturgy and homilies in the possession of the church of England; that the New Testament in the possession of the whole Christian world, were derived from the sources to which they are severally referred, proves with equal force that the writings of the Old Testament in the possession of the Jews are the productions of the ancient prophets. Jews and Christians now have them. They had them a century ago; they had them in the time of Christ. They were then universally acknowledged by the Israelites in Judea and elsewhere. They can be historically traced up centuries before the advent of Christ. Three hundred years before that event, they were translated into the Greek language and widely disseminated. They contain the history, laws, and literature of the people of

Judea, whose existence and peculiarities are as well ascertained as those of any people in the world. These writings are essential to account for the known character of that people, for it was in virtue of these sacred books they were what they were. Critics have indeed disputed about the particular dates of some of these productions, but no one has had the hardihood to deny that they existed centuries before the birth of Christ. This being admitted, we have a basis for another argument for the truth of Christianity, which cannot be resisted.

In these ancient writings, preserved in the hands of the open enemies of Christ, we find the advent of a deliverer clearly predicted. Immediately after the apostacy, it was foretold that the seed of the woman should bruise the serpent's head. This prediction is the germ of all the subsequent prophecies, which do but reveal its manifold meaning. Who the promised seed was to be, and how the power of evil was by him to be destroyed, later predictions gradually revealed. It was first made known that the Redeemer should belong to the race of Shem.[15] Then that he should be of the seed of Abraham, to whom the promise was made; In thee shall all the nations of the earth be blessed;[16] then that he should be of the tribe of Judah of whom it was foretold that, The sceptre shall not depart from Judah, or a law-giver from between his feet, until Shiloh come, and to him shall be the gathering of the people.[17] Subsequently it was revealed that he was to be of the lineage of David; There shall come forth a rod out of the stem of Jesse, and a branch shall grow out of his roots, and the Spirit of the Lord shall rest upon him, the spirit of wisdom and understanding, the spirit of knowledge and the fear of the Lord.[18]

It was foretold that his advent should be preceded by that of a special messenger. Behold I send my messenger, and he shall prepare the way before me; and the Lord whom ye seek shall suddenly come to his temple, even the messenger of the covenant whom ye delight in, behold he shall come saith the Lord of Hosts.[19] The time,

---

15. Gen. ix.26.
16. Gen. xviii. 18.
17. Gen. xlix. 10.
18. Is. xi. 1, 2.
19. Mal. iii. 1.

the manner, and the place of his birth were all predicted. As to the time, Daniel said, Know therefore and understand that from the going forth of the commandment to build and restore Jerusalem unto Messiah the prince, shall be seven weeks and three score and two weeks.[20] As to the miraculous manner of his birth, Isaiah said, Behold, a virgin shall conceive and bear a son, and shall call his name Immanuel.[21] As to the place, Micah said, But thou Bethlehem Ephratah though thou be little among the thousands of Judah, yet out of thee shall come forth unto me that is to be ruler in Israel.[22]

This deliverer was to be a poor man. Behold, O daughter of Zion, thy king cometh unto thee, poor, riding upon an ass and a colt foal of an ass.[23] He was to be a man of sorrows and acquainted with grief, despised and rejected of men,[24] and yet Immanuel, God with us,[25] Jehovah our righteousness,[26] Wonderful, Counsellor, The Mighty God, The everlasting Father, The Prince of Peace,[27] whose goings forth were of old, from the days of eternity.[28]

The Redeemer thus predicted was to appear in the character of a prophet or divine teacher. The Lord thy God, said Moses, will raise up unto thee a prophet from the midst of thee, of thy brethren, like unto me, unto him shall he hearken.[29] Behold my servant whom I uphold, mine elect in whom my soul delighteth, I have put my Spirit upon him, he shall bring forth judgment unto the Gentiles.[30] The Spirit of the Lord God is upon me, because he hath anointed me to preach good tidings unto the meek; he hath sent me to bind up the broken hearted, to proclaim liberty to the captives, and the opening of the prison to them that are bound.[31] In that day shall the deaf hear the words of the book, the eyes of the blind shall see out of obscurity

---

20. Daniel ix. 25.
21. Isaiah vii. 14.
22. Micah v. 2.
23. Zech. ix. 9.
24. Is. 53.
25. Is. vii. 14.
26. Jer. xxiii. 6.
27. Is. ix. 6.
28. Mich. v. 2.
29. Deut. xviii. 15.
30. Is. xlii. 1.
31. Is. lxi. 1.

and out of darkness; the meek also shall increase their joy in the Lord, and the poor among men shall rejoice in the Holy One of Israel.[32]

He was also to be a priest. The Lord hath sworn and will not repent, Thou art a priest forever after the order of Melchizedek.[33] He shall build the temple of the Lord, and he shall bear the glory, and shall sit and rule upon his throne, and he shall be a priest upon his throne.[34]

The regal character of this Redeemer is set forth in almost every page of the prophetic writings. I have anointed, (said God in reference to the Messiah,) my king on my holy hill of Zion.[35] Thy throne O God is forever and ever; the sceptre of thy kingdom is a sceptre of righteousness. Thou lovest righteousness and hatest wickedness, therefore God, thy God, hath anointed thee with the oil of gladness above thy fellows.[36] Unto us a child is born, and unto us a son is given, and the government shall be upon his shoulder. Of the increase of his government and peace there shall be no end, upon the throne of David and upon his kingdom to order it, and to establish it with judgment and justice from hence for even for ever.[37]

The characteristics of this kingdom of the Messiah were also clearly predicted. It was to be a spiritual, in distinction from the external and ceremonial character of the former dispensation. Behold the days shall come, saith the Lord, that I will make a new covenant with the house of Israel and with the house of Judah, not according to the covenant which I made with their fathers, &c. I will put my law in their inward parts and write it in their hearts, and will be their God, and they shall be my people.[38] Hence the effusion of the Holy Spirit is so constantly mentioned as attending the advent of the promised Redeemer. In that day I will pour out my Spirit upon all flesh, and your sons and your daughters shall prophesy, &c.[39]

---

32. Is. xxix. 18, 19.
33. Ps. cx. 4.
34. Zech. vi. 13.
35. Ps. ii. 6.
36. Ps. xlv. 6, 7.
37. Is. ix. 6, 7.
38. Jer. xxxi. 31, 32.
39. Joel ii. 28.

Again, this kingdom was not to be confined to the Jews, but was to include all the world. As early as in the book of Genesis it was declared that the obedience of all nations should be yielded to Shiloh, and that all the nations of the earth should be blessed in Abraham and his seed. God promised the Messiah the heathen for his inheritance and the utmost parts of the earth for his possession.[40] It shall come to pass in the last days, said Isaiah, that the mountain of the Lord's house shall be established upon the top of the mountains, and shall be exalted above the hills, and all nations shall flow unto it.[41] It is a light thing, said God, that thou shouldst be my servant to raise up the tribes of Jacob, and to restore the preserved of Israel, I will also give thee for a light to the Gentiles, that thou mayest be my salvation to the ends of the earth.[42] In that day there shall be a root of Jesse, which shall stand for an ensign of the people, and to it shall the Gentiles seek.[43] I saw in the night visions, said Daniel, and behold, one like the Son of man came with the clouds of heaven, and came to the Ancient of days, and they brought him near before him; and there was given to him dominion and glory, and a kingdom, that all people, nations and languages should serve him; his dominion is an everlasting dominion which shall not pass away, and his kingdom that which will not be destroyed.[44] Its progress however was to be gradual. The stone cut out of the mountains, without hands, was to break in pieces the iron, the brass, the clay, the silver and the gold, i.e. all other kingdoms, and become a great mountain and fill the whole earth.[45]

Though the prophets describe in such strong language the excellence, glory and triumph of this Redeemer, they did not the less distinctly predict his rejection, sufferings and death. Lord who hath believed our report, and to whom hath the arm of the Lord been revealed. For he shall grow up before him as a tender plant, and as a root out of a dry ground; he is despised and rejected of men, we hid as it were our faces from him, he was despised and we esteemed him

---

40. Ps. ii. 8.
41. Is. ii. 2.
42. Is. xlix. 6.
43. Is. xi. 10.
44. Dan. vii. 13, 14.
45. Dan. ii. 45.

not.[46] To him whom man despiseth, to him whom the nation abhorreth, to a servant of rulers, kings shall see and arise, and princes shall also worship.[47] The people whom he came to redeem, it was foretold, would not only reject him, but betray and sell him for thirty pieces of silver. If ye think good, give my price, and if not forbear. So they weighed for my price thirty pieces of silver. And the Lord said unto me, Cast it into the potter, the goodly price at which I was prized at of them.[48] He was to be grievously persecuted and put to death. He was, said the prophet, taken from prison and from judgment (cut off by an oppressive judgment) and who shall declare his generation; for he was cut off from the land of the living; for the transgression of my people was he stricken. And he made his grave with the wicked and with the rich in his death.[49] Even the manner and circumstances of his death were minutely foretold. The assembly of the wicked enclose me; they pierce my hands and my feet. They part my garments among them and cast lots upon my vesture.[50] He was not however to continue under the power of death. Thou wilt not leave my soul in hell; neither wilt thou suffer thy holy one to see corruption.[51]

The consequences of the rejection of the Messiah to the Jewish people were also predicted with great distinctness. The children of Israel, it is said, shall abide many days without a king, without a prince, and without a sacrifice, and without an image, and without teraphim. Afterwards shall the children of Israel return and seek the Lord and his goodness in the latter days.[52] Though the number of the children of Israel be as the sand of the sea, a remnant shall be saved.[53] Of the rebellious portion of the nation it was said, I will scatter them among all people, from one end of the earth to the other, and among those nations shalt thou find no ease, neither shall the soul of thy foot have rest;. . . . And thou shalt become an astonishment and proverb,

---

46. Is. liii.
47. Is. xlix. 7.
48. Zech. xi. 12.
49. Is. liii. 8, 9.
50. Ps. xxii. 16, 18.
51. Ps. xvi. 10, 11.
52. Hos. iii. 4, 5.
53. Is. x. 22, 23.

and a by-word among all nations, whither the Lord shall lead thee.[54] Though thus scattered and afflicted, they were not to be utterly destroyed, for God promised saying, When they are in the land of their enemies I will not cast them away, neither will I abhor them to destroy them utterly, and to break my covenant with them, for I am the Lord their God.[55] It was moreover predicted that after a long dispersion they should be brought to acknowledge their crucified king. I will pour upon the house of David and upon the inhabitants of Jerusalem, the spirit of grace and supplications, and they shall look upon me whom they have pierced, and they shall mourn for him, as one mourneth for his only son, and shall be in bitterness for him, as one is in bitterness for his first-born.[56] This same prophet foretold that after the people had rejected and betrayed the good shepherd, they should be given up to the oppression of their enemies, the greater portion should be destroyed, but the residue, after long suffering should be restored.[57]

This representation of the prophecies of the Jewish Scriptures, respecting Christ and his kingdom, is in the highest degree inadequate. It would be impossible to give a full exhibition of the subject, without unfolding the whole Old Testament economy. It is not in detached predictions merely, that the former dispensation was prophetic. In its main design it was prefigurative and preparatory. It had indeed its immediate purpose to answer, in preserving the Israelites a distinct people, in sustaining the true religion, and in exhibiting the divine perfections in his government of the church. But all this was subordinate to its grand purpose of preparing that people and the world for the advent of Christ, and to be a shadowy representation of the glories of the new dispensation, for the double purpose of affording an object of faith and hope to those then living, and that the new economy might be better understood, more firmly believed and more extensively embraced. Detached passages from such a scheme of history and prophecy are like the scattered ruins of an ancient temple. To form a just judgment the plan must be viewed as a whole as

---

54. Deut. xxviii. 66.
55. Lev. xxvi. 44.
56. Zech. xii. 10.
57. Zech. xiii. 7, 9.

well as in its details. It could then be seen that the history of the Jews was the history of the lineage of Christ; the whole sacrificial ritual a prefiguration of the Lamb of God who was to bear the sin of the world; that the tabernacle and the temple, with their complicated services, were types of things spiritual and heavenly; that the prophets, who were the teachers and correctors of the people, were sent, not merely nor principally to foretell temporal deliverances, but mainly to keep the eyes of the people directed upward and onward to the great deliverer and to the final redemption. Detached passages can give no adequate conception of this stupendous scheme of preparation and prophecy, running through thousands of years, and its thousand lines all tending to one comon centre,—the cross of Christ.

The argument from prophecy in support of the truth of Christianity, therefore, can be appreciated by those only who will candidly study the whole system. Still enough has been presented to show that it is impossible to account for the correspondence between the prophecies of the Old Testament and the events recorded in the New, upon any other assumption than that of divine inspiration. We have seen that it was predicted, centuries before the advent of Christ, that a great deliverer should arise, to be born of the tribe of Judah, and of the family of David, and at the village of Bethlehem; that he should be a poor and humble man and yet worthy of the highest reverence paid to God; that he should be a teacher, priest and king; that he should be rejected by his own people, persecuted and put to death; that he should rise again from the dead; that the Spirit of God should be poured out upon his followers, giving them holiness, wisdom and courage; that true religion, no longer confined to the Jews, should be extended to the Gentiles and in despite of all opposition should continue, triumph and ultimately cover the earth; that the Jews who rejected the Messiah, should be cast off and scattered and yet preserved; like a river in the ocean, divided but not dissipated, a standing miracle, a fact without a parallel or analogy. Here then is the whole history of Christ and his kingdom, written centuries before his advent. A history full of apparent inconsistencies; a history not written in one age or by one man, but in different ages and by different men, each adding some new fact or characteristic, yet all combining to form one consistent, though apparently contradictory whole.

Admitting then, what no one denies, the antiquity of the Jewish

Scriptures, there is no escape from the conclusion that they were written by divine inspiration, and that Jesus Christ to whom they so plainly refer, is the Son of God and the Saviour of the world. To suppose that Christ, knowing these ancient prophecies, set himself without divine commission, to act in accordance with them, is to suppose impossibilities. It is to suppose that Jesus Christ was a bad man, which no man, who reads the New Testament, can believe, any more than he can believe that the sun is the blackness of darkness. It is to suppose him to have had a control over the actions of others which no impostor could exert. Many of the most important predictions in reference to Christ were fulfilled by the acts of his enemies. Did Christ instigate the treachery of Judas, or prompt the priests to pay the traitor thirty pieces of silver? Did he plot with Pilate for his own condemnation? or so arrange that he should die by a Roman, instead of a Jewish, mode of capital infliction? Did he induce the soldiers to part his garments and cast lots upon his vesture, or stipulate with them that none of his bones should be broken? By what possible contrivance could the two great predicted events of the final destruction of the Jewish policy and the consequent dispersion of the Jews, on the one hand, and the rapid propagation of the new religion among the Gentiles, on the other, have been brought to pass? These events were predicted, their occurrence was beyond the scope of contrivance or imposture. There is no rational answer to this argument from prophecy. The testimony of the Scriptures to the messiahship of Jesus Christ, is the testimony of God. Search the Scriptures, said our Saviour himself, for in them ye think ye have eternal life, and they are they which testify of me.

God then has been pleased to hedge up the way to infidelity. Men must do violence to all their usual modes of argument; they must believe moral impossibilities and irreconcileable contradictions, and above all they must harden their hearts to the excellence of the Saviour, before they can intelligently become infidels.

This exposition of the grounds of faith is made in order to show that unbelief is a sin; and to justify the awful declaration of Christ, "He that believeth not, shall be damned." Men flatter themselves that they are not responsible for their faith. Belief being involuntary, cannot, it is said, be a matter of praise or blame. This false opinion arises from confounding things very different in their nature. Faith differs according to its object and the nature of the evidence on which it is founded. A man believes that two and two are four, or that Napoleon died in St. Helena, and is neither morally better, nor worse for such a faith. Disbelief, in such cases, would indicate insanity, not moral aberration. But no man can believe that virtue is vice or vice virtue, without being to the last degree depraved. No man can disbelieve in God, especially under the light of revelation, without thereby showing that he is destitute of all right moral and religious sentiments. And no man can disbelieve the record which God has given of his Son, without being blind to the glory of God and the moral excellence of the Saviour. He rejects the appropriate testimony of God, conveyed in a manner which proves it to be his testimony.

It is vain, therefore, for any man to hope that he can be innocently destitute of faith in God or of faith in Jesus Christ. If the external world retains such an impression of the hand of God, as to leave those without excuse, who refuse to regard it as his work; surely those who refuse to acknowledge the excellence of his word and the glory of his Son, will not be held guiltless. The evidence which has convinced millions, is before their eyes, and should convince them. Instead, therefore, of apologizing for their want of faith and complaining of the weakness of the evidence, to which nothing but neglect or blindness can render them insensible, let them confess their guilt in not believing, and humble themselves before God and pray that he would open their eyes to see the excellence of his word. They should dismiss their cavils, and be assured that if the Bible does not win their faith by its milder glories, it will one day, reveal itself by its terrors, to their awakened consciences, to be indeed the word of God.

Chapter II.

Sin

SECTION I.   *All men are sinners. The nature of man, since the fall, is depraved.*

Since then the Scriptures are undoubtedly the word of God, with what reverence should we receive their divine instructions; with what assiduity and humility should we study them; with what confidence should we rely upon the truth of all their declarations; and with what readiness should we obey all their directions. We are specially concerned to learn what they teach with regard to the character of men, the way of salvation, and the rule of duty.

With respect to the first of these points, (the character of men) the Bible very clearly teaches that all men are sinners. The apostle Paul not only asserts this truth, but proves it at length, in reference both to those who live under the light of nature, and those who enjoy the light of revelation. The former, he says, are justly chargeable with impiety and immorality, because the perfections of the divine Being, his eternal power and godhead, have, from the creation, been manifested by the things which are made. Yet men have not acknowledged their creator. They neither worshipped him as God, nor were thankful for his mercies, but served the creature more than the creator. In thus departing from the fountain of all excellence, they departed from excellence itself. Their foolish hearts were darkened and their corruption manifests itself not only by degrading idolatry, but by the various forms of moral evil both in heart and life. These sins are committed against the law which is written on every man's heart; so that they know that those who do such things are worthy of death, and are therefore without excuse even in their own consciousness.

With regard to those who enjoy a supernatural revelation of the character and requirements of God, the case is still more plain. Instead of rendering to this God the inward and outward homage which are his due, they neglect his service, and really prefer his creatures to himself. Instead of regulating their conduct by the perfect rule of duty contained in the Scriptures, by breaking that law they constantly dishonour God. It is thus the apostle shows that all classes of men, when judged by the light they have severally enjoyed, are found guilty before God. This universality of guilt moreover, he says, is confirmed by the clear testimony of the Scriptures, which declare, There is none righteous, no not one. There is none that understandeth; there is none that seeketh after God. They have all gone out of the way; they have altogether become unprofitable; there is none that doeth good, no not one.

This language is not used by the Holy Spirit in reference to the men of any one age or country, but in reference to the human race. It is intended to describe the moral character of man. It is in this sense that it is quoted and applied by the apostle. And we accordingly find similar declarations in all parts of the Bible, in the New Testament, as well as in the Old, in the writings of one age, as well as in those of another. And there are no passages of an opposite character; there are none which represent the race as being what God requires, nor any which speak of any member of that race as being free from sin. On the contrary, it is expressly said, If we say we have no sin, we deceive ourselves, and the truth is not in us.[58] In many things we all offend.[59] There is no man that sinneth not.[60] All have sinned and come short of the glory of God.[61] Hence the Scriptures proceed upon the assumption of the universal sinfulness of men. To speak, to act, to walk after the manner of men, is, in the language of the Bible, to speak or act wickedly. The world are the wicked. This present evil world, is the description of mankind, from whose character and deserved punishment, it is said to be the design of Christ's death to redeem his people.[62] The world cannot hate you, said our Saviour to those who refused to be his disciples, but me it hateth, because I testify of it that the works thereof are evil.[63] They are of the world, therefore they speak of the world and the world heareth them.[64] We are of God, and the whole world lieth in wickedness.[65]

This however is not a doctrine taught in isolated passages. It is one of those fundamental truths which are taken for granted in almost every page of the Bible. The whole scheme of redemption supposes that man is a fallen being. Christ came to seek and to save the lost. He was announced as the Saviour of sinners. His advent and work have no meaning or value but upon the assumption that we are guilty, for he came to save his people from their sins; to die the just for the unjust; to bear our sins in his own body on the tree. Those who have no sin, need no Saviour; those who do not deserve death, need no Redeemer. As the doctrine of redemption pervades the Scripture, so does the doctrine of the universal sinfulness of men.

---

58. 1 John i. 8.
59. James iii. 2.
60. 1 Kings viii. 46.
61. Rom. iii. 23.
62. Gal. i. 4.
63. John vii. 7.
64. 1 John iv. 5.
65. 1 John v. 19.

This doctrine is also assumed in all the Scriptural representations of what is necessary for admission into heaven. All men, everywhere, are commanded to repent. But repentance, supposes sin. Every man must be born again, in order to see the kingdom of God; he must become a new creature; he must be renewed after the image of God. Being dead in trespasses and in sins, he must be quickened, or made partaker of a spiritual life. In short it is the uniform doctrine of the Bible, that all men need both pardon and sanctification in order to their admission to heaven. It therefore teaches that all men are sinners.

The Scriptures moreover teach that the sinfulness of men is deep seated; or, consisting in a corruption of the heart, it manifests itself in innumerable forms in the actions of the life. All the imaginations of man's heart are only evil continually.[66] God says of the human heart that it is deceitful above all things and desperately wicked.[67] All men, by nature are the children of wrath.[68] And therefore the Psalmist says, Behold I was shapen in iniquity, and in sin did my mother conceive me.[69]

This corruption of our nature is the ground of the constant reference of every thing good in man to the Holy Spirit, and of everything evil, to his own nature. Hence in the language of the Bible, the natural man is a corrupt man; and the spiritual man alone is good. Hence too the constant opposition of the terms flesh and spirit; the former meaning our nature as it is apart from divine influence, and the latter the Holy Spirit, or its immediate effects. To be in the flesh, to walk after the flesh, to mind the things of the flesh, are all Scriptural expressions descriptive of the natural state of men. It is in this sense of the term that Paul says, In my flesh there dwelleth no good thing.[70] And that our Saviour said, That which is born of the flesh is flesh.[71]

This humbling doctrine is, moreover, involved in all the descriptions which the Bible gives of the nature of that moral change

---

66. Gen. vi. 5.
67. Jer. xvii. 9.
68. Eph. ii. 3.
69. Ps. li. 5.
70. Rom. vii. 18.
71. John iii. 6.

which is necessary to salvation. It is no mere outward reformation; it is no assiduous performance of external duties. It is a regeneration; a being born of the Spirit; a new creation; a passing from death into life. A change never effected by the subject of it, but which has its source in God. Of no doctrine, therefore, is the Bible more full than of that which teaches that men are depraved and fallen beings, who have lost the image of God, and who must be created anew in Christ Jesus before they can see the kingdom of heaven.

These Scriptural representations respecting the universality of sin and the corruption of our nature, are abundantly confirmed by experience and observation. Men may differ as to the extent of their sinfulness, or as to the ill desert of their transgressions, but they cannot be insensible to the fact that they are sinners, or that they have sustained this character as long as they have had any self-knowledge. As far back as they can go in the history of their being, they find the testimony of conscience against them. As this consciousness of sin is universal, and as it exists as soon as we have any knowledge of ourselves, it proves that we are fallen beings; that we have lost the moral image of God with which our first parents were created. It is a fact, of which every human being is a witness, that our moral nature is such that instead of seeking our happiness in God and holiness, we prefer the creature to the creator. It would be just as unreasonable to assert that this was the original, proper state of man, as to say our reason was sound, if it universally, immediately and infallibly led us into wrong judgments upon subjects fairly within its competency.

The proof, that man is a depraved being, is as strong as that he is a rational, a social, or a moral being. He gives no signs of reason at his birth; but he invariably manifests his intellectual nature as soon as he becomes capable of appreciating the objects around him or of expressing the operations of his mind. No one supposes reason to be the result of education, or the effect of circumstances, merely because its operations cannot be detected from the first moment of existence. The uniformity of its manifestation under all circumstances, is regarded as sufficient proof that it is an attribute of our nature.

The same remark may be made respecting the social affections. No one of them is manifested from the beginning of our course in this world; yet the fact that men in all ages and under all circumstances, evince a disposition to live in society; that all parents love their children, that all people have more or less sympathy in the joys and sorrows of their fellow men, is proof that these affections are not acquired but original, that they belong to our nature and are characteristic of it.

In like manner the apostle reasons from the fact that all men perform moral acts and experience the approbation or disapprobation of conscience, that they have, by nature, and not from example, instruction, or any other external influence, but in virtue of their original moral constitution, a law written on their hearts, a sense of right and wrong. But if the uniform occurence of any moral acts is a proof of a moral nature, the uniform occurrence of wrong moral acts is a proof of a corrupt moral nature. If the universal manifestation of reason and of the social affections, proves man to be by nature a rational and social being, the universal manifestation of sinful affections proves him to be by nature a sinful being. When we say that any one is a bad man, we mean that the predominant character of his actions proves him to have bad principles or dispositions. And when we say that man's nature is depraved we mean that it is a nature whose moral acts are wrong. And this uniformity of wrong moral action is as much a proof of a depraved nature, as the acts of a bad man are a proof of the predominance of evil dispositions in his heart. This is the uniform judgment of men, and is sanctioned by the word of God. A good tree cannot bring forth evil fruit, neither can a corrupt tree bring forth good fruit. Therefore by their fruits shall ye know them. This illustration was used by our Saviour with the express design of teaching that the predominant character of the acts of men, is to be taken as a certain index of the state of the heart; and hence the uniform occurrence of sin in all men is a certain evidence of the corruption of their nature. Indeed there is no one fact with regard to human nature, which consciousness and observation more fully establishes than that it is depraved.

SECTION II. *The sins of men are numerous and aggravated.*

The Bible not only teaches that all men are sinners, and that the evil is deeply seated in their hearts, but moreover that their sinfulness is very great. The clearest intimation which a law-giver can give of his estimate of the evil of transgression is the penalty which he attaches to the violation of his laws. If he is wise and good, the penalty will be a true index of the real demerit of transgression; and in the case of God, who is infinitely wise and good, the punishment which he denounces against sin, must be an exact criterion of its ill-desert. If we are unable to see that sin really deserves what God has declared to be its proper punishment, it only shows that our judgment differs from his; and that it should thus differ is no matter of surprise. We cannot know all the reasons which indicate the righteousness of the divine threatenings. We can have no adequate conception of the greatness, goodness and wisdom of the Being against whom we sin; nor of the evil which sin is suited to produce; nor of the perfect excellence of the law which we transgress. That sin therefore appears to us a less evil than God declares it to be, is no evidence that it is really undeserving of his wrath and curse.

There is still more operative cause of our low estimate of the evil of sin. The more depraved a man is, the less capable is he of estimating the heinousness of his transgressions. And the man who in one part of his career, looked upon certain crimes with abhorrence, comes at last to regard them with indifference. That we are sinners, therefore, is a sufficient explanation of the fact, that we look upon sin in a very different light from that in which it is presented in the word of God. Nothing then can be more reasonable than that we should bow before the judgment of God, that we should acknowledge that sin really deserves the punishment which he has declared to be its due. That punishment is so awful, that nothing but a profound reverence for God, and some adequate conception of the evil of sin, can produce a sincere acquiescence in its justice. Yet nothing can be more certain than that this punishment is the proper measure of the ill-desert of sin.

The term commonly employed to designate this punishment is death; death not merely of the body, but of the soul; not merely temporal but eternal. It is a comprehensive term therefore to express all the evils in this world and the world to come, which are the penal consequences of sin. In this sense it is to be understood in the threatening made to our first parents. In the day thou eatest thereof thou shalt surely die.[72] And when the prophet says, The soul that sinneth it shall die.[73] And when the Apostle says, The

---

72. Gen. ii. 17.
73. Ezek. xviii. 4.

wages of sin is death.[74] The same general idea is expressed by the word curse, As many as are of the law are under the curse; for it is written, cursed is every one that continueth not in all things written in the book of the law to do them;[75] and also by the word wrath. We were by nature the children of wrath,[76] The wrath of God is revealed from heaven against all ungodliness and unrighteousness of men.[77]

These and similar passages teach that sinners are the objects of the divine displeasure, and that this displeasure will certainly be manifested. As God is infinitely good and the fountain of all blessedness, his displeasure must be the greatest of all evils. The Scriptures, however, in order to impress this truth more deeply upon our minds, employ the strongest terms human language affords, to set forth the dreadful import of God's displeasure. Those who obey not the gospel, it is said, shall be punished with everlasting destruction from the presence of the Lord and from the glory of his power.[78] Our Saviour says, The wicked shall be cast into hell, into the fire that never shall be quenched; where their worm dieth not and the fire is not quenched.[79] At the last great day, he tells us, the judge shall say to those upon his left-hand, Depart from me ye cursed into everlasting fire, prepared for the devil and his angels.[80] The Son of man shall send forth his angels, and they shall gather out of his kingdom all things that offend, and them that do iniquity, and shall cast them into a furnace of fire; there shall be wailing and gnashing of teeth.[81] In the last day, all that are in their graves shall hear his voice and shall come forth; they that have done good unto the resurrection of life, and they that have done evil unto the resurrection of damnation;[82] or as it is expressed in Daniel,[83] to shame and everlasting contempt.

---

74. Rom. vi. 23.
75. Gal. iii. 10.
76. Eph. ii. 3.
77. Rom. i. 18.
78. 2 Thess. i. 9.
79. Mark. ix. 43, 44.
80. Matt. xxv. 41.
81. Matt. xiii. 41, 42.
82. John v. 29.
83. Daniel xii. 2.

Whatever explanation may be given of the terms employed in these and many similar passages, there can be no doubt that they are intended to convey the idea of endless and hopeless misery. Whence this misery shall arise, or wherein it shall consist, are questions of minor importance. It is sufficient that the Scriptures teach that the sufferings here spoken of, are in degree inconceivably great and in duration endless. The most fearful exhibition given of the future state of the impenitent, is that which presents them as reprobates, as abandoned to the unrestrained dominion of evil. The repressing influence of conscience, of a probationary state, of a regard to character, of good example, and above all of the Holy Spirit, will be withdrawn, and unmingled malignity, impurity and violence constitute the character and condition of those who finally perish. The wicked are represented as constantly blaspheming God, while they gnaw their tongues with pain.[84] The God who pronounces this doom upon sinners, is he who said, As I live I have no pleasure in the death of the wicked. The most fearful of these passages fell from the lips of the Lamb of God, who came to die that we might not perish, but have eternal life.

It must be remembered that it is not against the chief of sinners that this dreadful punishment is denounced. It is against sin, one sin, any sin. Cursed is every one that continueth not in all things written in the book of the law to do them.[85] Whosoever shall keep the whole law, and yet offend in one point, he is guilty of all.[86] As far as we know, the angels were punished for their first offence. Adam and his race fell by one transgression. Human governments act on the same principle. If a man commit murder, he suffers death for the one offence. If he is guilty of treason, he finds no defence in his freedom from other crimes. Sin is apostacy from God; it breaks our communion with him, and is the ruin of the soul.

The displeasure of God against sin and his fixed determination to punish it, are also manifested by the certain connexion which he has established between sin and suffering. It is the undeniable

---

84. Rev. xvi. 10.
85. Gal. iii. 10.
86. James ii. 10.

tendency of sin to produce misery; and although in this world the good are not always more happy than the wicked, this only shows that the present is a state of trial and not of retribution. It affords no evidence to contradict the proof of the purpose of God to punish sin, derived from the obvious and necessary tendency of sin to produce misery. This tendency is as much a law of nature as any other law with which we are acquainted. Men flatter themselves that they will escape the evil consequences of their transgressions by appealing to the mercy of God, and obtaining a suspension of this law in their behalf. They might as reasonably expect the law of gravitation to be suspended for their convenience. He that soweth to the flesh, shall of the flesh reap corruption, as certainly as he who sows tares shall reap tares. The only link which binds together causes and effects in nature, is the will of God; and the same will, no less clearly revealed, connects suffering with sin. And this is a connexion absolutely indissoluble save by the mystery of redemption.

To suspend the operation of a law of nature, (as to stop the sun in his course,) is merely an exercise of power. But to save sinners from the curse of the law required that Christ should be made a curse for us; that he should bear our sins in his own body on the tree; that he should be made sin for us and die the just for the unjust. It would be a reflection on the wisdom of God to suppose that he would employ means to accomplish an end more costly than that end required. Could our redemption have been affected by corruptible things, as silver or gold, or could the blood of bulls or of goats have taken away sin, who can believe that Christ would have died? The apostle clearly teaches that it is to make the death of Christ vain, to affirm that our salvation could have been otherwise secured.[87] Since, then, in order to the pardon of sin, the death of Christ was necessary, it is evident that the evil of sin in the sight of God must be estimated by the dignity of him who died for our redemption. Here we approach the most mysterious and awful doctrine of the Bible. In the beginning was the Word, and the Word was with God, and the Word was God. All things were made by him; and without him was not any thing made that was made. And the word was made flesh and dwelt among us,

---

87. Gal. ii. 21.

and we beheld his glory as the only begotton of the Father full of grace and truth.[88] God therefore was manifested in the flesh. He who being in the form of God, thought it not robbery to be equal with God made himself of no reputation, and took upon him the form of a servant, and was made in the likeness of men; and being found in fashion as a man, he humbled himself and became obedient unto death, even the death of the cross.[89] He hath also been exalted to be the brightness of the Father's glory and the express image of his person, upholding all things by the word of his power; whom all the angels are commanded to worship; of whom the Scriptures say, Thy throne O God is forever and ever, Thou Lord in the beginning hast laid the foundation of the earth, and the heavens are the work of thy hands; They shall perish, but thou remainest; they shall wax old as doth a garment; and as a vesture shalt thou fold them up, and they shall be changed; but thou art the same, and thy years shall not fail,— even He, who is God over all and blessed forever, inasmuch as the children were partakers of flesh and blood, himself also took part of the same; that through death he might destroy him that had the power of death, that is the Devil, and deliver them who through fear of death were all their lifetime subject to bondage.

It is the doctrine of the Bible that the infinite and eternal Son of God assumed our nature, that he might redeem us from the curse of the law by being made a curse for us. It is obvious that no severity of mere human suffering; no destroying deluge; no final conflagration, not hell itself can present such a manifestation of the evil of sin and of the justice of God as the cross of his incarnate Son. It declares in language which is heard by the whole intelligent universe, that sin deserves God's wrath and curse, and that none who refuse submission to the appointed method of pardon, can escape its condemnation.

The penalty then which God has attached to the violation of his law, the certainty with which that penalty is inflicted, the doom of the fallen angels, the consequences of Adam's sin, and above all the death of Christ, are manifestations of the evil of sin in the estimation of God, which it is the highest infatuation for us to disregard.

---

88. John i. 1, 3, 14.
89. Phil. ii. 6, 7.

However obdurate our hearts may be in reference to this subject, our reason is not so blind as not to see that our guilt must be exceedingly great. We cannot deny that all the circumstances which aggravate the heinousness of sin concur in our case. The law which we transgress is perfectly good. It is the law of God; the law of right and reason. It is the expression of the highest excellence; it is suited to our nature, necessary to our perfection and happiness. Opposition to such a law must be in the highest degree unreasonable and wicked.

This law is enforced not only by its own excellence but by the authority of God. Disregard of this authority is the greatest crime of which a creature is capable. It is rebellion against a being whose right to command is founded on his infinite superiority, his infinite goodness and his absolute propriety in us as his creatures. It is apostacy from the kingdom of God to the kingdom of Satan. There is no middle ground between the two. Every one is either the servant of God, or the servant of the devil. Holiness is the evidence of our allegiance to our maker, sin is the service of Satan. Could we form any adequate conception of these two kingdoms, of the intrinsic excellence of the one and the absolute evil of the other, of the blessedness attendant on the one and the misery connected with the other; could we in short bring heaven and hell in immediate contrast, we might have some proper view of the guilt of this apostacy from God. It is the natural tendency of our conduct to degrade ourselves and others, to make Eden like Sodom, and to kindle every where the fire that never shall be quenched. This cannot be denied, for moral evil is the greatest of all evils and the certain cause of all others. He therefore who sins is not only a rebel against God, but a malefactor, an enemy to the highest good of his fellow creatures.

Again, our guilt is great because our sins are exceedingly numerous. It is not merely outward acts of unkindness and dishonesty with which we are chargeable, our habitual and characteristic state of mind is evil in the sight of God. Our pride, vanity, indifference to his will and to the welfare of others, our selfishness, our loving the creature more than the Creator, are continuous violations of his law. We have never, in any one moment of our lives, been or done what the law requires us to be and to do. We have never had that delight in the divine perfections, that sense of dependence and obligation, that fixed purpose to do the will and promote the glory of God, which constitute the love which is our first and highest duty.

It is in this sense that men are said to be totally depraved; they are entirely destitute of supreme love to God. Whatever else they may have is as nothing while this is wanting. They may be affectionate fathers or kind masters, or dutiful sons and daughters, but they are not obedient children of God; they have not those feelings towards God which constitute their first and greatest duty, and without which they are always transgressors. The man who is a rebel against this righteous sovereign, and whose heart is full of enmity to his person and government, may be faithful to his associates and kind to his dependents, but he is always and increasingly guilty as it regards his ruler. Thus we are always sinners; we are at all times and under all circumstances in opposition to God, because we are never what his law requires us to be. If we have never loved him supremely; if we have never made it our governing purpose to do his will; if we have never been properly grateful for all his mercies; if we have never made his glory, but some other and lower object, the end of our actions; then our lives have been an unbroken series of transgressions. Our sins are not to be numbered by the conscious violations of duty; they are as numerous as the moments of our existence.

If the permanent moral dispositions of a man are evil, it must follow that his acts of transgression will be past counting up. Every hour there is some work of evil, some wrong thought, some bad feeling, some improper word, or some wicked act, to add to the number of his offences. The evil exercise of an evil heart is like the ceaseless swinging of the pendulum. The slightest review of life therefore is sufficient to overwhelm us with the conviction of the countless multitude of our transgressions. It is this which constitutes our exceeding sinfulness in the sight of God. While conscience sleeps, or our attention is directed to other subjects, the number of our transgressions grows like the unnoticed pulsations of our heart. It is not until we pause and call ourselves to an account, that we see how many feelings have been wrong; how great is the distance at which we habitually live from God, and how constant is our want of conformity to his will. It was this that forced the Psalmist to cry, Mine iniquities have taken hold upon me, so that I am not able to look up, they are more than the hairs on my head, therefore my heart faileth me.

Again, we may judge of the greatness of our guilt before God, by considering the numerous restraints of his truth, providence and spirit, which we habitually disregard. The simple fact that sin is wrong, that conscience condemns it, is a constant and powerful restraint. We cannot avail ourselves of the plea of ignorance, as we have a perfect standard of duty in the law of God. We cannot resist the conviction that his commands are righteous, yet, in despite of this conviction, we live in constant disobedience.

We are, moreover, fully aware of the consequences of sin. We know the judgment of God that those who do such things are worthy of death, and yet continue our transgressions. We are surprised at the drunkard who indulges his fatal passion in the very presence of ruin; yet are blind to our own infatuation in continuing to disobey God in despite of threatened death. We stupidly disregard the certain consequences of our conduct, and awake only in time to see that madness is in our hearts. This insensibility, notwithstanding the occasional admonitions of conscience and the constant warnings of the word of God, constitutes a peculiar aggravation of our guilt.

Nor are we more mindful of the restraining influence of the love of God. We disregard the fact that the Being against whom we sin, is He to whom we owe our existence and all our enjoyments; who has carried us in his arms, and crowned us with loving kindness and tender mercies; who is merciful and gracious, slow to anger and plenteous in mercy; who has not dealt with us after our sins, nor rewarded us according to our iniquities, but has borne with our provocations, waiting that his goodness might lead us to repentance. We have despised his forbearance, deriving from it a motive to sin, as though he were slack concerning his promises, and would not accomplish his threatenings; thus treasuring up for ourselves wrath against the day of wrath and revelation of the righteous judgment of God. Besides all this, we disregard the love of Christ. He came to save us from our sins, and we will not accept of his mediation, or reciprocate his love. There stands his cross, mutely eloquent; at once an invitation and a warning. It tells us both of the love and justice of God. It assures us that he who spared not his own Son, is ready to be gracious. All this we disregard. We count the blood of the covenant, an unholy thing; we act as if it were not the blood of the Son of God, shed for us for the remission of sins. Or, it may be, we turn the grace of God into licentiousness, and draw encouragement from the death of Christ to continue in sin. This unbelieving rejection of the Saviour involves guilt so peculiarly great, that it is often spoken of as the special ground of the condemnation of the world. He that believeth not is condemned already, because he hath not believed on the only begotten Son of God. When he, the Spirit of truth is come, he shall convince the world of sin, because they believe not in me. If he that despised Moses' law died without mercy, under two or three witnesses, of how much sorer punishment, suppose ye, shall he be thought worthy, who hath trodden under foot the Son of God.

This great sin of rejecting Jesus Christ as a Saviour, it must be remembered, is an often repeated and long continued sin. It is also one which is chargeable not on the openly wicked merely, but upon those whom the world calls moral. They too resist the claims of the Son of God; they too refuse his love and reject his offers. It was when all other messengers had failed, the Lord of the vineyard sent his Son to his disobedient servants, saying, They will reverence my Son. The guilt of thus rejecting Christ, will never be fully appreciated until the day when He shall sit on the throne and from his face the earth and heaven shall flee away and no place be found for them.

Besides these restraints from without, we resist the still more effectual influence of the Spirit of God. That Spirit strives with all men; suggesting truth and exciting conscience, expostulating and warning, and drawing men from sin to God. It is from Him that all good thoughts and right purposes do proceed. This spirit we quench; we resist his gracious influences, not once or twice, but a thousand times. Though he will not always strive with men, he strives long, and returns after many insulting rejections, repeating the warnings and invitations of mercy. All men are sensible of this divine influence, though they may not be aware of its origin. They know not whence proceed the serious thoughts, the anxious forebodings, the convictions of truth, the sense of the emptiness of the world, the longing after security and peace of which they are conscious. God sends these admonitions even to those who are most contented with the world and most happy in their estrangement from himself. He leaves no man without a witness and a warning. These strivings of the Spirit are not only frequent, but often urgent. Almost every man can look back and see many instances in which an unseen hand was upon him, when a voice, not from man, has sounded in his ears, when feelings to which he was before a stranger were awakened in his breast, and when he felt the power of the world to come. The shadow of the Almighty has passed over him, and produced the conviction that God is, and that He is an avenger.

From a review of what has been said it is plain that the Scriptures teach not only that all men are sinners, but that their corruption is radical, seated in their hearts, and that it is exceedingly great. The severity of the penalty which God has attached to transgression, the certainty of its infliction, the costliness of the sacrifice by which alone its pardon could be obtained, are all proofs of the evil of sin in the sight of God. The greatness of our personal guilt is plain from the excellence of the law which we have violated; from the authority and goodness of the Being whom we have offended, from the number of our sins, and from the powerful restraints which we have disregarded.

Chapter III.

Causes of Indifference to the Charge of Sin.

SECTION I. *Sin, want of consideration, striving against the Spirit.*

The charge of sin is brought so directly in the word of God against every human being, and is so fully sustained by observation and experience, that the general indifference of men under so weighty an accusation is a fact which needs explanation. Indifference is no proof of innocence, any more than insensibility to pain is a proof of health. In ordinary cases indeed, a man cannot be ill without knowing it, but his sensations are a very unsafe criterion of the nature or danger of his disease. He may be most free from pain, when most in peril. In like manner, the indifference of men to their own sinfulness affords no presumption that their guilt is not great in the sight of God. The absence of the immediate consciousness of guilt is no proof of innocence, unless attended by the joyful exercise of all right feelings. When accompanied by indifference to duty and the indulgence of sin, it is the evidence of the depth of our depravity. All men assume this to be true in their judgments of those more wicked than themselves. To say of a man, he is a hardened wretch, is not the language of extenuation or apology. It is the language of aggravated condemnation. Those who feel thus keenly with regard to others, that indifference is an aggravation of guilt, strangely imagine it to be, in their own case, a proof of comparative innocence.

This insensibility of men, therefore, to the moral turpitude of their character in the sight of God, so far from being an indication of goodness, is the result and evidence of the extent of their corruption. As in bodily disease when the seat of life is attacked, the sensibilities are weakened, so in the disease of sin, insensibility is one of its symptoms, and increases with the increase of the evil. Sin produces this effect both by blinding the mind and by hardening the heart. It obscures our apprehensions of the excellence of God and of his law, and it produces a callousness of feeling, so that what is seen is not regarded. Experience teaches us that a mere change in the state of the mind, produces an immediate and entire change in our apprehensions and feelings in reference to our own sins. The man who one hour was as indifferent as the most careless, the next, is filled with astonishment and remorse. Others think his feelings unreasonable and exaggerated; he knows them to be rational and even inadequate. This is not the result of any hallucination or mistaken apprehensions of God or of his own character. It is the natural effect of an enlightened mind and of an awakened conscience. The ease and frequency with which the indifference of men to their guilt in the sight of God, is destroyed, is of itself a proof that their insensibility is not based upon truth; that it is the effect of a darkened understanding and a hardened heart, and that though it may increase as sin gains the ascendancy, it vanishes the moment the light and power of truth are let in upon the soul.

Besides this general cause of the indifference of men to the declarations of God regarding their sinfulness, there are others which ought to be specified. When the prophet contemplated the impenitent unconcern of the people, he exclaimed, Israel doth not know, my people do not consider. And when god would rouse them to a sense of their guilt, he says, Now therefore thus saith the Lord of hosts, consider your ways. It is this want of consideration, more than any difficulty in arriving at the truth, which sets men in such opposition to God in their judgments of themselves, and which hardens them in their indifference. This inconsideration indeed is but an effect of the more general cause already referred to, but it becomes in its turn a cause both of ignorance and unconcern. Men learn little upon any subject by intuition, and the knowledge is the subject to which men generally devote the least attention. They are engrossed by the cares or pleasures of the world. They either float softly down the stream of life, or are hurried along its troubled course, with scarcely an hour given to serious reflection. That under such circumstances men should be ignorant of themselves and indifferent to their character in the sight of God, is not only natural but unavoidable. It is however a lamentable thing that they should make a judgment of themselves formed without consideration, the ground of their conduct, and confide in it in opposition to the judgment of God. If they will judge, let them at least consider. If they will act on their own conclusions respecting themselves, let them at least examine and decide deliberately, and not venture every thing on a hasty, unconsidered estimate of their character, which, it may be, could not stand, even in their own judgment, a moment's inspection.

Men, however, are not merely inconsiderate, they often make direct efforts to suppress the rising conviction of guilt and danger. The testimony of God against them is so plain; the authority of his law is so obvious; their want of conformity to it is so glaring, and the influences of the Spirit are so general and frequent, that the conviction of sin can hardly fail to obtrude itself even upon those who in general are the most unconcerned. It is, however, a painful conviction, and therefore, instead of being cherished, it is disregarded or suppressed. The mind refuses to dwell upon the subject, or to examine the evidence of guilt, but either turns to other objects, or, by some act of levity or transgression, grieves away the Spirit of God and hardens itself in unconcern. This is a frequently recurring experience in the history of most men. They have more anxious thoughts than they allow their most intimate friends to suspect; they often mask an aching heart with a smiling face. They have a quick foresight of what such feelings must lead to, if cherished. They see, at once, that they cannot cultivate such sentiments, and live as they have been accustomed to do. There are pleasures, and it may be sins, which must be abandoned. There are companions who must be avoided. There is the opposition of friends, the ridicule of associates, the loss of caste, to be encountered. All the horrors of a religious life present themselves to the imagination, and frighten the half awakened from considering their ways, which they know to be but the first step in what appears to be a long and painful journey. They therefore struggle against their convictions, and in general master them. This struggle is sometimes short; at others, it is protracted and painful. Victory however comes at last, and the soul regains its wonted unconcern. Such persons little know what they are doing. They little suspect that they are struggling to elude the grasp of mercy; that they are striving against the Spirit of God, who would draw them from the paths of destruction, and guide them into the way of life.

SECTION II.   *Sophistical objections against the doctrine of the Bible.*

Another cause of the indifference of men may be found in the objections which they urge against the truth. Such objections indeed are more frequently and effectually urged to perplex the advocates of religion, than to quiet the uneasiness of conscience. Still men endeavour to impose upon themselves as well as to embarrass others. And the objections referred to, doubtless are, often obstacles in the way of the inquirer; or opiates to the consciences of those who desire to be deceived. It is objected that we are what God made us; that our character is determined either by our original constitution, or by the circumstances in which we are placed, and therefore we cannot be responsible for it; that in as much as neither our belief nor our affections are under the control of the will, we cannot be accountable for either; that it is useless to use means to escape the judgment of God, since what is to be, will be; that we must wait till God sees fit to change our hearts, since it is declared in Scripture to be his work.

It will be observed that these and similar objections relate to the reconciliation of different truths, and not to their separate validity or evidence. The proposition that men are responsible for their moral character, taken by itself, is so capable of demonstration, that all men do in fact believe it. Every man feels it to be true with regard to himself, and knows it to be true with regard to others. All self-condemnation and self-approbation rest on the consciousness of this truth. All our judgments regarding the moral conduct of others are founded on the same assumption. It is, therefore, one of those truths which is included in the universal consciousness of men, and has in all ages and nations been assumed as certain. Men cannot really doubt it, if they would. On the other hand, it is no less certain that our character does depend in a measure upon circumstances beyond our control; upon our original constituton, upon education, upon prevalent habits and opinions, upon divine influence, &c. All this is proved by experience and observation. Hence then are two facts resting on independent evidence, each certain and each by itself securing general assent. Yet we see men constantly disposed to bring up the one against the other; and argue against their responsibility, because they are dependent, or against their dependence, because they are responsible.

In like manner the proposition that man is a free agent commands immediate and universal asset, because it is an ultimate fact of consciousness. It can no more be doubted than we can doubt our own existence. Side by side however with this intimate persuasion of our moral liberty, lies the conviction, no less intimate, of our inability to change, by merely willing to do so, either our belief or our affections, for which, as before stated, every man knows himself to be responsible. Perhaps few men,—perhaps no man,—can see the harmony of these truths; yet they are truths, and as such are practically acknowledged by all men.

Again, all experience teaches us that we live in a world of means, that knowledge, religion, happiness, are all to be sought in a certain way, and that to neglect the means is to lose the end. It is, however, no less true that there is no necessary or certain connection between the means and the end; that God holds the result in his own hands and decides the issues according to his sovereign pleasure. In all the ordinary affairs of life men submit to this arrangement and do not hesitate to use means, though the end is uncertain and beyond their control. But in religion, they think this uncertainty of the result a sufficient excuse for neglect.

It is obvious that this method of reasoning, or rather of cavilling, which consists of bringing up one well established truth against another, is unworthy of a rational being. We ought to, (and practically, we must) receive every truth on its own evidence. If we cannot reconcile one fact with another, it is because of our ignorance; better instructed men or higher orders of beings may see their perfect harmony. Our want of such knowledge does not in the least impair the force of the evidence on which they separately rest. In every department of knowledge the number of irreconcileable truths depends on the progress of the student. That loose matter flies off from revolving bodies, and that every thing adheres to the surface of the earth, notwithstanding its rapid revolution, are irreconcileable facts to one man, though not to another.

That two rays of light should produce darkness, or two sounds cause silence, are facts which many may be entirely unable to reconcile with other facts of which they are certain, while the philosopher sees not only their consistency, but that they are the necessary consequences of the same cause.

If the evidence of the constant revolution of the earth round its axis were presented to a man, it would certainly be unreasonable to him to deny the fact, merely because he could not reconcile it with the stability of every thing on the earth's surface. Or if he saw two rays of light made to produce darkness, must he resist the evidence of his senses because he knows that two candles give more light than one? Men do not commonly act thus irrationally in physical investigations. They let each fact stand on its own evidence. They strive to reconcile them and are happy when they succeed. But they do not get rid of difficulties by denying facts.

If in the department of physical knowledge we are obliged to act upon the principle of receiving every fact upon its own evidence, even when unable to reconcile one with another, it is not wonderful that this necessity should be imposed upon us in those departments of knowledge, which are less within the limits of our powers. It is certainly irrational for a man to reject all the evidence of the spirituality of the soul, because he cannot reconcile with that doctrine the fact that a disease of the body disorders the mind. Must I do violence to my nature in denying the proof of design afforded by the human body, because I cannot account for the occasional occurrence of deformities of structure? Must I harden my heart against all the evidence of the benevolence of God, which streams upon me in a flood of light from all his works, because I may not know how to reconcile that benevolence with the existence of evil? Must I deny my free agency, the most intimate of all convictions, because I cannot see the consistency between the freeness of an act and the certainty of its occurrence? Must I deny that I am a moral being, the very glory of my nature, because I cannot change my character at will?

It is impossible for any man to act, in any department of knowledge, upon the principle, on which these cavilling objections to religion are founded. From youth to age we are obliged to take each fact as it comes, upon its own evidence, and reconcile it with other facts, as best we may.

The unreasonableness of this method of arguing is further evident from the consideration that if it were universally adopted it would render all progress in knowledge impossible. It would be tantamount to a resolution to know nothing until we know all things; for our knowledge at first is confined to isolated facts. To classify and harmonize these facts, is the slow work of the student's life. This is a most benevolent arrangement of providence. It at once stimulates the desire of knowledge and imposes on us the constant exercise of faith. And it is in virtue of these two important principles of our nature that all valuable knowledge is obtained. The desire of knowing not merely facts, but their relations and harmony, leads to the constant effort to increase the number of known truths and to obtain an insight into their nature; and the necessity we are under of believing what we cannot understand, or cannot reconcile, cultivates the habit of faith; of faith in evidence, faith in the laws of our nature, faith in God. It is thus our heavenly Father leads us along the paths of knowledge; and he who refuses to be thus led, must remain in ignorance. God deals with us as children; though as rational children. He does not require us to believe without evidence; but he does require us to believe what we cannot understand, and what we cannot reconcile with other parts of knowledge. This necessity of implicit faith is not confined to any one department of knowledge, but as already stated, is constantly demanded with regard to all. The simplest objects in the physical world are surrounded with mysteries. A blade of grass has wonders about it which no philosopher can clear up; no man can tell what fixes the type of each species of plant or animal; by what process the materials of leaf and flower are selected and arranged; whence the beautiful tints are borrowed or how applied; what conducts the silent process of formation of the eye or hand. Every thing we see is, even to the most enlightened, the index of something unknown and inscrutable.

If the visible and tangible forms of matter are replete with things past finding out, what may we expect when we turn our eyes on the world of Spirits. Even that little world in our own bosoms which is pervaded by our own consciousness, the facts of which are most intimately known, is full of wonders; of phenomena which we can neither comprehend nor reconcile. Who can understand the secret union of the soul and body, which establishes their reciprocal influence? Why should the emotion of shame suffuse the cheek, or that of fear send the blood to the heart? Why does the soul suffer if the body be injured? What conception can we form either of matter or mind which is consistent with their mutual influence and communion? The operations of our rational and moral faculties are not less beyond our comprehension. We know certain facts, but the reason of them, or their consistency we cannot understand. We know that certain feelings follow certain perceptions; the feeling of confidence the perception of truth; the feeling of pleasure the perception of beauty; the feeling of approbation the perception of what is morally right. Why these feelings should thus rise no one can tell. Such are the laws of our being; laws which we did not originate and which we cannot control. That is, we cannot prevent the feeling of confidence or faith, attending the perception of truth, nor that of pleasure, the perception of beauty, nor that of approbation, the perception of moral rectitude. Yet the consciousness of self-agency mingles with all these operations. We are free in being subject to the laws of our own nature. The necessity under which we form such judgments or exercise such feelings produces no sense of bondage. In these involuntary or necessary judgments or feelings, however, our moral character is largely concerned. If two men see an act of cruelty, and the one smiles at it, and the other is indignant, no sophistry can prevent our condemning the former and approving the latter. The feeling excited by the act arises in each spontaneously and by an inward necessity which neither, at the moment, can control. The knowledge of this fact does not interfere with our judgment in the case. And that judgment is not merely that the feeling which produced the smile, is an indication of a state of mind, or of previous conduct worthy of disapprobation, but that the feeling itself was wrong. Moreover the feeling of disapprobation which arises thus spontaneously in our bosoms, at this delight in suffering, is itself a moral feeling. We should condemn ourselves if it did not arise, we approve ourselves because of it. There are therefore, in our own breasts, enigmas which we cannot solve, depths which we cannot fathom. Must we then, in order to be rational, deny these facts? Must we maintain that our nature is an illusion and our constitution a falsehood? Shall we, on the one hand, deny that we are subject to the laws of our being, or, on the other, that the acts which result from those laws are not our own, do not express our character nor involve responsibility? This happily cannot be done, for faith in our own consciousness is one of the laws of our nature from which we can never effectually emancipate ourselves.

If then there are in our own nature so many things which we cannot comprehend, how can we expect to understand God, to know the reasons and relations of his acts, or to be able to reconcile in all cases his works with his attributes? To do this would require a more thorough knowledge of God than we have of ourselves. It would require a comprehension of his purposes and of the mode in which he accomplishes them. It would require in short a knowledge which no creature can possess. For what man knoweth the things of a man, save the spirit of man that is in him? Even so the things of God knoweth no man, but the Spirit of God. We then, who are the least and lowest of God's rational creatures, may well expect to be required to live by faith; to receive, as true, on his authority, much that we cannot understand and cannot reconcile. It is not however blind belief which is required of us. We are not required to believe any thing without adequate evidence; but on the other hand we are not allowed to reject any thing simply because we cannot understand it. We must not reject the existence of God, because we cannot comprehend self-existence; we must not deny his eternity, because we cannot conceive of duration without succession, nor his omnipresence, because we cannot see how a being can be equally and entirely in all places at the same time; nor omniscience, because we cannot see how free acts can be foreknown. In like manner we are not required to believe in God's goodness without abundant evidence of his benevolence; but we are required to believe it, whether we can reconcile it with the existence of evil or not. We are not required to believe in the providence of God without evidence, but our being unable to reconcile his government with our liberty, is no rational ground of unbelief. The same remark might be made with regard to the apostacy of our race and the corruption of our nature; our inability and obligation to obedience; the necessity of divine influence and the use of means. We are required to believe nothing on these or any other subjects without adequate proof, but we are not allowed to make our ignorance of the relations of these truths an excuse for either misbelief or disobedience. God gives to the glow worm light enough to see its own path, though not enough to dispel the darkness of the night. Thus too he shows us where to put our foot down in each successive step towards heaven, though he may not enable us to comprehend the Almighty unto perfection.

It may be said that we have not answered one of all the objections to which reference has so often been made. We have done far better than answer them, if we have made the reader feel the necessity of an humble, trustful spirit towards God. This is the appropriate state of mind for every learner, whether in the school of nature or of Christ. It is that state which the feebleness of our powers and the difficulty of the things to be learned, render not only reasonable but indispensable. A second impression which we have laboured to produce is, that it is one of our primary duties to submit to the truth, to form the purpose and to cherish the habit of yielding the mind to evidence. Faith without evidence is irrational; but unbelief in despite of evidence is not less so. There is a great difference, in the temper of different men in relation to this subject. Some resist the truth as long as they can; they cavil at it and oppose it. Others are candid and docile; they are willing to admit the force of proof as far as they perceive it. This is the only way in which true knowledge can be obtained. It is thus the philosopher is accustomed to act. He carefully interrogates nature for facts; these facts are received; they are classified and harmonized as far as the investigator is able thus to reconcile them. But he rejects none because he cannot make it fit into a system. He waits for further light. It is thus we are bound to act. We too are called upon to receive every truth upon its own evidence; to harmonize our knowledge where we can, but to reject nothing simply because of our ignorance of its consistency with other truths.

A third lesson which it is very important for us to learn is, what is adequate evidence of truth and when we are bound to rest satisfied. This may be a question which it is difficult to decide; but as far as religion is concerned the case is sufficiently plain. By the laws of our being we are imperatively required to confide in the well ascertained testimony of our senses; to rely upon the veracity of our own consciousness; to receive the unimpeachable testimony of our fellow men, and to abide by those truths which are matters of intuitive perception, or the necessary conclusions of reason. These are laws of belief impressed upon our constitution by our creator; and are therefore the authoritative expressions of his will. To refuse obedience to these laws is, then, not only unreasonable, it is rebellion against God. They are the adamantine bars by which he has closed up the way to universal scepticism; and those who break through them do but prematurely enter upon the outer darkness. We are obliged then as rational beings to receive every truth which rests upon the testimony of our senses, upon the authority of consciousness, the un-impeachable testimony of witnesses, or the intuitive peceptions or necessary deductions of reason. Whether we can systematize and reconcile all the truths thus arrived at, is a very different question. Our obligation to receive them does not rest upon this power, but upon the evidence afforded for each separate truth. Our conscious-ness tells us that we are sinners; it also informs us of our helpless-ness. We may fight against one or the other of these truths as the ocean chafes the rocks. They cannot be moved. When the mind has been drugged with false philosophy, it may for a time disbelieve. But the infidelity lasts no longer than the intoxication. As soon as the man is sober, the truth re-appears in greater clearness and authority than ever. Nothing therefore can be eventually gained by resistance to the truth, and it is the part of wisdom to submit at once to the laws of belief which God has impressed upon our nature.

Besides this rule of faith, (if it may be so called,) which God has given us in the constitution of our nature, we have his word and his providence, authenticated by all kinds of adequate testimony. There can be no higher ground of faith than the authority of God. Even confidence in the testimony of our senses or the dictates of con-sciousness, resolves itself into confidence in the veracity of God, by whom the laws of nature have been established. Any truth therefore which is sustained by a well authenticated revelation of God, or upon the actual dispensations of his providence, must be considered as fully established; and every objection which can be shown to militate against either, must be considered as fully answered. It was thus that the sacred writers answered objections. It was enough for them that God asserted any truth, or actually exercised any prerogative. Any further vindication they deemed unnecessary. We should act on the same principle and quietly submit to all that God says and to all he does. Some men complainingly ask, Why were we born? Surely it is enough that they are born. The fact cannot be denied, whether they can see the wisdom and design of their creation or not. Or they ask, Why were we born in a state of sin, or in a world in which sin is universal and inevitable? This, to human reason, may be a question impossible to answer. But as the fact stares us in face, is there any use in denying it? But it is further asked, If we are born in such a state that either from our nature or circumstances sin is inevitable and universal, how can we be responsible? Whatever difficulty there may be in showing how we are responsible, there is no doubt as to the fact. We feel ourselves to be responsible, and can no more free ourselves of the conviction than we can get rid of the consciousness of existence. Where then is the wisdom of quarrelling with facts? Why should we spend our lives like a wild beast in a cage forever chafing against the bars of its prison, which nevertheless remain? Let us learn to submit to what we see to be true; let us remember that our knowledge does not embrace all truth; that things may be perfectly consistent with each other and with the attributes of God, though we may not see how. Our knowledge will continually increase; and those facts which give us most difficulty will be found to be so analogous to others, the justice of which we are able to recognise, that if we never come to see all things in their harmony, we shall at least see that they must be consistent, being parts of that system which is every where luminous with the manifestations of the wisdom and love of God. Let us remember that we are children, the children of God, that he gives us abundant evidence of every thing which he requires us to believe, though he renders it necessary for us to exercise confidence in him, to feel assured that what he says is true and that what he does is right; that though clouds and darkness may be round about him, justice and judgment are the habitation of his throne.

The last general remark to be made in reference to these objections, is, that they are almost always dishonestly urged; that is, they are urged with an inward conviction of their fallacy. As in many cases we know things to be true, which we cannot prove, so we often know objections to be fallacious which we cannot answer. If a man denies his own existence, or the distinction between right and wrong, it is in vain to argue with him. There can be nothing plainer than the truth denied, and therefore there can be no means of proving it. So also, if, to escape the charge of guilt, he denies his responsibility, he denies a fact of consciousness, which cannot possibly be made plainer. Or if he plead his inability as an excuse for not repenting and obeying God, he presents a plea which he knows has no validity. He knows that however real this inability may be, it is of such a nature as to afford no excuse for his continuing in sin, because the conviction of its reality co-exists in his own consciousness, with a sense of guilt. It is a plea therefore that does not avail at the bar of his own conscience, and he knows that it will not avail at the bar of God. In like manner, when men object to the strictness of the divine law, they do so with the inward persuasion of the righteousness of that law. Its requirements commend themselves to their conscience. They know that as God is infinitely wise and good, it is right that we should regard him with supreme affection, and implicitly submit to all his directions.

All such cavilling objections, men know to be false. God has not left himself without a witness. His voice has an authority which we cannot resist. When he tells us we are sinners, we know it to be true. When he tells us that we are worthy of death, we know it to be a righteous judgment. When he tells us that we have no strength to save ourselves and that our salvation depends upon his will, we know it to be even so. Whenever he reveals himself our mouths are shut, not from fear merely, but from an intimate persuasion of the justice of all his ways. It is, then, both foolish and wicked to urge objections against the truth, which we ourselves know to be futile, whether this be done with a view to perplex our fellow-men, or in the vain endeavor to silence the accusations of conscience and the word of God.

Such is the power of truth that neither the natural insensibility of the heart, nor the want of consideration, nor the direct efforts which men make to suppress serious thoughts, nor the whole array of sophisticated objections, can avail to counteract the secret conviction in the breast of the impenitent that they are in the road to eternal death. This conviction is often very weak. When men are engrossed in the concerns of this world, it is overlooked. Still it is there; and it is ever and anon waking up to trouble them. Nor can the suggestion that God is merciful and, peradventure, will not be strict to mark iniquity, quiet this uneasy apprehension. This suggestion, therefore, avails but little. It is counteracted by the sense of ill-desert, by the irrepressible conviction that those who commit sin are worthy of death; by the plain declarations of Scripture, and by the evidence which even providence affords that God is righteous. The vague apprehension of coming wrath, therefore, in despite of all their efforts, still haunts the path of the impenitent. It chills their joys and gathers strength whenever the world seems to be receding from their grasp.

Most men are driven to enter the plea of guilty before the bar of conscience, and content themselves with praying for a delay of judgment. They are forced to admit that they are not fit to die in their present state; that they are bound to comply with the requirement of the gospel, but they plead for time. Go thy way for this time; when I have a more convenient season I will call for thee. Conscience is more easily deluded by this plea, which seems to admit its demands, than by any other. It is, therefore, the most dangerous snare for souls. Men do not reflect on the wickedness of pleading with God for liberty to continue, a little longer in sin; to be allowed to break his commandments, to disregard his mercies, to slight his love, and to injure the cause of truth and righteousness. They do not think of the indignation with which they would reject such a plea from an ungrateful and disobedient son or servant. Nor do they remember that every such act of procrastination is a great aggravation of their guilt, as it supposes a consciousness of the evil of their present course and a recognition of the righteousness of all the demands of God. Nor do they consider that the difficulties which beset the path of their return to God are all increased by delay. If the work of repentance be irksome to-day, it will be more irksome to-morrow. If the heart be now hard, it will become yet harder by neglect. If the power of sin be now too strong for us to resist, it will become still stronger by indulgence. If the motives to repentance now fail to secure obedience, they will act with constantly increasing disadvantage hereafter. If God be justly displeased now, he will be more and more displeased by continued disobedience. Every day's procrastination therefore increases, at a fearful rate, the probability of our final perdition.

Chapter IV.

Conviction of Sin.

Section I.   *Knowledge of sin. Sense of personal ill-desert.*

Though men are generally so indifferent to their sinfulness and danger, it often pleases God to arouse their attention, and to produce a deep conviction of the truth of all that the Bible teaches on these subjects. The effects of such conviction are very various, because they are modified by the temperament, the knowledge, the circumstances and concomitant exercises of those who experience it. A sentence of death, if passed upon a hundred men, would probably affect no two of them alike. The mind of one might fasten particularly on the turpitude of his crime; that of another upon the disgrace which he had incurred; that of a third on the sufferings of his friends on his account; that of a fourth upon the horrors of death, or upon the fearfulness of appearing before God. All these and many other views, in endless combination, might operate with still different degrees of force on each, and the result be still further modified by their physical and moral temperament, their knowledge and previous history. The endless diversity, therefore, in the experience of men when convinced of sin, is what might be expected; and shows it to be impossible to give any description of such experience that shall be applicable to all cases. It will be sufficient briefly to state, what the Scriptures teach to be necessary on this subject.

There must be some correct knowledge of sin. It is clearly the doctrine of the Scriptures, confirmed by universal experience, that men are naturally exceedingly blind on this subject. They have very inadequate ideas of the nature of this evil. Being ignorant of the holiness of God, they do not regard the opposition of sin to his nature so much as its effects upon themselves, or upon society. They judge of it by a wrong standard, and hence all their judgments respecting it are either erroneous or defective. Its real nature, or the real source of its evil in a great measure escapes their notice. Hence a thousand things which are unquestionably sinful, they in general overlook or disregard. It is not so much the state of the heart towards God, as the temper and deportment of one man towards his fellow men, that they consider. And therefore they often regard themselves and others as really good, though they may be destitute of any one right sentiment towards their maker. Being ignorant of the true nature of sin, they have no conception of the number of their transgressions. They are disposed to estimate them by the number of positive or overt acts of disobedience to the moral law; overlooking the habitual state of the heart, the uniform want of love, faith, and due reverence towards God. Nor have they any adequate idea of the guilt of sin. It is to them, as it exists in themselves, comparatively a trifle. Any great concern about it, they consider unreasonable; and when manifested by others, hypocritical or fanatical. There is a deceitfulness in sin by which men are deluded so as to form wrong judgments as to its nature, its extent, its turpitude and power. This delusion must be dispelled. The eyes must be opened to see sin as it is represented in the word of God, as an exceedingly evil and bitter thing, as extending not merely to overt acts or out-breaks of passion, but as deeply seated in the heart, polluting at the fountain the streams of life; as really deserving the punishment which God has denounced against it; and as having such hold upon the inward principles of our nature, that its power cannot be broken by any ordinary exertion.

This insight into the Scriptural account of sin is attended with a firm conviction of its truth; and this conviction is inseparable from the kind of knowledge of which we are now speaking; because it is in fact nothing but an insight into the nature of the Scriptural doctrine as true, or as accordant with the moral nature which God has given us. Men therefore are not thus convinced either by argument or authority. They see and feel what God has declared concerning the nature and evil of sin to be true. Hence the conviction is irresistible even when most unwelcome. We often see it taking sudden and powerful possession of the soul, when conscience is roused from its torpor and assents to the declarations of God, with a force not to be resisted. When Paul reasoned of righteousness, temperance and judgment to come, Felix trembled. The truth, externally presented, found such a response in the bosom of the Roman governor that he could not disbelieve. This is in accordance with daily experience. The cavils of men against the unreasonable strictness of the divine law and their objections against the justice of its awful penalty vanish, in a moment, when their eyes are open to see what the law and its violation really are. And so long as the perception lasts, the conviction remains. If they can succeed in shutting out the light, and in quieting conscience aroused by its intrusion, they become as skeptical as ever on all these subjects. In many cases they succeed in closing their eyes on what they hate to see; and regain their former unbelief. But often this is found to be impossible, especially on the near approach of death, or when God is about to pluck them as brands from the burning. Probably a day does not pass without some illustration of the truth of these remarks. Men who have long lived in unbelief or carelessness are arrested by an influence which they can neither understand nor resist. There is no new revelation, no novel arguments, no conscious process of reasoning. There is simply a perception of the truth of the declarations of God concerning sin. Against the conviction thence arising, their old cavils, the arguments and assurances of their friends have no effect. They do not reach the point. They are addressed to something quite foreign to the ground of the conviction, and therefore do not affect it. Though this persuasion of the truth of the Scriptural doctrine respecting sin, is often temporary, it forms an essential part of those convictions which are abiding and saving. Men may have this persuasion who never accept the offers of salvation, but those who do accept them cannot be entirely without it.

This knowledge of sin, which enters so essentially into the nature of true conviction, is derived from the law, for by the law is the knowledge of sin. I had not known sin, said the apostle, but by the law. For without the law, sin was dead. I was alive without the law once; but when the commandment came sin revived and I died. It is clearly taught in these and similar passages, that the apostle was at one time ignorant of the extent and spirituality of the law, and consequently ignorant of sin. He thought himself to be as good as could be reasonably expected. He was contented and at ease. But when the law was revealed to him in its true character, his views of sin were at once changed. He came to know what it was, and to feel its power over him. A thousand things which before had appeared indifferent or trivial, he now saw to be aggravated offences; and especially the secret, deep-seated evil of his heart, which had escaped his knowledge or regard, was detected as the great source of all other sin.

The law is the means of communicating this knowledge, because it is an expression of the perfect holiness of God. So long as men judge themselves by themselves, and compare themselves among themselves, they will be in the dark as to their true character. It is not until they judge themselves by the perfect standard of duty contained in the law of God, that they can have any proper knowledge of their real character. It is in his light that we see light. It is only when we look away from the sinful beings by whom we are surrounded, and feel ourselves in the presence of the perfect purity of God, that we are sensible of the extent of our departure from the standard of excellence. It is therefore both the doctrine of the Bible and the experience of the people of God, that the knowledge of sin arises from the apprehension of the divine excellence as revealed in the law.

There is no doubt great diversity in the experience of Christians as to the clearness of their views on this subject. In some cases every thing is seen as through a glass, darkly; in others there is such a discovery of the infinite excellence of God and of his law, as to fill the mind with the greatest reverence and self-abasement. Sometimes this knowledge steals upon the mind as imperceptibly as the opening day; at others, in a moment, the truth stands disclosed in all its awful purity. The man who one hour was unconcerned, the next is full of astonishment at his former blindness. He wonders how it was possible he could be so ignorant of the excellence of God and the perfection of his law. He is amazed at his infatuation in thinking that he was to be judged by the common standard of man's judgment, by the low demands of the world or of his associates. He now sees that the rule by which he is to be tried is infinitely pure, and cannot over-look the least transgression. We are no where taught what degree of clearness of this knowledge is necessary to salvation. We only know that men must have such a knowledge of sin as to bring their judgments respecting it into accordance with the declarations of God; that instead of that perpetual opposition to the doctrine of the Scriptures respecting the evil and extent of sin, which men so generally evince, they must be brought to acquiesce in the truth and justice of all God's representations on the subject.

Besides this knowledge of sin and assent to the Scriptural doctrine on the subject, there is, in genuine conviction, a sense of personal unworthiness. This perhaps has been in a measure anticipated, but it deserves particular consideration. Holy beings may have a clear perception of the truth as presented in the word of God respecting the nature of sin, but they can have no sense of moral turpitude. And among men there is often a clear understanding of the doctrine on this subject, and a general assent to its truth, without any adequate conviction that what the Bible says of sinners is applicable to us. It is not enough therefore that we should know and believe what the Scriptures teach respecting sin, we must feel that it is all true as it regards ourselves. There must be an assent of our own consciousness to the declaration that the heart is deceitful above all things and desperately wicked; that in us, that is, in our flesh, there dwelleth no good thing. This sense of personal unworthiness is the principal part of conviction of sin. It is the opposite of that false notion of our own excellence, which we are so prone to indulge. It destroys our self-complacency and eradicates the disposition to justify ourselves, or extenuate our guilt.

The most certain concomitant of this sense of moral turpitude in the sight of God, is shame. O my God, cried Ezra under a sense of sin, I am ashamed and blush to lift up my face to thee my God, for our iniquities are increased over our head, and our trespass is grown up unto the heavens. And Daniel said: O Lord, righteousness belongeth unto thee, but unto us confusion of face as at this day. I have heard of thee, said Job, with the hearing of the ear, but now my eye seeth thee, and I abhor myself and repent in dust and ashes. And in another place he says: Behold I am vile, what shall I answer thee? I will lay my hand upon my mouth. The same feeling is expressed by the Psalmist, when he says, Mine iniquities have taken hold upon me, so that I cannot look up; they are more than the hairs on my head, therefore, my heart faileth me. The same emotion filled the bosom of the Publican, when he would not so much as lift up his eyes to heaven, but smote upon his breast and said, God be merciful to me a sinner.

With this sense of unworthiness are mingled, in a greater or less degree, the feelings of contrition and remorse; sorrow for our innumerable offences, and bitter self-condemnation. To these are often added perplexity and fear of the wrath of God; a dread lest our sins never can be forgiven, lest our defilement never can be washed away. No suffering in this world can exceed what the soul often endures under the pressure of these feelings. It cries out with Paul, O wretched man that I am, who shall deliver me from the body of this death? Or it is forced to say with Job, The arrows of the Almighty are within me, the poison whereof drinketh up my spirits; and the terrors of God do set themselves in array against me. Or with David, While I suffer thy terrors I am distracted; thy fierce wrath goeth over me; thy terrors have cut me off.

With the inspired record of the experience of God's people on this subject, we find the langauge of his more eminent servants in the later times remarkably coincident. The confessions of Augustin are full of similar expressions of humiliation and anguish under a sense of sin. And even the stout heart of Luther was so broken by his inward sufferings, that his life was long a burden almost too heavy for him to bear. But while it is no doubt true that it is the natural tendency of correct apprehensions of our real character in the sight of God to produce these strong emotions of humiliation and sorrow; and while it is no less true that those who have made the most eminent attainments in holiness, have generally had the largest share of these inward trials, it is not to be supposed that they are necessary to the character of a Christian. On the contrary a believing apprehension of the mercy of God in Jesus Christ, while it would not prevent humiliation and penitential sorrow on account of sin, would effectually extract the bitterness of remorse and fear from the cup of repentance. There is no true religion in these terrors and fearful apprehensions. The death-bed of the impenitent often exhibits this sense of guilt, humiliation, remorse, dread of punishment and other indications of an enlightened and awakened conscience. And in many cases those who have suffered all this distress, lose their serious impressions and sink into their former carelessness. Though, therefore, the pain of remorse and dread of the wrath of God often attend conviction of sin, they do not constitute it. In many cases there is little of this agitation of feeling. Perhaps the most frequent form of religious experience on this subject is a deep distress on account of the want of an excitement of feeling corresponding with the judgment of the understanding and conscience. The common complaint with many is that they cannot feel; that their hearts are like ice; that the knowledge and perception of their ingratitude and disobedience produce little or no emotion. Such persons would gladly exchange their insensibility for the keenest anguish; their constant prayer is that God would take from them their heart of stone, and give them a heart of flesh. This form of experience is just as consistent with the nature of conviction of sin as the other. All that is necessary is the testimony of conscience to the justice of the divine representations of our character and conduct; the consciousness and acknowledgment that we are what God declares us to be. Where this judgment of the conscience, or this sense of personal unworthiness exists, leading the sinner to lay his hand upon his mouth in the presence of God, and to bow at his feet as undeserving of mercy, there, as far as this point is concerned, is genuine conviction.

This state of mind may be produced in very different ways. Sometimes it is the result of a calm review of life and a comparison of the habitual state of the heart and general course of our conduct with the law of God. Sometimes, some one offence more than commonly aggravated seizes upon the conscience; some broken vow, some neglected call, some open sin, is made the means of revealing the man to himself. Whatever may be the particular occasion, the mind is led to fix itself on its responsibility to God and the conviction of its guilt becomes settled and confirmed. This is necessary to the sinner's return to God. So long as he thinks himself whole, he will not apply to the physician. So long as he regards his sins as either few or trivial, he will feel no concern for pardon or sanctification. But when his eyes are opened and his conscience aroused, he feels that his case demands immediate and earnest attention; he knows himself to be unprepared to meet his God, that his sins are so great that they cannot be forgiven, unless he obtains an interest in the redemption that is in Christ Jesus. Every true Christian is in some way brought to this conviction and acknowledgment of personal ill-desert in the sight of God.

In the third place, conviction of sin includes a conviction of our condemnation before God. A sense of sin is a sense of unworthiness and a sense of unworthiness involves a sense of just exposure to the divine displeasure. It may be proper to notice three very distinct states of mind in reference to this subject. It is very obvious that our views of the punishment due to sin, must depend upon our views of sin itself. If we have inadequate apprehensions of the evil of sin, we shall have inadequate apprehensions of the punishment which it deserves. Hence in the great majority of men there is a secret disbelief of the Scriptural representations on this subject. They cannot reconcile the declarations of God respecting the doom of the impenitent with their views of his justice and mercy, and, therefore, they cannot believe them. And it very often happens that the sense of sin which serious people experience is insufficient to overcome this unbelief, or at least, the strong opposition of the heart to what the Bible teaches on this subject. They feel that they are sinners, they feel that they deserve the displeasure of God, but they still experience a secret revolting against the dreadful denunciations of the Scriptures against all sin. "To submit to the condemning power of the holy law of God," says Dr. Milner, "is a hard matter, a very hard matter indeed to do this thoroughly. My understanding has shown me, for many years, that this was the touch-stone of a sound conversion; and I have been busy enough in noting the defect of it in others; but as to myself, if I have got on at all in this respect, it is very lately indeed. The heart is sadly deceitful here; for, with Christ's salvation before one's eye, one may easily fancy that God is just and equitable in condemning sinners; when if you put the case, only for a moment, to your own heart seriously, as a thing likely to happen, the heart will rise against such a dispensation; perhaps indeed with a smothered sort of opposition and dislike, but which is very steady and determined. Nothing less than the Holy Ghost himself can cure this, by showing us the glory of God in the face of Jesus Christ.''[90] That the soul should revolt at the idea of its own misery, is the law of our nature, and never can be eradicated. This is not the sentiment which it is intended to condemn, but the opposition of the heart to the truth and justice of God's declarations respecting the punishment due to sin. It is this opposition, this disposition to criminate God, to regard him as unjustly severe, which ought to be subdued; because it shows that our hearts are not in harmony with his word; that we regard as unjust what he pronounces just. All experience shows that this is a very common state of mind. And its existence proves that our views of the ill-desert of sin have not been sufficiently clear to bring us to submit to the plan which God has revealed for our redemption from deserved condemnation.

The opposite extreme to this is the feeling that our sins are so great that they cannot be forgiven. This is no uncommon persuasion. When there is a clear discovery of the evil of sin, with no comcomitant apprehension of the true plan of salvation, despair is the natural result. The judgment of conscience is known to be true when it pronounces our sins to be deserving of death. And unless the soul sees how God can be just and yet justify the sinner, it cannot hope for mercy. Nothing can be more pitiable than a soul in this condition. Its views of the justice of God and of the evil of sin, are neither false nor exaggerated. It is their truth which gives them power, and which renders futile the soothing assurance of friends that God will not be so strict in marking iniquity, or that the sinner's guilt is not so great as he imagines. An enlightened conscience cannot be thus appeased, and if such be the only sources of consolation to which it has access, it must despair.

In a Christian country, however, the knowledge of the plan of salvation is so generally diffused, that it seldom fails, even when imperfectly understood, to calm or restrain the apprehensions of God's displeasure. It is known that God can pardon sin, that there is salvation at least for some, for some have been saved. And although the sinner is often disposed to think that his is an excepted case, or that there is some peculiar aggravation in his guilt, which puts him

---

90. Wilberforce's Correspondence.

beyond the reach of mercy, yet he cannot be sure that this is the case. And in his darkest hours the belief in the possibility of salvation is not entirely destroyed.

Between these extremes of inimical opposition of the truth of God as to the just exposure of the sinner to condemnation and the despair of mercy which arises from unbelief, lies genuine conviction of ill-desert. If religious experience is the conformity of our judgments and feelings to the truths that are revealed in the Scriptures and if it is there revealed that the wages of sin is death, our judgment and feeling must assent to that truth; we must admit that such is the just desert of sin and of our sins. There must be no disposition to complain of the extent or severity of the law; but such a sense of ill-desert in the sight of God as shall lead us to lie at his feet, sensible that he can neither do nor threaten wrong and that forgiveness must be a matter entirely of grace. It is obvious that there can be no intelligent acceptance of Christ as a saviour without this conviction of our exposure to condemnation and there can be no conviction of such exposure, without a perception of the justice of the penalty of the law. It is, however, to be remembered that there are many things involved in Christian experience, which may not be the object of distinct attention. It may, therefore, well happen that many pass from death unto life, without any lively apprehension of the wrath of God, or any very distinct impression that all that he has threatened against sin might be justly inflicted upon them. Their attention may have been arrested and their hearts moved by the exhibition of the love of God in Christ, and they may have been conscious, at the time, of little more than a cordial acquiescence in the gospel, and the desire and purpose to live for the service of God. Still, even in such persons, as soon as their attention is directed to the subject, there is a full recognition of ill-desert, a readiness to acknowledge that salvation is a matter of grace, and that they would have no right to complain had they been left to perish in their sins. Diversified, therefore, as may be the experience of God's people on this subject, they agree in acknowledging the justice of God in his demands and his threatenings and in regarding themselves as unworthy of the least of all his favours.

SECTION II.   *Insufficiency of our own righteousness and of our own strength.*

Another essential characteristic of genuine conviction is the persuasion that our own good works are entirely insufficient to recommend us to God, or to be the ground of our acceptance before him. Since the Scriptures declare that we are justified freely, not by works, lest any man should boast, but by faith in Jesus Christ, our experience must accord with this declaration. We must have such views of the holiness of God, of the extent of his law and of our own unworthiness as shall make us fully sensible that we cannot by our own works secure either pardon or acceptance. It is easy to profess that we do not trust to our own righteousness, but really to divest ourselves of all reliance upon our supposed excellence, is a difficult task. When a man is roused to a sense of his guilt and danger, his first impulse is almost always to fly to any other refuge than that provided in the gospel. The most natural method of appeasing conscience is the promise of reformation. Particular sins are therefore forsaken, and a struggle, it may be, is maintained against all others. This conflict is often long and painful, but it is always unsuccessful. It is soon found that sin, in one form or other, is constantly getting the mastery, and the soul feels that something more must be done if it is ever to make itself fit for heaven. It is, therefore, ready to do, or to submit to any thing which appears necessary for this purpose. What particular form of works it may be which it endeavours to weave into a robe of righteousness, depends on the degree of knowledge which it possesses, or the kind of religious instruction which it receives. When greatly ignorant of the gospel, it endeavours by painful penances, self-imposed, or prescribed by priestly authority, to make satisfaction for its sins. Experience teaches that there is no extremity of self-denial to which a conscience-stricken man will not gladly submit as a means of satisfying the demands of God. If heaven were really to be gained by such means, we should see the road crowded by the young and old, the rich and poor, the learned and ignorant, in multitudes as countless as those which throng the cruel temples of the Hindoos, or which perish on the burning sands of Arabia. This is the easiest, the pleasantest, the most congenial of all the methods of salvation, taught by the cunning craftiness of men. It is no wonder that those who teach it as the doctrine of the gospel, should find submissive hearers. If men can be allowed to purchase heaven, or make atonement for past transgressions, by present suffering, they will gladly undertake it. This is so congenial to the human heart, that men who are well informed, and who pride themselves on their independence of mind, are scarcely less apt to be caught in the meshes of this net, than their more ignorant brethren. We see, therefore, statesmen and philosophers, as well as peasants, wearing sack-cloth, or walking barefoot, at the bidding of their religious teachers.

In Protestant countries, where the Bible is generally accessible, it is rare to see any such gross exhibitions of the spirit of self-righteousness. The Scriptures so clearly teach the method of salvation, that almost every one knows that at least mere external works of morality or discipline cannot avail to our justification before God. We must have a finer robe, a robe composed of duties of a higher value. Prayers are multiplied, the house of God is frequented, the whole routine of religious duties is assiduously attended to, under the impression that thus we shall satisfy the demands of God and secure his favour. Multitudes are contented with this routine. Their apprehensions of the character and requirements of God, of the evil of sin, and of their own ill-desert are so low, that this remedy is adequate for all the wounds their consciences feel. The performance of their social and religious duties seems sufficient, in their view, to entitle them to the character of religious men; and they are satisfied. Thus it was with Paul, who considered himself, as touching the righteousness which is of the law to be blameless. But all his strictness of moral duty and religious observance, was discovered to be worthless, so far as satisfying the demands of God is concerned. And every man, who is brought to accept the offer of salvation as presented in the gospel, is made to feel that it is not for any thing which he either does or abstains from doing, that his sins are pardoned and his person accepted before God. Nay, he sees that what men call their good works are so impure, as to be themselves a ground of condemnation. What are cold, wandering, selfish, irreverent prayers, but offences against God, whom we pretend to propitiate, by services which are but a mockery of his holiness? And what is any routine of heartless observances, or if not heartless, at least so imperfect as to fail of securing even our own approbation, in the eyes of him before whom the heavens are unclean? What approach can such services make either towards satisfying the present demands of God, or atoning for years of neglect and sin? It requires but little insight into the state of his own heart, or the real character of the divine law, to convince the sinner that he must have a better righteousness than that which consists of his own duties or observances.

From this foundation of sand the convinced sinner is, therefore, soon driven, but he betakes himself to another refuge nearer the cross, as he supposes, and which seems to require more self-renunciation. He ceases to think of establishing his own righteousness, but he still wishes to be made worthy to receive the righteousness of God. He knows that he can never cancel his debt of guilt, that his best services are unworthy of acceptance, that with all his circumspection he never lives a day in full compliance with the just demands of the law, and consequently that his salvation must be of grace, but he still thinks he must in some way merit that grace, or at least, be prepared by some observance or some experience for its reception. The distressed soul imagines that if it could be more distressed, more humbled, more touched with sorrow or remorse, it might then find acceptance. It sees that its long course of disobedience and ingratitude, its rejection of Christ, its disregard of mercies and warnings, its thousand sins of commission and omission, if forgiven at all, must be gratuitously pardoned, but this hardness of heart, this want of due tenderness and penitence, is a sin which must first be got out of the way, before the others can be remitted. It is, however, only one of the long, black catalogue. It can no more be separately conquered or atoned for, before coming to Christ, than any other sin of heart or life. It is often long before the soul is brought to see this, or to feel that it is really endeavouring to make itself better before applying to the physician; to accomplish at least some preparatory part of salvation for itself, so as not to be entirely indebted to the Redeemer. At last, however, the soul discovers its mistake; it finds that Christ does not save sinners for their tenderness or conviction, that tears are not more worthy of acceptance, than fasting, or almsgiving; that it is the unworthy, the hard-hearted, the ungodly, those who have nothing to recommend them, that Christ came to save, and whom he accepts in order to render them contrite and tenderhearted and obedient. These graces are his gifts, and if we stay away from him until we get them ourselves, we must perish in our sins. To this entire self-renunciation, this absolute rejection of every thing in itself as the ground, or reason of its acceptance, must the soul be brought before it embraces the offers of the gospel.

It is included in what has been said that a consciousness of our own weakness is a necessary ingredient, or consequence of true conviction. There is not only a giving up of our own righteousness, but of our own strength. All that is necessary here as on other points, is that we should feel what is true. If it is the doctrine of the Bible that the sinner can change his own heart, subdue his sins, excite all right affections in his heart, then genuine religious experience requires that this truth should be known, not merely as a matter of speculation, but as a matter of consciousness. But if the Scriptures teach that this change of heart is the work of the Holy Spirit; that we are born not of the will of man but of God; that it is the exceeding greatness of the divine power that operates in them that believe, quickening those who were dead in trespasses and sins, creating them anew in Christ Jesus, so that they are his workmanship, created unto good works; if from one end of the Scriptures to the other, the internal work of salvation is declared to be not by the might, or power of man, but by the Spirit of the Lord, then is this one of the great truths of revelation of which we must be convinced. Our experience must accord with this representation and we must feel that to be true in our case, which God declares to be true universally.

When a man is brought to feel that he is a sinner, that his heart is far from being right in the sight of God, he as naturally turns to his own strength to effect a change and to bring himself up to the standard of the law, as he turns to his own works as a compensation for his sins, or as a ground of confidence towards God. His efforts, therefore, are directed to subdue the power of sin, and to excite religious feelings in his heart. He endeavours to mortify pride, to subdue the influence of the body, to wean himself from the world. He gives up his sinful, or worldly associates; he strengthens his purposes against evil; he forces himself to discharge the most ungrateful duties and exercises himself in self-denial. At the same time he tries to force himself into a right state of mind, to make himself spiritual, repent, love and exercise all the Christian graces of meekness, humility, brotherly kindness and charity; that is, he tries to make himself religious. He does every thing in his own strength and to save himself. Sometimes this course is pursued to the end of life. At others, it is continued for years and then found to be all in vain. Wesley tells us this was the kind of religion which he had, until his visit to America and his intercourse with the Moravians. This is the religion of ascetics, which may be persevered in, through stress of conscience, or fear of perdition, with great strictness and constancy. Almost every man makes trial of it. He will be his own saviour, if he can. It is found, however, by those who are taught of God, to be a hopeless task. The subtle evil of the heart is not to be subdued by any such efforts. If we force ourselves to forego the pleasures of sin, we cannot destroy the desire of forbidden joys. If we refuse to gratify pride, we cannot prevent its aspirations. If we relinquish the pursuit of worldly things, we still retain the love of the world. If we force ourselves to perform religious duties, we cannot make those duties a delight. If we compel ourselves to think of God, we cannot force ourselves to love him, to desire communion with him, to take pleasure in his service, and to delight in all his requirements. No one can tell the misery arising from these painful and ineffectual struggles; these vain attempts to subdue sin and excite the Christian graces. If any thing could be taken as a substitute for them; if making many prayers, or submitting to any suffering, could be taken as an equivalent, it would be gladly acceded to. But to change the heart, to delight in God, to be really spiritual and holy, is a work the sinner finds to be above his strength and yet absolutely necessary. Repeated failures do not destroy his delusion; he still thinks that this is his work and that he must do it, or be lost. He, therefore, struggles on, he collects all his strength, and at length suddenly discovers it to be perfect weakness. He finds that if he is ever renewed and made holy, it must be the work of God and he cries in the depth of his distress, Lord save me, or I perish. He gives up working in his own strength and sees, what he wonders he never saw before, that the Christian virtues are really graces, i.e. gifts; that they are not excellencies to be wrought out by ourselves; but favours bestowed through Christ and for Christ's sake; that it is the Holy Spirit purchased and sent by Him that is to change the heart and convince of sin, righteousness and judgment; that faith, repentance, joy, peace, humility and meekness are the fruits of that Spirit and not the products of our own evil hearts; that if we could make ourselves holy we should scarcely need a Saviour; and that it is the greatest of all delusions to suppose that we must be holy before we come to God through Christ, instead of holiness being the result of our reconciliation. While we are under the law, we bring forth fruit unto death. It is not until we are free from the law and reconciled to God by the death of his Son, that we bring forth fruit unto righteousness. This great truth, though written on every page of the Bible, every man has to learn for himself. He cannot be made to understand it by reading it in the Scriptures, or by being told it by others. He must try his own strength until he finds it to be nothing, before he submits to be saved by grace of God and bowing at the feet of Jesus, in utter despair of any other helper, says, Lord if thou wilt, thou canst make me clean.

The man, therefore, whom the Holy Ghost convinces of sin, he causes to understand and believe what God has revealed on this subject. He makes him feel that what He declares to be true of all men, is true of him; that he deserves what God declares all men to deserve; that he has no merit to recommend him to God and no strength to change his own heart. This knowledge the Spirit communicates through the law, which by presenting the perfect rule of duty, shows us how far short we come of the glory of God, and how often and justly we have incurred its penalty; which convinces us that we are entirely unable to comply with its righteous demands, and that no mere objective presentation of what is holy, just and good can change the heart, or destroy the power of indwelling sin; since even when we see the excellence of the law we do not conform to it and cannot do the things that we would, but ever find a law in our members warring against the law of our minds and bringing us into subjection of the law of sin. It is thus that the law is a school-master to bring us to Christ; to drive us from every refuge of our own righteousness and strength, to Him who is made of God, unto those that believe, both justification and sanctification.

Chapter V.

Justification.

SECTION I.   *Importance of the doctrine. Explanation of the Scriptural terms relating to it. Justification is not by works.*

The state of mind described in the preceding chapter, cannot be long endured. Some way of satisfying the demands of conscience must be adopted. When the mind is enlightened by divine truth and duly impressed with a sense of guilt, it cannot fail anxiously to enquire, How can a man be just with God? The answer given to this question decides the character of our religion, and if practically adopted, our future destiny. To give a wrong answer, is to mistake the way to heaven. It is to err where error is fatal, because it cannot be corrected. If God require one thing and we present another, how can we be saved? If he has revealed a method in which he can be just and yet justify the sinner, and if we reject that method and insist upon pursuing a different way, how can we hope to be accepted? The answer, therefore, which is given to the above question should be seriously pondered by all who assume the office of religious teachers, and by all who rely upon their instructions. As we are not to be judged by proxy, but every man must answer for himself, so every man should be satisfied for himself what the Bible teaches on this subject. All that religious teachers can do, is to endeavour to aid the investigations of those who are anxious to learn the way of life. And in doing this, the safest method is to adhere strictly to the instructions of the Scriptures, and exhibit the subject as it is there presented. The substance and the form of this all-important doctrine are so intimately connected, that those who attempt to separate them, can hardly fail to err. What one discards as belonging merely to the form, another considers as belonging to its substance. All certainty and security are lost, as soon as this method is adopted, and it becomes a matter to be decided exclusively by our own views of right and wrong, what is to be retained and what rejected from the Scriptural representations. Our only security, therefore, is to take the language of the Bible in its obvious meaning, and put upon it the construction which the persons to whom it was addressed must have given, and which, consequently, the sacred writers intended it should bear.

As the doctrine of justification is not only frequently stated in the sacred Scriptures, but formally taught and vindicated, all that will be attempted in this chapter, is to give, as faithfully as possible, a representation of what the inspired writers inculcate on this subject; that is, to state what positions they assume, by what arguments they sustain those positions, how they answer the objections to their doctrine and what application they make of it to the hearts and conscience of their readers.

It is one of the primary doctrines of the Bible, everywhere either asserted or assumed, that we are under the law of God. This is true of all classes of men, whether they enjoy a divine revelation or not. Every thing which God has revealed as a rule of duty enters into the constitution of the law which binds those to whom that revelation is given, and by which they are to be ultimately judged. Those who have not received an external revelation of the divine will, are a law unto themselves. The knowledge of right and wrong, written upon their hearts, is of the nature of a divine law, having its authority and sanction, and by it the heathen are to be judged in the last day.

God has seen fit to annex the promise of life to obedience to his law. The man that doeth these things shall live by them,[91] is the language of Scripture on this subject. To the lawyer who admitted that the law required love to God and man, our Saviour said, Thou hast answered right. This do, and thou shalt live.[92] And to one who asked him, What good thing shall I do that I may have eternal life? he said, If thou wouldst enter into life, keep the commandments.[93] On the other hand, the law denounces death as the penalty of transgression. The wages of sin is death. Such is the uniform declaration of Scripture on this subject.

The obedience which the law demands, is called righteousness; and those who render that obedience are called righteous. To ascribe righteousness to any one, or to pronounce him righteous, is the scriptural meaning of the word to justify. The word never means to make good in a moral sense, but always to pronounce just or righteous. Thus God says, I will not justify the wicked.[94] Judges are commanded to justify the righteous and to condemn the wicked.[95] Woe is pronounced on those who justify the wicked for a reward.[96] In the New Testament it is said, By the deeds of the law shall no flesh be justified in his sight.** It is God who justifieth, who is he that condemneth.[97] There is scarcely a word in the Bible the meaning of

---

91. Rom. x. 5.
92. Luke x. 28.
93. Matt. xix. 17.
94. Ex. xxiii. 7.
95. Deut. xxv. 1.
96. Is. v. 23.
** Rom. iii. 20.
97. Rom. viii. 33, 34.

which is less open to doubt. There is no passage in the New Testament in which it is used out of its ordinary and obvious sense.[98] When God justifies a man, he declares him to be righteous. To justify never means to render one holy. It is said to be sinful to justify the wicked; but it could never be sinful to render the wicked holy. And as the law demands righteousness, to impute or ascribe righteousness to any one, is in scriptural language to justify. To make (or constitute) righteous, is another equivalent form of expression. Hence to be righteous before God, and to be justified, mean the same thing; as in the following passage, Not the hearers of the law are righteous before God, but the doers of the law shall be justified.[99] The attentive, and especially the anxious reader of the Bible cannot fail to observe that these various expressions, to be righteous in the sight of God, to impute righteousness, to constitute righteous, to justify, and others of similar import, are so interchanged as to explain each other, and to make it clear that to justify a man is to ascribe or impute to him righteousness. The great question then is, How is this righteousness to be obtained? We have reason to be thankful that the answer which the Bible gives to this question is so perfectly plain.

In the first place, that the righteousness by which we are to be justified before God is not of works, is not only asserted but proved. The apostle's first argument on this point is derived from the consideration that the law demands a perfect righteousness. If the law was satisfied by an imperfect obedience, or by a routine of external duties, or by any service which men are competent to render, then indeed justification would be by works. But since it demands perfect obedience, justification by works is, for sinners, absolutely impossible. It is thus the apostle reasons.[100] As many as are of the works of the law, are under the curse. For it is written, cursed is every one that continueth not in all things written in the book of the law to do them. As the law pronounces its curse upon every man who continues not to do all that it commands, and as no man can pretend to this perfect obedience, it follows that all who look to the law for justi-

---

98. Revelation xxii. 11, is probably no exception to this remark, as the text in that passage is uncertain.
99. Rom. ii. 13.
100. Gal. iii. 10.

fication must be condemned. To the same effect in the following verse, he says, The law is not of faith, but the man that doeth them shall live by them. That is, the law is not satisfied by any single grace or imperfect obedience. It knows and can know no other ground of justification than complete compliance with its demands. Hence in the same chapter, Paul says, If there had been a law which could have given life, verily righteousness would have been by the law. Could the law pronounce righteous, and thus give a title to the promised life to those who had broken its commands, there would have been no necessity of any other provision for the salvation of men; but as the law cannot thus lower its demands, justification by the law is impossible. The same truth is taught in a different form, when it is said, If righteousness come by the law, Christ is dead in vain.[101] There would have been no necessity for the death of Christ, if it had been possible to satisfy the law by the imperfect obedience which we can render. Paul therefore warns all those who look to works for justification that they are debtors to do the whole law.[102] It knows no compromise; it cannot demand less than what is right, and perfect obedience is right, and therefore its only language is as before, Cursed is every one that continueth not in all things written in the book of the law to do them; and, The man that doeth those things shall live by them. Every man, therefore, who expects justification by works, must see to it, not that he is better than other men, or that he is very exact and does many things, or that he fasts twice in the week, and gives tithes of all he possesses, but that he is sinless.

That the law of God is thus strict in its demands, is a truth which lies at the foundation of all Paul's reasoning in reference to the method of justification. He proves that the Gentiles have sinned against the law written on their hearts; and that the Jews have broken the law revealed in their Scriptures; both Jews and Gentiles therefore are under sin, and the whole world is guilty before God. Hence he infers that by the deeds of the law there shall no flesh be justified in his sight. There is however no force in this reasoning, except on the assumption, that the law demands perfect obedience. How many men, who freely acknowledge that they are sinners, depend upon

---

101. Gal. ii. 21.
102. Ibid v. 3.

their works for acceptance with God? They see no inconsistency between the acknowledgment of sin, and the expectation of justification by works. The reason is, they proceed upon a very different principle from that adopted by the apostle. They suppose that the law may be satisfied by very imperfect obedience. Paul assumes that God demands perfect conformity to his will, that his wrath is revealed against all ungodliness and unrighteousness of men. With him therefore it is enough that men have sinned, to prove that they cannot be justified by works. It is not a question of degrees, more or less, for as to this point there is no difference, since all have sinned, and come short of the glory of God.

This doctrine, though so plainly taught in scripture, men are disposed to think very severe. They imagine that their good deeds will be compared with their evil deeds, and that they will be rewarded or punished as the one or the other preponderates; or that the sins of one part of life may be atoned for by the good works of another; or that they can escape by mere confession and repentance. They could not entertain such expectations, if they believed themselves to be under a law. No human law is administered as men seem to hope the law of God will be. He who steals or murders, though it be but once, though he confesses and repents, though he does any number of acts of charity, is not less a thief or murderer. The law cannot take cognizance of his repentance and reformation. If he steals or murders the law condemns him. Justification by the law is for him impossible. The law of God extends to the most secret exercises of the heart. It condemns whatever is in its nature evil. If a man violate this perfect rule of right, there is an end of justification by the law; he has failed to comply with its conditions; and the law can only condemn him. To justify him, would be to say that he had not transgressed. Men however think that they are not to be dealt with on the principles of strict law. Here is their fatal mistake. It is here that they are in most direct conflict with the Scriptures, which proceed upon the uniform assumption of our subjection to the law. Under the government of God, strict law is nothing but perfect excellence; it is the steady exercise of moral rectitude. Even conscience, when duly enlightened and roused, is as strict as the law of God. It refuses to be appeased by repentance, reformation, or penance. It enforces every command and every denunciation of our Supreme Ruler, and teaches, as plainly as do the Scriptures themselves, that justification by an imperfect obedience is impossible. As conscience however is fallible, no reliance on this subject is placed on her testimony. The appeal is to the word of God; which clearly teaches that it is impossible a sinner can be justified by works, because the law demands perfect obedience.

The apostle's second argument to show that justification is not by works, is the testimony of the Scriptures of the Old Testament. This testimony is urged in various forms. In the first place, as the apostle proceeds upon the principle that the law demands perfect obedience, all those passages which assert the universal sinfulness of men, are so many declarations that they cannot be justified by works. He therefore quotes such passages as the following: There is none righteous, no not one. There is none that understandeth, there is none that seeketh after God. They are all gone out of the way; they are altogether become unprofitable; there is none that doeth good, no not one.[103] The Old Testament, by teaching that all men are sinners, does, in the apostle's view, thereby teach that they can never be accepted before God on the ground of their own righteousness. To say that a man is a sinner, is to say that the law condemns him; and of course it cannot justify him. As the ancient Scriptures are full of declarations of the sinfulness of men, so they are full of proof that justification is not by works.

But in the second place, Paul cites their direct affirmative testimony in support of his doctrine. In the Psalms it is said, Enter not into judgment with thy servant; for in thy sight shall no man living be justified.[104] This passage he often quotes; and to the same class belong all those passages which speak of the insufficiency or worthlessness of human righteousness in the sight of God.

In the third place, the apostle refers to those passages which imply the doctrine for which he contends; that is, to those which speak of the acceptance of men with God as a matter of grace, as something which they do not deserve, and for which they can urge no claim founded upon their own merit. It is with this view that he refers to the language of David; Blessed are they whose

---

103. Rom. iii. 10, 12.
104. Ps. cxliii. 2.

iniquities are forgiven, and whose sins are covered. Blessed is the man to whom the Lord will not impute sin.[105] The fact that a man is forgiven implies that he is guilty; and the fact that he is guilty, implies that his justification cannot rest upon his own character or conduct. It need hardly be remarked, that in this view, the whole Scriptures, from beginning to the end, are crowded with condemnations of the doctrine of justification by works. Every penitent confession, every appeal to God's mercy, is a renunciation of all personal merit, a declaration that the penitent's hope was not founded on any thing in himself. Such confessions and appeals are indeed often made by those who still rely upon their good works, or inherent righteousness, for acceptance with God. This, however, does not invalidate the apostle's argument. It only shows that such persons have a different view of what is necessary for justification, from that entertained by the apostle. They suppose that the demands of the law are so low, that although they are sinners and need to be forgiven, they can still do what the law demands. Whereas, Paul proceeds on the assumption that the law requires perfect obedience, and therefore every confession of sin, or appeal for mercy, involves a renunciation of justification by the law.

Again, the apostle represents the Old Testament as teaching that justification is not by works, by showing that they inculcate a different method of obtaining acceptance with God. This they do by the doctrine which they teach concerning the Messiah as a Redeemer from sin. Hence Paul says that the method of justification without works, (not founded upon works) was testified by the law and the prophets, that is, by the whole of the Old Testament. The two methods of acceptance with God, the one by works the other by a propitiation for sin, are incompatible. And as the ancient Scriptures teach the latter method, they repudiate the former. But they moreover, in express terms, assert, That the just shall live by faith. And the law knows nothing of faith; its language is, The man that doeth them shall live by them.[106] The law knows nothing of any thing but obedience as the ground of acceptance. If the Scriptures say we are

---

105. Rom. iv. 7, 8.
106. Gal. iii. 11, 12.

accepted through faith, they thereby say that we are not accepted on the ground of obedience.

Again, the examples of justification given in the Old Testament, show that it was not by works. The apostle appeals particularly to the case of Abraham, and asks, Whether he attained justification by works? and answers, No, for if he were justified by works he had whereof to glory, but he had no ground of glorying before God, and, therefore, he was not justified by works. And the Scriptures expressly assert. Abraham believed God and it was imputed to him for righteousness. His acceptance, therefore, was by faith and not by works.

In all these various ways, does the apostle make the authority of the Old Testament sustain his doctrine that justification is not by works. This authority is as decisive for us as it was for the ancient Jewish Christians. We also believe the Old Testament to be the word of God, and its truths come to us explained and enforced by Christ and his apostles. We have the great advantage of an infallible interpretation of these early oracles of truth, and the argumentative manner in which their authority is cited and applied prevents all obscurity as to the real intentions of the sacred writers. That by the deeds of the law no flesh shall be justifed before God, is taught so clearly and so frequently in the New Testament, it is so often asserted, so formally proved, so variously assumed, that no one can doubt that such is indeed the doctrine of the word of God. The only point on which the serious inquirer can even raise a question, is what kind of works do the Scriptures mean to exclude as the foundation for acceptance with God. Does the apostle mean works in the widest sense, or does he merely intend ceremonial observances, or works of mere formality performed without any real love to God.

Those who attend to the nature of his assertions and to the course of his argument, will find that there is no room for doubt on this subject. The primary principle on which his argument rests precludes all ground for mistaking his meaning. He assumes that the law demands perfect obedience, and as no man can render that obedience, he infers that no man can be justified by the law. He does not argue that because the law is spiritual it cannot be satisfied by mere ceremonies or by works flowing from an impure motive. He no where says, that though we cannot be justified by external rites, or by works having the mere form of goodness, we are justified by our sincere though imperfect obedience. On the contrary he constantly teaches, that since we are sinners and since the law condemns all sin, it condemns us, and justification by the law is, therefore, impossible. This argument applies to the Jews and the Gentiles without distinction, to the whole world, whether they knew any thing of the Jewish Scriptures or not. It was the moral law, the law which he pronounced holy, just and good, which says, Thou shalt not covet, it is this law, however revealed, whether in the writings of Moses, or in the human heart, of which he constantly asserts that it cannot give life, or teach the way of acceptance with God. As most of those to whom he wrote had enjoyed a divine revelation, and as that revelation included the law of Moses and all its rites, he of course included that law in his statement and often specially refers to it; but never in its limited sense as a code of religious ceremonies, but always in its widest scope as including the highest rule of moral duty made known to men. And hence he never contrasts one class of works with another, but constantly works and faith, excluding all classes of the former, works of righteousness as well as those of mere formality. Not by works of righteousness which we have done, but according to his mercy he hath saved us.[107] Who hath saved us not according to our works.[108] We are saved by faith, not by works.[109] Nay, men are said to be justified without works; to be in themselves ungodly when justified; and it is not until they are justified that they perform any really good works. It is only when united to Christ that we bring forth fruit unto God. Hence we are said to be his workmanship, created in Christ Jesus unto good works. All the inward excellence of the Christian and the fruits of the spirit are the consequences and not the causes of his reconciliation and acceptance with God. They are the robe of beauty, the white garment, with which Christ arrays those who come to him poor and blind and naked. It is then the plain doctrine of the word of God that our justification is not founded upon our own obedience to the law. Nothing done by us or wrought in us can for a moment stand the test of a rule of righteousness which pronounces

---

107. Titus iii. 5.
108. 2 Tim. i. 9.
109. Eph. ii. 9.

a curse upon all those, who continue not in all things written in the book of the law to do them.

SECTION II. *The demands of the Law are satisfied by what Christ has done.*

We have thus seen that the Scriptures teach first that all men are naturally under the law as prescribing the terms of their acceptance with God, and secondly, that no obedience which sinners can render is sufficient to satisfy the demands of that law. It follows then that unless we are freed from the law, not as a rule of duty, but as prescribing the conditions of acceptance with God, justification is for us impossible. It is, therefore, the third great point of Scriptural doctrine on this subject, that believers are free from the law in the sense just stated. Ye are not under the law, says the apostle, but under grace.[110] To illustrate this declaration he refers to the case of a woman who is bound to her husband as long as he lives, but when he is dead, she is free from her obligation to him, and is at liberty to marry another man. So we are delivered from the law as a rule of justification, and are at liberty to embrace a different method of obtaining acceptance with God.[111] Paul says of himself,[112] that he had died to the law, i.e. become free from it. And the same is said of all believers.[113] He insists upon this freedom as essential not only to justification but to sanctification. For while under the law, the motions of sin, which were by the law, brought forth fruit unto death, but now we are delivered from the law that we may serve God in newness of spirit.[114] Before faith came we were kept under the law, which he compares to a schoolmaster, but now we are no longer under a schoolmaster.[115] He regards the desire to be subject to the law as the greatest infatuation. Tell me, he says, ye that desire to be under the law, Do ye not hear then law? and then shows that those who are under the demands of a legal system, are in the condition of slaves

110. Rom. vi. 14.
111. Rom. vii. 1, 6.
112. Gal. ii. 19.
113. Rom. vii. 6.
114. Rom. vii. 5, 6.
115. Gal. iii. 24, 25.

and not of sons and heirs. Stand fast, therefore, he exhorts, in the
liberty wherewith Christ hath made us free. Behold I Paul say unto
you, that if ye be circumcised Christ shall profit you nothing. For I
testify to everyone that is circumcised that he is a debtor to do the
whole law. Christ has become of no effect to you; whosoever of you
are justified by the law, ye are fallen from grace.[116] This infatuation
Paul considered madness, and exclaims, O foolish Galatians, that ye
should not obey the truth, who hath bewitched you, before whose
eyes Jesus Christ hath evidently set forth, crucified among you? This
only would I learn of you, Received ye the Spirit by the works of the
law, or by the hearing of faith?[117] This apostasy was so fatal, the
substitution of legal obedience for the work of Christ as the ground
of justification, was so destructive, that Paul pronounces accursed
any man or angel who should preach such a doctrine for the gospel
of the grace of God.

It was to the law, as revealed in the books of Moses, that the
fickle Galatians were disposed to look for justification. Their apostacy, however, consisted in going back to the law, no matter in what
form revealed, to works, no matter of what kind, as the ground of
justification. The apostle's arguments and denunciations, therefore,
are so framed as to apply to the adoption of any form of legal obedience, instead of the work of Christ, as the ground of our confidence
towards God. To suppose that all he says relates exclusively to a relapse into Judaism, is to suppose that we Gentiles have no part in the
redemption of Christ. If it was only from the bondage of the Jewish
economy that he redeemed his people, then those who were never
subject to that bondage have no interest in his work. And of course
Paul was strangely infatuated in preaching Christ crucified to the
Gentiles. We find, however, that what he taught in the Epistle to the
Galatians, in special reference to the law of Moses, he teaches in the
Epistle to the Romans in reference to that law which is holy, just and
good, and which condemns the most secret sins of the heart.

The nature of the apostle's doctrine is, if possible, even more
clear from the manner in which he vindicates it, than from his direct
assertions. What then? he asks, shall we continue in sin, because we

116. Gal. v. 1, 4.
117. Gal. iii. 1, 2.

are not under the law, but under grace? God forbid. Had Paul taught that we are freed from the ceremonial, in order to be subject to the moral law, there could have been no room for such an objection. But if he taught that the moral law itself could not give life, that we must be freed from its demands as the condition of acceptance with God, then indeed, to the wise of this world, it might seem that he was loosing the bands of moral obligation, and opening the door to the greatest licentiousness. Hence the frequency and earnestness with which he repels the objection, and shows that so far from legal bondage being necessary to holiness, it must cease before holiness can exist; that it is not until the curse of the law is removed, and the soul reconciled to God, that holy affections rise in the heart, and the fruits of holiness appear in the life. Do we then make void the law through faith? God forbid: yea, we establish the law.[118]

It is then clearly the doctrine of the Bible that believers are freed from the law as prescribing the conditions of their acceptance with God; it is no longer incumbent upon them, in order to justification, to fulfil its demand of perfect obedience, or to satisfy its penal exactions. But how is this deliverance effected? How is it that rational and accountable beings are exempted from the obligations of that holy and just law, which was originally imposed upon their race as the rule of justification? The answer to this question includes the fourth great truth respecting the way of salvation taught in the Scriptures. It is not by the abrogation of the law, either as to its precepts or penalty; it is not by lowering its demands, and accommodating them to the altered capacities or inclinations of men. We have seen how constantly the apostle teaches that the law still demands perfect obedience, and that they are debtors to do the whole law who seek justification at its hands. He no less clearly teaches that death is as much the wages of sin in our case, as it was in that of Adam. If it is neither by abrogation nor relaxation that we are freed from the demands of the law, how has this deliverance been effected? By the mystery of vicarious obedience and suffering. This is the gospel of the grace of God. This is what was a scandal to the Jews, and foolishness to the Greeks, but, to those that are called, the power of God and the wisdom of God.

---

118. Rom. iii. 31.

The Scriptures teach us that the Son of God, the brightness of the Father's glory, and the express image of his person, who thought it not robbery to be equal with God, became flesh, and subjected himself to the very law to which we were bound; that he perfectly obeyed the law, and suffered its penalty, and thus, by satisfying its demands, delivered us from its bondage and introduced us into the glorious liberty of the sons of God. It is thus that the doctrine of redemption is presented in the Scriptures. God, says the apostle, sent forth his Son, made of a woman, made under the law, that he might redeem those that were under the law.[119] Being made under the law, we know that he obeyed it perfectly, and brought in everlasting righteousness, and is therefore declared to be the Lord our righteousness, since, by his obedience, many are constituted righteous.[120] He, therefore, is said to be made righteousness unto us.[121] And those who are in him are said to be righteous before God, not having their own righteousness, but that which is by the faith of Christ.[122]

That we are redeemed from the curse of the law by Christ's enduring that curse in our place, is taught in every variety of form from the beginning to the end of the Bible. There was the more need that this point should be clearly and variously presented, because it is the one on which an enlightened conscience immediately fastens. The desert of death begets the fear of death. And this fear of death cannot be allayed, until it is seen how, in consistency with divine justice, we are freed from the righteous penalty of the law. How this is done the Scriptures teach in the most explicit manner. Christ hath redeemed us from the curse of the law, being made a curse for us.[123] Paul had just said, As many as are of the law are under the curse. But all men are naturally under the law, and therefore all are under the curse. How are we redeemed from it? By Christ's being made a curse for us. Such is the simple and sufficient answer to this most important of all questions.

The doctrine so plainly taught in Gal. iii. 13, that Christ has

---

119. Gal. iv. 4, 5.
120. Rom. v. 19.
121. 1 Cor. i. 30.
122. Phil. iii. 9.
123. Gal. iii. 13.

redeemed us from the curse of the law by bearing it in our stead, is no less clearly presented in 2 Cor. v. 21. He hath made him to be sin for us, who knew no sin, that we might be made the righteousness of God in him. This is represented as the only ground on which men are authorised to preach the gospel. We are ambassadors for Christ, says the apostle, as though God did beseech you by us, we pray you in Christ's stead, be ye reconciled to God. Then follows a statement of the ground upon which this offer of reconciliation is presented. God has made effectual provision for the pardon of sin, by making Christ, though holy, harmless, and separate from sinners, sin for us, that we might be made righteous in him. The iniquities of us all were laid on him; he was treated as a sinner in our place, in order that we might be treated as righteous in him.

The same great truth is taught in all those passages in which Christ is said to bear our sins. The expression to bear sin, is one which is clearly explained by its frequent occurrence in the sacred Scriptures. It means to bear the punishment due to sin. In Lev. xx. 17, it is said, He that marries his sister, shall bear his iniquity. Again, Whosoever curseth his God, shall bear his sin. Of him that failed to keep the passover, it was said, that man shall bear his sin.[124] If a man sin he shall bear his iniquity. It is used in the same sense when one man is spoken of as bearing the sin of another. Your children shall wander in the wilderness forty years, and bear your whoredoms.[125] Our fathers have sinned and are not, and we have borne their iniquities.[126] And when, in Ezekiel xviii. 20, it is said that the son shall not bear the iniquity of the father, it is obviously meant that the son shall not be punished for the sins of the father. The meaning of this expression being thus definite, of course there can be no doubt as to the manner in which it is to be understood when used in reference to the Redeemer. The prophet says, The Lord hath laid on him the iniquity of us all. My righteous servant shall justify many, for he shall bear their iniquities. He was numbered with transgressors, and bore the sins of many.[127] Language more explicit could not be used. This

124. Numbers ix. 13.
125. Ibidem xiv. 33.
126. Lam. v. 7.
127. Is. liii. 6, 11, 12.

whole chapter is designed to teach one great truth, that our sins were to be laid on the Messiah, that we might be freed from the punishment which they deserved. It is therefore said, He was wounded for our transgressions; he was bruised for our iniquities; the chastisement of our peace was upon him; for the transgression of my people was he smitten. In the New Testament, the same doctrine is taught in the same terms. Who his ownself bare our sins in his own body on the tree.[128] Christ was offered to bear the sins of many.[129] Ye know that he was manifested to take away (to bear) our sins.[130] According to all these representations, Christ saves us from the punishment due to our sins, by bearing the curse of the law in our stead.

Intimately associated with the passages just referred to, are those which describe the Redeemer as a sacrifice, or propitiation. The essential idea of a sin-offering is propitiation by means of vicarious punishment. That this is the Scriptural idea of a sacrifice, is plain from the laws of their institution, from the effects ascribed to them, and from the illustrative declarations of the sacred writers. The law prescribed that the offender should bring the victim to the altar, lay his hands upon its head, make confession of his crime; and that the animal should then be slain, and its blood sprinkled upon the altar. Thus, it is said, He shall put his hand upon the head of the burnt-offering, and it shall be accepted for him to make atonement for him.[131] And he brought the bullock for a sin-offering, and Aaron and his sons laid their hands upon the head of the bullock of the sin-offering.[132] The import of this imposition of hands, is clearly taught in the following passage: And Aaron shall lay his hands upon the head of the live goat, and confess over him all the iniquities of the children of Israel, and all their transgressions in all their sins, putting them upon the head of the goat, and the goat shall bear upon him all their iniquities unto a land not inhabited.[133] The imposition of hands, therefore, was designed to express symbolically the ideas of substitution and transfer of the liability to punishment. In the case just re-

---

128. 1 Peter, ii. 24.
129. Heb. ix. 28.
130. 1 John iii. 5.
131. Lev. i. 4.
132. Ib. viii. 11.
133. Lev. xvi. 21, 22.

ferred to, in order to convey more clearly the idea of the removal of the liability to punishment, the goat on whose head the sins of the people were imposed, was sent into the wilderness, but another goat was slain and consumed in its stead.

The nature of these offerings is further obvious from the effects attributed to them. They were commanded in order to make atonement, to propitiate, to make reconciliation, to secure the forgiveness of sins. And this effect they actually secured. In the case of every Jewish offender, some penalty connected with the theocratical constitution under which he lived, was removed by the presentation and acceptance of the appointed sacrifice. This was all the effect, in the way of securing pardon, that the blood of bulls and of goats could produce. Their efficacy was confined to the purifying of the flesh and to securing, for those who offered them, the advantages of the external theocracy. Besides, however, this efficacy, which, by divine appointment, belonged to them considered in themselves, they were intended to prefigure and predict the true atoning sacrifice which was to be offered when the fulness of time should come. Nothing, however, can more clearly illustrate the Scriptural doctrine of sacrifices, than the expressions employed by the sacred writers to convey the same idea as that intended by the term sin-offering. Thus all that Isaiah taught by saying of the Messiah that the chastisement of our peace was upon him; that by his stripes we are healed; that he was smitten for the transgression of the people; that on him was laid the iniquity of us all, and that he bore the sins of many, he taught by saying, he made his soul an offering for sin. And in the epistle to the Hebrews it is said, He was offered (as a sacrifice) to bear the sins of many. The same idea, therefore, is expressed by saying, either he bore our sins, or he was made an offering for sin. But to bear the sins of any one, means to bear the punishment of those sins; and, therefore, to be a sin-offering conveys the same meaning.

Such being the idea of a sacrifice which pervades the whole Jewish Scriptures, it is obvious that the sacred writers could not teach more distinctly and intelligibly the manner in which Christ secures the pardon of sin, than by saying he was made an offering for sin. With this mode of pardon all the early readers of the Scriptures were familiar. They had been accustomed to it from their earliest years. No one of them could recall the time when the altar, the victim and the blood were unknown to him. His first lessons in religion contained the ideas of confession of sin, substitution and vicarious sufferings and death. When, therefore, the inspired penmen told men imbued with these ideas that Christ was a propitiation for sin, that he was offered as a sacrifice to make reconciliation, they told them, in the plainest of all terms, that he secures the pardon of our sins by suffering in our stead. Jews could understand such langauge in no other way, and therefore, we may be sure it was intended to convey no other meaning. And in point of fact, it has been so understood by the Christian church from its first organization to the present day.

If it were merely in the way of casual allusion that Christ was declared to be a sacrifice, we should not be authorized to infer from it the method of redemption. But this is far from being the case. This doctrine is presented in the most didactic form. It is exhibited in every possible mode. It is asserted, illustrated, vindicated. It is made the central point of all divine institutions and instructions. It is urged as the foundation of hope, as the source of consolation, the motive to obedience. It is in fact the gospel. It would be vain to attempt a reference to all the passages in which this great doctrine is taught. We are told that God set forth Jesus Christ as a propitiation for our sins through faith in his blood.[134] Again he is declared to be a propitiation for our sins, and not for our's only but for the sins of the whole world.[135] He is called the Lamb of God that taketh away (beareth) the sins of the world.[136] Ye were not redeemed, says the apostle Peter, with corruptible things as silver and gold from your vain conversation received by tradition from your fathers, but with the precious blood of Christ as of a lamb without blemish and without spot.[137] In the epistle to the Hebrews this doctrine is more fully exhibited than in any other portion of Scripture. Christ is not only repeatedly called a sacrifice but an elaborate comparison is made between the offering which he presented and those which were offered under the old dispensation. If the blood of bulls and of goats, says the apostle, and the ashes of a heifer sprinkling the unclean, sanctifieth to the purifying of the flesh, how much more shall the

---

134. Rom. iii. 25.
135. 1 John ii. 2.
136. John i. 29.
137. i Pet. i. 18, 19.

blood of Christ, who through the eternal spirit (possessing an eternal spirit) offered himself without spot unto God, purge your conscience from dead works to serve the living God.[138] The ancient sacrifices in themselves could only remove ceremonial uncleanness. They could not purge the conscience or reconcile the soul to God. They were mere shadows of the true sacrifice for sins. Hence they were offered daily. Christ's sacrifice being really efficacious, was offered but once. It was because the ancient sacrifices were ineffectual, that Christ said, when he came into the world, Sacrifice and offering thou wouldst not, but a body hast thou prepared me. In burnt offerings and sacrifices for sin thou hast no pleasure, Then said I, Lo I come to do thy will, O God. By the which will, adds the apostle, that is, by the accomplishing purpose of God, we are sanctified (or atoned for) through the offering of the body of Jesus Christ once for all; and by that one offering he hath perfected for ever them that are sanctified, and of all this, he adds, the Holy Ghost is witness.[139] The Scriptures, therefore, clearly teach that Jesus Christ delivers us from the punishment of our sins, by offering himself as a sacrifice in our behalf; that as under the old dispensation, the penalties attached to the violations of the theocratical covenant, were removed by the substitution and sacrifice of bulls and of goats, so under the spiritual theocracy, in the living temple of the living God, the punishment of sin is removed by the substitution and death of the Son of God. As no ancient Israelite, when by transgression he had forfeited his liberty of access to the earthly sanctuary, was ignorant of the mode of atonement and reconciliation; so now, no conscience-stricken sinner, who knows that he is unworthy to draw near to God, need be ignorant of that new and living way which Christ hath consecrated for us, through his flesh, so that we have boldness to enter into the holiest blood of Jesus.

In all the forms of expression hitherto mentioned, viz: Christ was made a curse for us; he was made sin for us; he bore our sins, he was made a sin offering, there is the idea of substitution. Christ took our place, he suffered in our stead, he acted as our representative. But as the act of a substitute is in effect the act of the principal,

---

138. Heb. ix. 13, 14.
139. Heb. x. 5, 15.

all that Christ did and suffered in that character, every believer is regarded as having done and suffered. The attentive and pious reader of the Bible will recognise this idea in some of the most common forms of Scriptural expression. Believers are those who are in Christ. This is their great distinction and most familiar designation. They are so united to him, that what he did in their behalf they are declared to have done. When he died, they died; when he rose, they rose; as he lives, they shall live also. The passages in which believers are said to have died in Christ are very numerous. If one died for all, says the apostle, then all died (not, were dead.)[140] He that died (with Christ) is justified from sin, i.e. freed from its condemnation and power; and if we died with Christ, we believe, that we shall live with him.[141] As a woman is freed by death from her husband, so believers are freed from the law by the body (the death) of Christ, because his death is in effect their death.[142] And in the following verse, he says, having died, (in Christ) we are freed from the law. Every believer, therefore, may say with Paul, I was crucified with Christ.[143] In like manner the resurrection of Christ secures both the spiritual life and future resurrection of all his people. If we have been united to him in his death, we shall be in his resurrection. If we died with him, we shall live with him.[144] God, says the apostle, hath quickened us together with Christ; and hath raised us up together, and made us to sit together in heavenly places in Christ Jesus.[145] That is, God hath quickened, raised, and exalted us together[146] with Christ. It is on this ground also that Paul says that Christ rose as the first fruits of the dead; not merely the first in order, but the earnest and security of the resurrection of his people. For as in Adam all die, so in Christ shall all be made alive.[147] As our union with Adam secures our death, union with

---

140. 2 Cor. v. 14.
141. Rom. vi. 7, 8.
142. Rom. vii. 4.
143. Gal. ii. 20.
144. Rom. vi. 5, 8.
145. Eph. ii. 5. 6.
146. There is no separate word in the original to answer to the word *together*, which is not to be understood of the union of believers with one another in the participation of these blessings. It is their union with Christ that the passage asserts.
147. 1 Cor. xv. 20, 22.

Christ secures our resurrection. Adam is a type of him that was to come, that is Christ, inasmuch as the relation in which Adam stood to the whole race is analogous to that in which Christ stands to his own people. As Adam was our natural head, the poison of sin flows in all our veins. As Christ is our spiritual head, eternal life which is in him, descends to all his members. It is not they that live, but Christ that liveth in them.[148] This doctrine of the representative and vital union of Christ and believers, pervades the New Testament. It is the source of the humility, the joy, the confidence which the sacred writers so often express. In themselves they were nothing and deserved nothing, but in Him they possessed all things. Hence they counted all things but loss that they might be found in Him. Hence they determined to know nothing, to preach nothing, to glory in nothing but in Christ and him crucified.

The great doctrine of the vicarious sufferings and death of Jesus Christ, is further taught in those numerous passages which refer our salvation to his blood, his death, or his cross. Viewed in connection with the passages already mentioned, those now referred to not only teach the fact that the death of Christ secures the pardon of sin, but how it does it. To this class belong such declarations as the following. The blood of Jesus Christ cleanses us from all sin.[149] We have redemption through his blood.[150] He has made peace through the blood of his cross.[151] Being justified by his blood.[152] Ye are made nigh by the blood of Christ.[153] Ye are come to the blood of sprinkling.[154] Elect unto obedience and sprinking of the blood of Jesus Christ.[155] Unto him who loved us and washed us from our sins in his own blood.[156] He hath redeemed us unto God by his blood.[157] This cup, said the Son of God himself, is the New Testament in my blood,

---

148. Gal. ii. 20.
149. 1 John i. 7.
150. Eph. i. 7.
151. Col. i. 20
152. Rom. v. 9.
153. Eph. ii. 13.
154. Heb. xii. 24.
155. 1 Pet. i. 2.
156. Rev. 1. v.
157. Rev. v. 9.

which is shed for many for the remission of sins.[158] The sacrificial character of the death of Christ is taught in all these passages. Blood was the means of atonement, and without the shedding of blood, there was no remission; and, therefore, when our salvation is so often ascribed to the blood of the Saviour, it is declared that he died as a propitiation for our sins.

The same remark may be made in reference to those passages, which ascribe our redemption to the death, the cross, the flesh of Christ; for these terms are interchanged as being of the same import. We are reconciled unto God by the death of his Son.[159] We are reconciled by his cross.[160] We are reconciled by the body of his flesh through death.[161] We are delivered from the law by the body of Christ;[162] he abolished the law in his flesh;[163] he took away the hand-writing, which was against us, nailing it to his cross.[164] The more general expressions respecting Christ's dying for us, receive a definite meaning from their connection with the more specific passages above mentioned. Every one, therefore, knows what is meant, when it is said that Christ died for the ungodly;[165] that he gave himself a ransom for many;[166] that he died the just for the unjust that he might bring us unto God.[167] Not less plain is the meaning of the Holy Spirit when it is said, God spared not his own son, but delivered him up for us all;[168] that he was delivered for our offences;[169] that he gave himself for our sins.[170]

Seeing then that we owe everything to the expiatory sufferings of the blessed Saviour, we cease to wonder that the Cross is rendered

---

158. Matt. xxvi. 28.
159. Rom. v. 10.
160. Eph. ii. 16.
161. Col. i. 22.
162. Rom. vii. 4.
163. Eph. ii. 15.
164. Col. ii. 14.
165. Rom. v. 6.
166. Matt. xx. 28.
167. 1 Pet. iii. 18.
168. Rom. viii. 32.
169. Rom. iv. 25.
170. Gal. i. 4.

so prominent in the exhibition of the plan of salvation. We are not surprised at Paul's anxiety lest the cross of Christ should be made of none effect; or that he should call the preaching of the gospel the preaching of the cross; or that he should preach Christ crucified, both to Jews and Greeks, as the wisdom of God and the power of God, or that he should determine to glory in nothing save in the Cross of Christ.

As there is no truth more necessary to be known, so there is none more variously or plainly taught than the method of escaping the wrath of God due to us for sin. Besides all the clear exhibitions of Christ as bearing our sins, as dying in our stead, as making his soul an offering for sin, as redeeming us by his blood, the Scriptures set him forth in the character of a Priest, in order that we might more fully understand how it is that he effects our salvation. It was predicted long before his advent that the Messiah was to be a priest. Thou art a priest forever after the order of Melchizedeck, was the declaration of the Holy Spirit by the mouth of David.[171] Zachariah predicted that he should sit as a priest upon his throne.[172] The apostle defines a priest to be a man ordained for men in things pertaining to God, that he may offer both gifts and sacrifices for sins.[173] Jesus Christ is the only real priest in the universe. All others were either pretenders, or the shadow of the great High Priest of our profession. For this office he had every necessary qualification. He was a man. For inasmuch as the children were partakers of flesh and blood he also took part of the same in order that he might be a merciful and faithful high priest; one who can be touched with a sense of our infirmities, seeing he was tempted in all points like as we are, yet without sin. He was sinless. For such a high priest became us who was holy, harmless and separate from sinners. He was the Son of God. The law made men having infirmity, priests. But God declared his Son to be a priest, who is consecrated for evermore.[174] The sense in which Christ is declared to be the Son

---

171. Ps. cx. 4.
172. Zechariah, vi. 13.
173. Heb. v. 1.
174. Heb. vii. 28.

of God, is explained in the first chapter of this epistle. It is there said, that he is the express image of God; that he upholds all things by the word of his power; that all the angels are commanded to worship him; that his throne is an everlasting throne; that in the beginning he laid the foundations of the earth; that he is from everlasting, and that his years fail not. It is from the dignity of his person, as possessing this divine nature, that the apostle deduces the efficacy of his sacrifice,[175] the perpetuity of his priesthood,[176] and his ability to save to the uttermost all who come unto God through him.[177] He was duly constituted a priest. He glorified not himself to be made a high priest, but he that said to him, Thou art my Son, said also, Thou art a priest for ever. He is the only real priest and, therefore, his advent superseded all others, and put an immediate end to all their lawful ministrations, by abolishing the typical dispensation with which they were connected. For the priesthood being changed, there was of necessity a change of the law. There was a disannulling of the former commandment for the weakness and unprofitableness thereof, and there was the introduction of a better hope.[178] He has an appropriate offering to present. As every high priest is appointed to offer sacrifices, it was necessary that this man should have somewhat to offer. This sacrifice was not the blood of goats or of calves, but his own blood; it was himself he offered unto God, to purge our conscience from dead works.[179] He has put away sin by the sacrifice of himself, which was accomplished when he was once offered to bear the sins of many.[180] He has passed into the heavens. As the high priest was required to enter into the most holy place with the blood of atonement, so Christ has entered not into the holy place made with hands, but into heaven itself, now to appear in the presence of God for us,[181] and where he ever lives to make intercession for us.[182]

---

175. Heb. ix. 14.
176. Ibid. vii. 16.
177. Ibid. vii. 25.
178. Ibid. vii. 12, 19.
179. Heb. ix. 12, 14.
180. Ibid. ix. 26, 28.
181. Ibid. ix. 24.
182. Ibid. vii. 25.

Seeing then we have a great High Priest, that is passed into the heavens, Jesus the Son of God (let the reader remember what that means), who is set down on the right hand of the Majesty on high, having by himself purged our sins and made reconciliation for the sins of the people, every humble believer who commits his soul into the hands of this High Priest, may come with boldness to the throne of grace, assured that he shall find mercy and grace to help in time of need.

SECTION III.   *The righteousness of Christ the true ground of our Justification. The practical effects of this doctrine.*

The Bible, as we have seen, teaches, first, that we are under a law which demands perfect obedience and which threatens death in case of transgression; secondly, that all men have failed in rendering that obedience, and therefore, are subject to the threatened penalty; thirdly, that Christ has redeemed us from the law by being made under it and in our place, satisfying its demands. It only remains to be shown that this perfect righteousness of Christ is presented as the ground of our justification before God.

In scriptural language condemnation is a sentence of death pronounced upon sin; justification is a sentence of life pronounced upon righteousness. As this righteousness is not our own, as we are sinners, ungodly, without works, it must be the righteousness of another, even of him who is our righteousness. Hence we find so constantly the distinction between our own righteousness and that which God gives. The Jews, the apostle says, being ignorant of God's righteousness, and going about to establish their own righteousness, would not submit themselves unto the righteousness of God.[183] This was the rock on which they split. They knew that justification required a righteousness; they insisted on urging their own, imperfect as it was, and would not accept of that which God had provided in the merits of his Son, who is the end of the law for righteousness to every one that believes. The same idea is presented in Rom. ix. 30, 32, where Paul sums up the case of the rejection of the Jews and the acceptance of believers. The Gentiles have attained

---

183. Rom. x. 3.

righteousness, even the righteousness which is of faith. But Israel hath not attained it. Wherefore? Because they sought it not by faith, but as it were by the works of the law. The Jews would not receive and confide in the righteousness which God had provided, but endeavoured, by works, to prepare a righteousness of their own. This was the cause of their ruin. In direct contrast to the course pursued by the majority of his kinsmen, we find Paul renouncing all dependence upon his own righteousness, and thankfully receiving that which God had provided. Though he had every advantage and every temptation to trust in himself, that any man could have; for he was one of the favoured people of God, circumcised on the eighth day, and touching the righteousness which is in the law, blameless, yet all these things he counted but loss, that he might win Christ, and be found in him, not having his own righteousness, which is of the law, but that which is through the faith of Christ, the righteousness which is of God by faith.[184] Here the two righteousnesses are brought distinctly into view. The one was his own, consisting in obedience to the law; this Paul rejects as inadequate, and unworthy of acceptance. The other is of God and received by faith; this Paul accepts and glories in as all sufficient and as alone sufficient. This is the righteousness which the apostle says God imputes to those without works. Hence it is called a gift, a free gift, a gift by grace, and believers are described as those who receive this gift of righteousness.[185] Hence we are never said to be justified by any thing done by us or wrought in us, but by what Christ has done for us. We are justified through the redemption that is in him.[186] We are justified by his blood.[187] We are justified by his obedience.[188] We are justified by him from all things.[189] He is our righteousness.[190] We are made the righteousness of God in him.[191] We are justified in his name.[192] There is no con-

184. Phil. iii. 9.
185. Rom. v. 17.
186. Rom. iii. 24.
187. Rom. v. 9.
188. Rom. v. 19.
189. Acts xiii. 39.
190. 1 Cor. i. 30.
191. 2 Cor. v. 21.
192. 1 Cor. vi. 11.

demnation to those who are in him.[193] Justification is, therefore, by faith in Christ, because faith is receiving and trusting to him as our Saviour, as having done all that is required to secure our acceptance before God.

It is thus then the Scriptures answer the question, How can a man be just with God? When the soul is burdened with a sense of sin, when it sees how reasonable and holy is that law which demands perfect obedience and which threatens death as the penalty of transgression; when it feels the absolute impossibility of ever satisfying these just demands by its own obedience and sufferings, it is then that the revelation of Jesus Christ as our righteousness, is felt to be the wisdom and power of God unto salvation. Destitute of all righteousness in ourselves, we have our righteousness in him. What we could not do he has done for us. The righteousness, therefore, on the ground of which the sentence of justification is passed upon the believing sinner, is not his own but that of Jesus Christ.

It is one of the strongest evidences of the divine origin of the Scriptures that they are suited to the nature and circumstances of man. If their doctrines were believed and their precepts obeyed, men would stand in their true relation to God, and the different classes of men to each other. Parents and children, husbands and wives, rulers and subjects, would be found in their proper sphere, and would attain the highest possible degree of excellence and happiness. Truth is in order to holiness. And all truth is known to be truth, by its tendency to promote holiness. As this test when applied to the Scriptures generally, evinces their divine perfection, so when applied to the cardinal doctrine of justification by faith in Jesus Christ, it shows that doctrine to be worthy of all acceptation. On this ground it is commended by the sacred writers. They declare it to be in the highest degree honorable to God and beneficial to man. They assert that it is so arranged as to display the wisdom, justice, holiness and love of God, while it secures the pardon, peace and holiness of men. If it failed in either of these objects; if it were not suited to the divine character, or to our nature and necessities, it could not answer the end for which it was designed.

It will be readily admitted that the glory of God in the exhibition

---

193. Rom. viii. 1.

or revelation of the divine perfections is the highest conceivable end of creation and redemption; and consequently that any doctrine which is suited to make such exhibition is, on that account, worthy of being universally received and gloried in. Now the inspired writers teach us that it is peculiarly in the plan of redemption that the divine perfections are revealed; that it was designed to show unto principalities and powers the manifold wisdom of God; that Christ was set forth as a propitiatory sacrifice to exhibit his righteousness or justice; and especially that in the ages to come he might show forth the exceeding riches of his grace and his kindness towards us in Christ Jesus. It is the love of God, the breadth and length and depth and heighth of which pass knowledge, that is here most conspicuously displayed. Some men strangely imagine that the death of Christ procured for us the love of God; whereas it was the effect and not the cause of that love. Christ did not die that God might love us; but he died because God loved us. God commendeth his love towards us in that while we were sinners Christ died for us. He so loved the world that he gave his only begotten Son, that whosoever believeth on him might not perish, but have eternal life. In this was manifested the love of God towards us, because God sent his only begotten Son into the world, that we might live through him. Herein is love, not that we loved God, but that he loved us, and sent his Son to be the propitiation for our sins.

As this love of God is manifested towards the unworthy, it is called grace, and this it is what the Scriptures dwell upon with such peculiar frequency and earnestness. The mystery of redemption is, that a Being of infinite holiness and justice should manifest such wonderful love to sinners. Hence the sacred writers so earnestly denounce every thing that obscures this peculiar feature of the gospel; everything which represents men as worthy, as meriting, or, in any way by their own goodness, securing the exercise of this love of God. It is of grace lest any man should boast. We are justified by grace; we are saved by grace; and if of grace it is no more of works, otherwise grace is no more grace. The apostle teaches us not only that the plan of salvation had its origin in the unmerited kindness of God, and that our acceptance with him is in no way or degree founded in our own worthiness, but moreover, that the actual administration of the economy of mercy is so conducted as to magnify this attribute of the divine character. God chooses the foolish, the base, the weak, yea those who are nothing, in order that no flesh should glory in his presence. Christ is made everything to us, that those who glory, should glory only in the Lord.[194]

It cannot fail to occur to every reader that unless he sincerely rejoices in this feature of the plan of redemption, unless he is glad that the whole glory of his salvation belongs to God; his heart cannot be in accordance with the gospel. If he believes that the ground of his acceptance is in himself, or even wishes that it were so, he is not prepared to join in those grateful songs of acknowledgment to Him, who hath saved us and called us with an holy calling, not according to our works, but according to his own purpose and grace, which it is the delight of the redeemed to offer unto him that loved them and gave himself for them. It is most obvious that the sacred writers are abundant in the confession of their unworthiness in the sight of God. They acknowledged that they were unworthy absolutely and unworthy comparatively. It was of grace that any man was saved; and it was of grace that they were saved rather than others. It is, therefore, all of grace, that God may be exalted and glorified in all them that believe.

The doctrine of the gratuitous justification of sinners by faith in Jesus Christ, not only displays the infinite love of God, but it is declared to be peculiarly honourable to him, or peculiarly consistent with his attributes, because it is adapted to all men. Is he the God of the Jews only? Is he not also of the Gentiles? Yes of the Gentiles also; seeing it is one God who shall justify the circumcision by faith, and the uncircumcision through faith. For the same Lord over all is rich unto all that call upon him. For whosoever shall call on the name of the Lord shall be saved. This is no narrow, national, or sectarian doctrine. It is as broad as the earth. Wherever men, the creatures of God can be found, there the mercy of God in Christ Jesus, may be preached. The apostle greatly exults in this feature of the plan of redemption, as worthy of God; and as making the gospel the foundation of a religion for all nations and ages. In revealing a salvation sufficient for all and suited for all, it discloses God in his true character, as the God and Father of all.

The Scriptures, however, represent this great doctrine as not less suited to meet the necessities of man, than it is to promote the

---

194. 1 Cor. i. 27,, 31.

glory of God. If it exalts God, it humbles man. If it renders it manifest that he is a Being of infinite holiness, justice and love, it makes
us feel that we are destitute of all merit, nay are most ill-deserving;
that we are without strength; that our salvation is an undeserved favour. As nothing is more true than the guilt and helplessness of men,
no plan of redemption which does not recognise these facts could
ever be in harmony with our inward experience, or command the full
acquiescence of the penitent soul. The ascription of merit which we
are conscious we do not deserve, produces of itself severe distress;
and if this false estimate of our deserts is the ground of the exhibition
of special kindness towards us, it destroys the happiness such kindness would otherwise produce. To a soul, therefore, sensible of its
pollution and guilt in the sight of God, the doctrine that it is saved
on account of its own goodness, or because it is better than other
men, is discordant and destructive of its peace. Nothing but an absolutely gratuitous salvation can suit a soul sensible of its ill-desert.
Nothing else suits its views of truth, or its sense of right. The opposite doctrine involves a falsehood and a moral impropriety in
which neither the reason nor conscience can acquiesce. The scriptural doctrine, which assumes what we know to be true, viz: our guilt
and helplessness, places us in our proper relation to God; that relation
which accords with the truth, with our sense of right, with our inward
experience, and with every proper desire of our hearts. This is one
of the reasons why the Scriptures represent peace as the consequence
of justification by faith. There can be no peace while the soul is not
in harmony with God, and there can be no such harmony until it will-
ingly occupies its true position in relation to God. So long as it does
not acknowledge its true character, so long as it acts on the assumption of its ability to merit or to earn the divine favour, it is in a false
position. Its feelings towards God are wrong, and there is no manifestation of approbation or favour on the part of God towards the
soul. But when we take our true place and feel our ill-desert, and
look upon pardoning mercy as a mere gratuity, we find access to God
and his love is shed abroad in our hearts, producing that peace which
passes all understanding. The soul ceases from its legal strivings; it
gives over the vain attempt to make itself worthy, or to work out a
righteousness wherewith to appear before God. It is contented to be
accepted as unworthy, and to receive as a gift a righteousness which
can bear the scrutiny of God. Peace, therefore, is not the result of

the assurance of mere pardon, but of pardon founded upon a righteousness which illustrates the character of God, which magnifies the law and makes it honorable; which satisfies the justice of God while it displays the infinite riches of divine tenderness and love. The soul can find no objection to such a method of forgiveness. It is not pained by the ascription of merit to itself, which is felt to be undeserved. Its utter unworthiness is not only recognised but openly declared. Nor is it harrassed by the anxious doubt whether God can consistently with his justice forgive sin. For justice is as clearly revealed in the cross of Christ, as love. The whole soul, therefore, however enlightened, or however sensitive, acquiesces with humility and delight in a plan of mercy which thus honours God, and which, while it secures the salvation of the sinner, permits him to hide himself in the radiance which surrounds his Saviour.

The apostles moreover, urge on men the doctrine of justification by faith with peculiar earnestness because it presents the only method of deliverance from sin. So long as men are under the condemnation of the law, and feel themselves bound by its demands of obedience as the condition and ground of their acceptance with God, they do and must feel that he is unreconciled, that his perfections are arrayed against them. Their whole object is to propitiate him by means which they know to be inadequate. Their spirit is servile, their religion a bondage, their God is a hard master. To men in such a state, true love, true obedience and real peace are alike impossible. But when they are brought to see that God, through his infinite love, has set forth Jesus Christ as a propitiation for our sins, that he might be just, and yet justify those that believe; that it is not by works of righteousness which we have done, but according to his mercy he saveth us; they are emancipated from their former bondage and made the sons of God. God is no longer a hard master, but a kind Father. Obedience is no longer a task to be done for a reward; it is the joyful expression of filial love. The whole relation of the soul to God is changed, and all our feelings and conduct change with it. Though we have no works to perform in order to justification, we have every thing to do in order to manifest our gratitude and love. Do we, therefore, make void the law through faith? God forbid; yea, we establish the law. There is no such thing as real, acceptable obedience until we are thus delivered from the bondage of the law as the rule of justification, and reconciled to God by the death of his Son. Till then we are slaves and enemies, and have the feelings of slaves. When we have accepted the terms of reconcilation we are the sons of God and have the feelings of sons.

It must not, however, be supposed that the filial obedience rendered by the children of God, is the effect of the mere moral influence arising from a sense of his favour. Though perhaps the strongest influence which any external consideration can exert, it is far from being the source of the holiness which always follows faith. The very act by which we become interested in the redemption of Christ, from the condemnation of the law, makes us partakers of his spirit. It is not mere pardon, or any other isolated blessing, that is offered to us in the gospel, but complete redemption, deliverance from evil and restoration to the love and life of God. Those, therefore, who believe, are not merely forgiven, but are so united to Christ, that they derive from and through him, the Holy Spirit. This is his great gift, bestowed upon all who come to Him and confide in Him. This is the reason why he says, Without me, ye can do nothing. As the branch cannot bear fruit of itself, except it abide in the vine; no more can ye, except ye abide in me. I am the vine, ye are the branches. He that abideth in me, and I in him, the same bringeth forth much fruit.

The gospel method of salvation, therefore, is worthy of all acceptation. It reveals the divine perfections in the clearest and most affecting light, and it is in every way suited to the character and necessities of men. It places us in our true position as undeserving sinners; and it secures pardon, peace of conscience and holiness of life. It is the wisdom and the power of God unto salvation. It cannot be a matter of surprise that the Scriptures represent the rejection of this method of redemption, as the prominent ground of the condemnation of those who perish under the sound of the gospel. That the plan should be so clearly revealed and yet men should insist upon adopting some other better suited to their inclinations, is the height of folly and disobedience. That the Son of God should come into the world; die the just for the unjust, and offer us eternal life, and yet we should reject his proffered mercy, proves such an insensibility to his excellence and love, such a love for sin, such a disregard of the approbation and enjoyment of God, that could all other grounds of condemnation be removed, this alone would be sufficient. He that believeth not, is condemned already, because he hath not believed in the name of the only begotten Son of God.

Chapter VI.

Faith.

SECTION I.   *Faith is the condition of salvation. The nature of saving Faith.*

However abundant and suitable may be the provision which God has made for the salvation of men, there are many who fail of attaining eternal life. There are those whom Christ shall profit nothing. Nay, there are those whose condemnation will be greatly aggravated, because they have known and rejected the Son of God, the Saviour of the world. It is, therefore, not less necessary that we should know what we must do in order to secure an interest in the redemption of Christ, than that we should understand what he has done for our salvation.

If God has revealed a plan of salvation for sinners, they must, in order to be saved, acquiesce in its provisions. By whatever name it may be called, the thing to be done, is to approve and accept of the terms of salvation presented in the gospel. As the plan of redemption is designed for sinners, the reception of that plan on our part, implies an acknowledgment that we are sinners, and justly exposed to the displeasure of God. To those who have no such sense of guilt, it must appear foolishness and an offence. As it proceeds upon the assumption of the insufficiency of any obedience of our own to satisfy the demands of the law, acquiesence in it, involves the renunciation of all dependence upon our own righteousness as the ground of our acceptance with God. If salvation is of grace, it must be received as such. To introduce our own merit, in any form or to any degree, is to reject it; because grace and works are essentially opposed; in trusting to the one we renounce the other.

As justification is pardon and acceptance dispensed on the ground of the righteousness of Christ, acquiesence in the plan of salvation involves the recognition and acceptance of the work of Christ as the only ground of justification before God. However much the child of God may be perplexed with anxious doubts, and vain endeavours, he is brought at last to see and admire the perfect simplicity of the plan of mercy; he finds that it requires nothing on his part but the acceptance of what is freely offered; the acceptance of it as free and unmerited. It is under the consciousness of ill-desert and helplessness that the soul embraces Jesus Christ as he is presented in the gospel. This it is that God requires of us in order to our justification. As soon as this is done, we are united to Christ; he assumes our responsibilities; he pleads our cause; he secures our pardon and acceptance on the ground of what he has done; so that there is no condemnation to them that are in Christ Jesus.

The nature of the duty required of us in order to our justification, is made, if possible, still more plain by the account which the Bible gives of those who are condemned. They are described as those who reject Christ, who go about to establish their own righteousness, and refuse to submit to the righteousness of God; as those who look to the law of their own works, instead of relying on the work of Christ. They are those who reject the counsel of God against themselves, who, ignorant of their character and of the requirements of God, refuse to be saved by grace through the redemption that is in Christ Jesus.

The word by which this acceptance of Christ is commonly expressed in the Bible, is faith. God so loved the world that he gave his only begotten Son, that whosoever believeth in him might not perish but have eternal life. He that believeth on him is not condemned; but he that believeth not is condemned already. He that believeth on the Son hath everlasting life; he that believeth not the Son shall not see life, but the wrath of God abideth on him. Verily, verily, I say unto you, he that believeth on me hath everlasting life. Go ye into the world and preach the gospel to every creature; he that believeth and is baptized shall be saved, he that believeth not shall be damned. Sirs, what must I do to be saved? and they said, Believe on the Lord Jesus Christ and thou shalt be saved. God is just and the justifier of him that believeth in Jesus. The Gentiles have attained righteousness, even the righteousness which is by faith; but Israel hath not attained it, because they sought it not by faith. Knowing that a man is not justified by works of the law, but by the faith of Jesus Christ, even we have believed in Jesus Christ, that we might be justified by the faith of Christ and not by the works of the law. By grace are ye saved through faith, and that not of yourselves, it is the gift of God. This is his commandment, That we should believe on his son Jesus Christ. He that believeth on the Son of God hath the witness in himself.

Language so plain and so varied as this, cannot be misunderstood. It teaches every serious inquirer after the way of life, that in order to salvation, he must believe in Jesus Christ. Still, though he knows what it is to believe, as well as any one can tell him, yet as he reads of a dead, as well as a living faith, a faith of devils and a faith of God's elect; as he reads on one page that he that believes shall be saved, and on another, that Simon himself believed, and yet remained in the gall of bitterness and the bonds of iniquity, he is often greatly perplexed and at a loss to determine what that faith is which is connected with salvation. This is a difficulty which is inseparable from the use of language. The soul of man is so wonderful in its operations; its perceptions, emotions, and affections are so various and so complicated, that it is impossible there should be a different word for every distinct exercise. It is therefore absolutely necessary that the same word should be used to express different states of mind, which have certain prominent characteristics in common. The definite, in distinction from the general or comprehensive meaning of the word, is determined by the context; by explanatory or equivalent expressions; by the nature of the thing spoken of, and by the effects ascribed to it. This is found sufficient for all the purposes of intercourse and instruction. We can speak without being misunderstood, of loving our food, of loving an infant, of loving a parent, of loving God, though in each of these cases the word love represents a state of mind peculiar to itself, and different from all the others. There is in all of them a pleasurable excitement on the perception of certain qualities, and this we call love, though no two states of mind can well be more distinct, than the complacent fondness with which a parent looks upon his infant, and the adoring reverence with which he turns his soul towards God.

We need not be surprised, therefore, that the word faith is used in Scripture to express very different exercises, or states of mind. In its widest sense, faith is an assent to truth upon the exhibition of evidence. It does not seem necessary that this evidence should be of the nature of testimony; for we are commonly and properly said to believe whatever we regard as true. We believe in the existence and attributes of God, though our assent is not founded upon what is strictly called testimony. But if faith means assent to truth, it is obvious that its nature and attendants must vary with the nature of the truth believed, and especially with the nature of the evidence upon which our assent is founded. A man may assent to the proposition, that the earth moves round its axis, that virtue is good, that sin will be punished, that to him, as a believer, God promises salvation. In all these cases there is assent, and therefore faith, but the state of mind expressed by the term, is not always the same. Assent to a speculative or abstract truth is a speculative act,; assent to a moral truth, is a moral act; assent to a promise made to ourselves, is an act of trust. Our belief that the earth moves round its axis is a mere assent. Our belief in the excellence of virtue is, in its nature, a moral judgment. Our belief of a promise is an act of trust. Or if any choose to say that trust is the result of assent to the truth of the promise, it may be admitted as a mere matter of analysis, but the distinction is of no consequence, because the two things are inseparable, and because the Scriptures do not make the distinction. In the language of the Bible, faith in the promises of God is a believing reliance, and no blessing is connected with mere assent as distinguished and separated from reliance.

It is, however, of more consequence to remark that the nature of the act by which we assent to truth, is modified by the kind of evidence upon which our assent is founded. The blind may believe, on the testimony of others, in the existence of colours and the deaf in the harmony of sounds, but their faith is very different from the faith of those who enjoy the exercise of the sense of sight or hearing. The universal reputation of such men as Bacon and Newton and the acknowledged influence of their writings, may be the foundation of a very rational conviction of their intellectual superiority. But a conviction, founded upon the perusal and appreciation of their own works, is of an essentially different character. We may believe on the testimony of those in whose veracity and judgment we confide, that a man of whom we know nothing has great moral excellence. But if we see for ourselves the exhibition of his excellence, we believe for other reasons, and in a different way. The state of mind, therefore, which, in the language of common life and in that of the sacred Scriptures, is expressed by the word faith, varies essentially with the nature of the evidence upon which our belief rests.

One man believes the Bible to be the word of God, and the facts and doctrines therein contained to be true, simply on the testimony of others. Born in a Christian land and taught by his parents to regard the Scriptures as a revelation from God, he yields a general assent to the truth, without troubling himself with any personal examination into the evidence upon which it rests. Another believes because he has investigated the subject. He sees that there is no rational way of accounting for the miracles, the accomplishment of predictions, the success and influence of the gospel, except upon the assumption of its divine origin. Others, again, believe because the truths of the Bible commend themselves to their reason and conscience, and accord with their inward experience. Those, whose faith rests upon this foundation, often receive the word with joy, they do many things, and have much of the appearance of true Christians; or, like Felix, they believe and tremble. This is the foundation of the faith which often surprises the wicked in their last hours. Men who all their lives have neglected or reviled the truth and who may have accumulated a treasury of objections to the authority of the Scriptures, are often brought to believe by a power which they cannot resist. An awakened conscience affirms the truth with an authority before which they quail. Their doubts and sophistries fly affrighted before the majesty of this new revealed witness for the truth. To disbelieve is now impossible. That there is a God, that he is holy and just, and that there is a hell, they would give the world to doubt, but cannot. Here is a faith very different in its origin, nature, and effects from that which rests upon the authority of men, or upon external evidence and argument. Though the faith just described, is generally most strikingly exhibited at the approach of death, it often happens that men who are habitually careless, are suddenly arrested in their career. Their conscience is aroused and enlightened. They feel those things to be true, which before they either denied or disregarded. The truth, therefore, has great power over them. It destroys their former peace. It forces them to self-denial and the performance of religious duties. Sometimes this influence soon wears off, as conscience subsides into its accustomed slumber. At others it continues long, even to the end of life. It then constitutes that spirit of bondage and fear under which is unhappy subjects endeavour to work out a way to heaven, without embracing the gospel of the grace of God. The effects produced by a faith of this kind, though specifically different from the fruits of the Spirit, are not always easily detected by the eye of man. And hence many who appear outwardly as the children of God, are inwardly under the dominion of a spirit the opposite of the loving, confiding, filial temper of the gospel.

There is a faith different from any of those forms of belief which have yet been mentioned. It is a faith which rests upon the manifestation by the Holy Spirit, of the excellence, beauty, and suitableness of the truth. This is what Peter calls the precious faith of God's elect. It arises from a spiritual apprehension of the truth, or from the testimony of the Spirit with and by the truth in our hearts. Of this faith the Scriptures make frequent mention. Christ said, I thank thee, O Father, Lord of heaven and earth, that thou hast hid these things from the wise and prudent, and hast revealed them unto babes.[195] The external revelation was made equally to the wise and to the babes. To the latter, however, was granted an inward illumination which enabled them to see the excellence of the truth, which commanded their joyful assent. Our Saviour therefore added, No man knoweth who the Son is, but the Father; and who the Father is, but the Son, and he to whom the Son will reveal him. When Peter made his confession of faith in Christ, our Saviour said to him, Blessed art thou, Simon Bar-jona: for flesh and blood hath not revealed it unto thee, but my Father which is in heaven.[196] Paul was a persecutor of the church; but when it pleased God to reveal his Son in him, he at once preached the faith which he before destroyed. He had an external knowledge of Christ before; but this internal revelation he experienced on his way to Damascus, and it effected an instant change in his whole character. There was nothing miraculous or peculiar in the conversion of the apostle, except in the more incidental circumstances of his case. He speaks of all believers as having the same divine illumination. God, he says, who commanded the light to shine out of darkness, hath shined into our hearts, to give us the light of the knowledge of the glory of God, as it shines in the face of Jesus Christ.[197] On the other hand, he speaks of those whose minds the god of this world hath blinded, lest the light of the glorious gospel of Christ, who is the image of God, should shine unto them. In the second chapter of his first epistle to the Corinthians, he dwells much upon this subject, and teaches not only that the true divine wisdom of the gospel was undiscoverable by human wisdom, but that when externally re-

---

195. Luke x. 21.
196. Matthew xvi. 17.
197. 2 Cor. iv. 6.

vealed, we need the Spirit that we may know the things freely given to us of God. For the natural man receiveth not the things of the Spirit of God, for they are foolishness unto him, neither can he know them for they are spiritually discerned. Hence the apostle prays for his readers, that the eyes of their understandings (hearts) might be opened, that they might know the hope of their calling, the riches of their inheritance, and the greatness of the divine power of which they were the subjects.[198] And in another place, that they might be filled with the knowledge of his will, in all wisdom and spiritual understanding.[199] By spiritual understanding is meant that insight into the nature of the truth which is the result of the influence of the Spirit upon the heart. Since faith is founded on this spiritual apprehension, Paul says, he preached not with the enticing words of man's wisdom, because a faith which resulted from such preaching could be at best a rational conviction; but in the demonstration of the Spirit and of power, that the faith of his hearers might stand, not in the wisdom of men, but in the power of God.[200] Hence faith is said to be one of the fruits of the Spirit, the gift of God, the result of his operation.[201] These representations of the Scriptures accord with the experience of a people of God. They know that their faith is not founded upon the testimony of others, or exclusively or mainly upon external evidence. They believe because the truth appears to them both true and good; because they feel its power and experience its consolations.

It is obvious that a faith founded upon the spiritual apprehension of the truth, as it differs in its origin, must also differ in its effects, from every other kind of belief. Of the multitudes who believe the Scriptures upon authority or on the ground of external evidence, how large a portion disregard their precepts and warnings. To say that such persons do not believe, though true in one sense, is not true in another. They do believe; and to assert the contrary is to contradict their consciousness. The state of mind which they exhibit, is in the Bible called faith, though it is dead. This rational conviction, in other cases, combined with other causes, produces that decorous attention

---

198. Eph. i. 18, 19.
199. Colossians, i. 9.
200. 1 Cor. ii. 4, 5.
201. Eph. ii. 8.   Col. ii. 12.

to the duties of religion and that general propriety of conduct, which are so often exhibited by the hearers of the gospel. The faith which is founded on the power of conscience produces still more marked effects; either temporary obedience and joy, or the despair and opposition manifested by the convinced, the dying, and the lost; or that laborious slavery of religion of which we have already spoken. But that faith which is the gift of God, which arises from his opening our eyes to see the excellence of the truth, is attended with joy and love. These feelings are as immediately and necessarily attendant on this kind of faith, as pleasure is on the perception of beauty. Hence faith is said to work by love. And as all revealed truth is the object of the faith of which we now speak, every truth must, in proportion to the strength of our faith, produce its appropriate effect upon the heart. A belief of the being and perfections of God, founded upon the apprehension of his glory, must produce love, reverence and confidence, with a desire to be conformed to his image. Hence the apostle says: We all, with open face, beholding, as in a glass, the glory of God, are changed into the same image from glory to glory, as by the spirit of the Lord.[202] Faith in his threatenings, founded upon a perception of their justice, their harmony with his perfections, and the ill-desert of sin, must produce fear and trembling. His people, therefore, are described as those who tremble at his word. Faith in his promises, founded upon the apprehension of his faithfulness and power, their harmony with all his revealed purposes, their suitableness to our nature and necessities, must produce confidence, joy and hope. This was the faith which made Abraham leave his own country, to go to a strange land; which led Moses to esteem the reproach of Christ greater riches than the treasures of Egypt. This was the faith of David also, of Samuel, and of all the prophets, who through faith subdued kingdoms, wrought righteousness, obtained promises, stopped the mouths of lions, quenched the violence of fire, escaped the edge of the sword, out of weakness were made strong, waxed valiant in fight, turned to flight the armies of the aliens. This is the faith which leads all people of God to confess that they are strangers and pilgrims upon earth, and that they look for a city which hath foundations, whose builder and maker is God. This is the faith which

---

202. 2 Cor. iii. 18.

overcomes the world, which leads the believer to set his affections on things above, where Christ sitteth at the right hand of God; which enables him to glory even in tribulation, while he looks not at the things which are seen, but at the things which are not seen; for the things that are seen are temporal, but the things that are not seen are eternal.

And what shall we say of a faith in Jesus Christ founded upon the apprehension of the glory of God, as it shines in him; which beholds that glory as the glory of the only begotten of the Father full of grace and truth; which contemplates the Redeemer as clothed in our nature; the first born of many brethren; as dying for our sins, rising again for our justification, ascending into heaven and as now seated at the right hand of God, where he ever liveth to make intercession for us? Such a faith the apostle tells us, must produce love, for he says, Whom having not seen ye love, and in whom, though now ye see him not, yet believing, ye rejoice with joy unspeakable and full of glory. The soul gladly receives him as a Saviour in all the characters and for all the purposes for which he is revealed; and naturally desires to be conformed to his will, and to make known the unsearchable riches of his grace to others.

It is no less obvious that no one can believe the representations given in the Scriptures respecting the character of man and the ill-desert of sin, with a faith founded upon right apprehension of the holiness of God and the evil of his own heart, without experiencing self-condemnation, self-abhorrence, and a constant hungering and thirsting after righteousness. Thus of all the truths in the word of God, it may be said, that so far as they are believed in virtue of this spiritual apprehension, they will exert their appropriate influence upon the heart and consequently upon the life. That such a faith should not produce good fruits is as impossible as that the sun should give light without heat. This faith is the living head of all right affections and of all holy living; without it all religion is a dull formality, a slavish drudgery, or at best a rationalistic homage. Hence we are said, to live by faith, to walk by faith, to be sanctified by faith, to overcome by faith, to be saved by faith. And the grand characteristic of the people of God is, that they are Believers.

SECTION II.   *Faith as connected with justification.*

What has been said hitherto is designed to illustrate the nature of saving faith, as it is represented in the Scriptures. It differs from all other acts of the mind to which the term faith is applied, mainly on account of the nature of the evidence on which it is founded. The Bible, however, is more definite in its instructions on this subject. Besides teaching us that there is a faith which receives as true all declarations of God, in virtue of an evidence exhibited and applied by the Holy Spirit, it tells us what those particular acts of faith are, which secure our justification before God. It plainly teaches that we are justified by those acts of faith which have a special reference to Christ and his mediatorial work. Thus we are said to be justified by faith in his blood.[203] The righteousness of God is said to be by faith of Jesus Christ; that is, by faith of which he is the object.[204] This expression occurs frequently; Knowing, says the apostle, that a man is not justified by the works of the law, but by the faith of Jesus Christ, even we have believed in Jesus Christ, that we might be justified by the faith of Christ.[205] Not having my own righteousness which is of the law, but that which is by the faith of Christ.[206] In all these places and in many others of a similar kind, it is expressly stated that Christ is the object of justifying faith. The same doctrine is taught in those numerous passages, in which justification or salvation is connected with believing in Christ. Whosoever believeth in him shall not perish but have eternal life.[207] He that believeth in the Son hath everlasting life.[208] Whosoever believeth on him shall receive remission of sins.[209] Believe in the Lord Jesus Christ and thou shalt be saved.[210] The same truth is involved in all the representations of the method of justification given in the word of God. We are said to be justified by the death of Christ, by the blood of his cross, by the redemption that is in him, by the sacrifice of himself, by his bearing our sins, by his obedience, or righteousness. All these representations imply that Christ in his mediatorial character, is the special

---

203. Rom. iii. 25.
204. Rom. iii. 22.
205. Gal. ii. 16.
206. Phil. iii. 9.
207. John iii. 16.
208. Ibid. 36.
209. Acts x. 43.
210. Acts xvi. 31.

object of justifying faith. It is indeed impossible that any man should believe the record which God has given of his Son, without believing every other record which he has given, so far as it is known and apprehended; still the special act of faith, which is connected with our justification, is belief in Jesus Christ as the Saviour from sin. And when we are commanded to believe in Jesus Christ, the Scriptural meaning of the expression is that we should trust, or confide in him. It does not express mere assent to the proposition that Jesus is the Christ, which angels and devils exercise; but it expresses trust which involves knowledge and assent. To believe in Christ as a propitiation for sin, is to receive and confide in him as such.

From this representation it is clear what we must do to be saved. When the mind is perplexed and anxious from a sense of sin and the accusations of conscience; when the troubled spirit looks round for some way of escape from the just displeasure of God, the voice of mercy from the lips of the Son of God is, come unto me, believe upon me, submit to be saved by me. Till this is done, nothing is done. And when this cordial act of faith in Christ is exercised, we are accepted for his sake, and he undertakes to save us from the dominion and condemnation of our sins. The experience of the people of God, when they are made the recipients of that divine illumination which reveals to them the glory of God, their own unworthiness, and the plan of salvation by Jesus Christ, is no doubt very various. It is modified by their previous knowledge, by their peculiar state of mind, by the particular truth which happens to attract their attention, by the clearness of the manifestation and by many other circumstances. This diversity is readily admitted, yet since no man can come unto the Father but by the Son; since without faith in him there is no forgiveness and no access to God, it must still be true that, with greater or less distinctness of apprehension, Christ and his mediatorial work constitute the object of the first gracious exercises of the renewed soul. Any approach to God, any hope of his favour, any peace of conscience or confidence of pardon, not founded upon him, must be delusive. Having, (that is, because we have) such an High Priest we come with boldness to the throne of grace; and this is the only ground on which we can venture to draw near. The whole plan of redemption shows that there is no pardon, no access to God, no peace or reconciliation except through Jesus Christ. And this idea is so constantly presented in the Bible, that all genuine religious experience must be in accordance with it.

It is, however, of such vital importance for the sinner distinctly to understand what it is that is required of him, that God has graciously so illustrated the nature of saving faith that the most illiterate reader of the Scriptures may learn the way of life. It is not merely by the term faith, or believing, that this act of the soul is expressed, but by many others of equivalent import. The consideration of a few of these will serve to explain more distinctly the plan of salvation, by showing at once the nature, object and office of justifying faith.

One of the most comprehensive and intelligible of these equivalent terms is that of receiving. To as many as received him, to them gave he power to become the sons of God.[211] As ye have therefore received Christ Jesus the Lord so walk ye in him.[212] Believers are therefore described as those who receive the gift of righteousness;[213] as those who gladly receive the word.[214] To receive Jesus Christ is to accept and recognise him in the character in which he presents himself, as the Son of God, the Saviour of sinners, as a propitiation for our sins, as a ransom for our souls, as the Lord our righteousness. He came to his own and his own received him not. The Jews would not recognise him as the Messiah, the only mediator between God and man, as the end of the law for righteousness. They denied the Holy One, and put far from them the offer of life through him. Could the nature, the object, or the office of faith be presented more clearly than they are by this representation? Can the soul, anxious about salvation, doubt what it has to do? Jesus Christ is presented to him in the gospel as the Son of God, clothed in our nature, sent by the Father to make reconciliation for iniquity, to bring in everlasting righteousness, to redeem us from the curse of the law by being made a curse for us. All that we have to do, is to receive him in this character; and those who thus receive him he makes the sons of

---

211. John i. 12.
212. Col. ii. 6.
213. Rom. v. 17.
214. Acts ii. 41.

God, that is, the objects of his favour, the subjects of his grace and the heirs of his kingdom.

A still more simple illustration of the nature of faith is contained in those passages in which we are commanded to look unto God. Look unto me and be ye saved, all ye ends of the earth.[215] Our Saviour avails himself of this figure, when he says, As Moses lifted up the serpent in the wilderness, even so must the Son of Man be lifted up, that whosoever believeth on him should not perish but have eternal life.[217] The dying Israelite, who was commanded to turn his feeble eye on the brazen serpent, was surely at no loss to know the nature of the duty required of him. He knew there was no virtue in the act of looking. He might look in vain all round the wide horizon. He was healed, not for looking, but because the serpent was placed there by the command of God, and salvation made to depend upon submitting to the appointed method of relief. Why then should the soul convinced of sin and misery be in doubt as to what it has to do? Christ has been set forth as crucified; and we are commanded to look to him and be saved. Can any thing be more simple? Must not every attempt to render more intelligible the Saviour's beautiful illustration, serve only to darken counsel by words without wisdom?

Another striking illustration of this subject, may be found in Heb. vi. 18, where believers are described as those who have fled for refuge to lay hold of the hope set before them. As of old, the manslayer, when pursued by the avenger of blood, fled to the city of refuge, whose gates were open night and day, and whose highways were always unincumbered; so the soul, under the sense of its guilt and convinced that it must perish if it remains where it is, flees to Jesus Christ, as the appointed refuge and finds peace and security in him. There the avenger cannot touch him; there the law which before denounced vengeance, spreads its ample shield around him and gives him the assurance of safety.

A still more common method of expressing the act of saving faith, is to be found in such passages as John vi. 35. He that cometh to me shall never hunger, and he that believeth on me shall never

---

215. Is. xlv. 22.
216. John iii. 14, 15.

thirst. All that the Father giveth to me shall come to me; and him that cometh to me I will in no wise cast out. Here coming and believing are interchanged as expressing the same idea. So also in the following chapter, where our Saviour says, If any man thirst let him come unto me and drink. He that believeth on me, as the Scripture hath said, out of his belly shall flow rivers of living waters. Hence the invitations and commands of the gospel are often expressed by this word. Come unto me all ye that labour and are heavy laden, and I will give you rest. And in the closing invitation of the sacred volume, The Spirit and the bride say, Come; and let him that heareth, say, Come; and let him that is athirst come; and whosoever will, let him take the water of life freely.

Though this language is so plain that nothing but the illumination of the Spirit can render it plainer, yet the troubled soul perplexes itself with the inquiry, what is it to come to Christ? Though assured that he is not far from any one of us, we are often forced to cry out, O that I knew where I might find him! that I might come even to his seat. Behold, I go forward, but he is not there; and backward, but I cannot perceive him; on the left hand, where he doth work, but I cannot behold him; he hideth himself on the right hand, that I cannot see him. It is often the very simplicity of the requirement that deceives us. We think we must do some great thing, which shall bear a certain proportion to the blessing connected with it. We cannot believe that it is merely looking, merely receiving, merely coming as the prodigal came to his father, or as the Israelite came to the high priest who was appointed to make atonement for the sins of the people. Yet is it even thus that we must come to the High Priest of our profession, with confession of sin, and submit to the application of his blood as the appointed means of pardon, and rejoice in the assurance of the divine favour. Or still more impressively as the Hebrew believer came to the altar, laid his hand with confession upon the head of the victim, and saw it die in his stead, so does the trembling soul come to Christ as its propitiatory sacrifice, and confiding in the efficacy of his death, looks up to God and says, My Father! Coming to Christ, therefore, is the confiding reception of him in the offices and for the purposes for which he is presented in the word of God, as our mediator and priest, as our advocate with the Father, as our Redeemer and Lord.

Another term by which faith is expressed is submitting. This is not to be understood as meaning a submission to the will of God as a sovereign ruler, a giving up all our controversy with him and resigning ourselves into his hands. All this is duty, but it is not saving faith. The submission required is submission to the revealed plan of salvation; it is the giving up all excuses for our sins, all dependence upon our own righteousness, and submitting to the righteousness which God has provided for our justification. This is what the Jews refused to do, and perished in unbelief.[217] This is what we must do, in order to be saved. Men, when sensible of their guilt and danger, are perplexed and anxious about many things. But there is only one thing for them to do. They must submit to be saved as ungodly, as sinners, as entirely undeserving, solely for Christ's sake. They must consent to allow the robe of his righteousness to be cast over all their nakedness and blood, that they may be found in him, not having their own righteousness, but the righteousness which is by faith in Jesus Christ. Then will they be prepared to join that great multitude which stand before the throne and before the Lamb, clothed in white robes and palms in their hands, crying with a loud voice, Salvation to our God who sitteth upon the throne, and to the Lamb, for thou wast slain, and hast redeemed us unto God by thy blood, out of every kindred, and people, and tongue, and nation, and has made us unto our God kings and priests.

It is thus that the Bible answers the question, What must we do to be saved? We are told to believe on the Lord Jesus Christ, and to set forth the nature, the object and office of this faith, the Scriptures employ the most significant terms and illustrations, in order that we may learn to renounce ourselves and our works, and to be found in Christ depending solely upon what He has done and suffered as the ground of our acceptance with God. Those who thus believe, have passed from death unto life; they are no longer under condemnation; they have peace with God and rejoice in hope of his glory. As this faith unites them with Christ, it makes them not only partakers of his death, but of his life. The Holy Spirit, given without measure to him, is through him given unto

---

217. Rom. x. 3. and xi. 20.

them, and works in them the fruits of holiness, which are unto the praise and glory of God.

Chapter VII.

Repentance.

Clearly as the Scriptures teach that whosoever believes shall be saved, they teach no less clearly that except we repent we shall all perish. These graces are not only alike indispensable, but they cannot exist separately. Repentance is a turning from sin unto God, through Jesus Christ, and faith is the acceptance of Christ in order to our return to God. Repentance is the act of a believer; and faith is the act of a penitent. So that whoever believes repents; and whoever repents believes.

The primary and simple meaning of the word commonly used in the New Testament to express the idea of repentance, is a change of mind, as the result of reflection. In this sense, it is said, There is no repentance with God. He is not a man that he should repent. In the same sense it is said, that Esau found no place for repentance, when he was unable to effect a change in the determination of his father. In the ordinary religious sense of the term, it is a turning from sin unto God. This is the account commonly given of it in the word of God. I thought upon my ways, said the Psalmist, and turned my feet unto thy testimonies.[218] When the wicked man turneth away from his wickedness, that he hath committed, and doeth that which is lawful and right, he shall save his soul alive.[219] Let the wicked forsake his way, and the unrighteous man his thoughts, and let him return unto the Lord, and he will have mercy upon him, and to our God, for he will abundantly pardon.[220] And Solomon, in his prayer at the dedication of the temple, said, If the people shall bethink themselves in the land whither they were carried away captives, and shall repent and make supplication unto thee, saying, We have sinned and done perversely, we have committed wickedness, and so return unto

---

218. Ps. cxix. 59.
219. Ezek. xviii. 27.
220. Is. lv. 7.

thee with all their heart and with all their soul; then hear their prayer and their supplication in heaven thy dwelling place, and maintain their cause.[221] To repent, then, is to turn from sin unto God. But as there is a repentance which has no connection with salvation, it becomes us to search the Scriptures that we may learn the characteristics of that repentance which is unto life.

As conviction of sin is an essential part of repentance and as that point has already been considered, it will not be necessary to dwell long upon this general subject. The pre-eminence, however, given to it in the Scriptures, and the large space which it occupies in the experience of Christians, demand that the nature of this turning from sin, which is so often enjoined, should be carefully studied.

There is one general truth in relation to this point which is clearly taught in the Bible; and that is, that all true repentance springs from right views of God. The language of Job may with more or less confidence be adopted by every Christian: I have heard of thee by the hearing of the ear, but now mine eye seeth thee; wherefore I abhor myself in dust and ashes.[222]

The discovery of the justice of God serves to awaken conscience, and often produces a fearful looking for of judgment and fiery indignation. This is the natural and reasonable effect of a clear apprehension of the rectitude of the divine character, as of a judge who renders to every one his due. There are accordingly many illustrations of the effects of this apprehension recorded in the Scriptures. Fearfulness and trembling, said the Psalmist, are fallen upon me; and horror hath overwhelmed me.[223] While I suffer thy terrors I am distracted. Thy fierce wrath goeth over me. Thy terrors have cut me off.[224] There is no rest in my bones because of my sins. For my iniquities have gone over my head, as a heavy burden they are too heavy for me.[225] These fearful forebodings are so common in the experience of the people of God, that the earlier writers make terror of conscience a prominent part of repentance. There are, however,

---

221. 1 Kings, viii, 47, 49.
222. Job xlii, 5, 6.
223. Ps. lv. 5.
224. Ibid. lxxxviii. 15, 16.
225. Ibid. xxxviii. 3.

two remarks upon this subject, which should be borne in mind. The first is, that these exercises vary in degree from the intolerable anguish of despair, to the calm conviction of the judgment that we are justly exposed to the displeasure of God. And secondly, that there is nothing discriminating in these terrors of conscience. They are experienced by the righteous and the unrighteous. If they occurred in the repentance of David, they did also in that of Judas. Sinners in Zion are often afraid; and fearfulness often surprises the hypocrite. These fearful apprehensions, therefore, are not to be desired for their own sake; since there is nothing good in fear. It is reasonable that those should fear who refuse to repent and to accept of the offers of mercy. But there is nothing reasonable in those fears which arise from unbelief, or distrust of the promises of God. It so often happens, however, in the experience of the people of God, that they are made sensible of their guilt and danger, before they have any clear apprehensions of the plan of redemption, that, in fact, fear of the wrath of God enters largely into the feelings which characterise their conversion. The apprehension of the holiness of God produces awe. The angels in heaven are represented as veiling their faces, and bowing with reverence before the Holy One. Something of the same feeling must be excited in the minds of men by the discovery of His infinite purity. It cannot fail, no matter what may be the state of his mind, to excite awe. This, however, may be mingled with love, and express itself in adoration; or it may co-exist with hatred, and express itself in blasphemy. Very often the effect is simply awe; (or at least this is the prominent emotion,) and the soul is led to prostrate itself in the dust. The moral character of this emotion can only be determined by observing whether it is attended with complacency in the contemplation of infinite purity, and with a desire of larger and more constant discoveries of it; or whether it produces uneasiness and a desire that the vision may be withdrawn and we be allowed to remain at ease in our darkness.

In the next place, this discovery of the holiness of God cannot fail to produce a sense of our own unworthiness. It is in his light that we see light. It is by the apprehension of his excellence that we learn our own vileness. And as no man can be aware that he appears vile in the sight of others, without a sense of shame, we find that this emotion is described as being one of the most uniform attendants upon repentance. Thus Ezra, in his penitential prayer, says, O my

God! I am ashamed and blush to lift up my face to thee my God; for our iniquities are increased over our head, and our trespass is grown up unto the heavens.[226] Daniel expresses the same feeling when he says, O Lord, righteousness belongeth unto thee, but unto us confusion of face, as at this day.[227] And God when describing the restoration of his people, even when assuring them of pardon, says, Thou shalt know that I am the Lord, that thou mayst be confounded and never open thy mouth any more because of thy shame, when I am pacified towards thee, for all that thou hast done, saith the Lord God.[228]

As the consciousness of unworthiness when we think of others, produces shame, so, when we think of ourselves, it produces self-abhorrence. This latter feeling, therefore, also enters into the nature of true repentance. In the strong language of the suffering patriarch already quoted, the sinner abhors himself and repents in dust and ashes. In another passage the same distinguished servant of God says, Behold I am vile; what shall I answer thee? I will lay my hand upon my mouth.[229] And the prophet describing the repentance of the people says, Ye shall remember your ways and all your doings, wherein ye have been defiled; and ye shall loathe yourselves in your own sight, for all the evil that ye have committed.[230] It is not the strength, but the nature of these feelings, which determines the character of our repentance. Their nature is the same in all true penitents; their strength varies in every particular case. In all, however, the sense of sin destroys that self-complacency with which sinners soothe themselves, thanking God they are not as other men. It humbles them before God, and places them in the position which he would have them occupy. To this man will I look, saith the Lord, even to him that is poor and of a contrite spirit and trembleth at my word.[231] With such a soul God condescends to take up his abode. For thus saith the High and Lofty One who inhabiteth eternity, whose name is Holy; I dwell in the high and holy place, with him also who

---

226. Ezra ix. 6.
227. Dan. ix. 7.
228. Ezek. xvi. 63.
229. Job xl. 4.
230. Ezek. xx. 43.
231. Is. lxvi. 2.

is of a contrite and humble spirit, to revive the spirit of the humble, and to revive the heart of the contrite ones.[232]

This humbling sense of our unworthiness, which produces true contrition and self-abasement, is essential to repentance. Most men are willing to acknowledge themselves to be sinners; but they are at the same time disposed to extenuate their guilt; to think they are as good as could be reasonably expected; that the law of God demands too much of beings so frail as man, and that it would be unjust to visit their short-comings with any severe punishment. The change which constitutes repentance destroys this disposition to self-justification. The soul bows down before God under the consciousness of inexcusable guilt. It stands self-condemned, and, instead of regarding God as a hard master, it acknowledges that he is righteous in all his demands, and in all his judgments. Such were the feelings of David, when he said, I acknowledge my transgressions, and my sin is ever before me. Against thee, thee only have I sinned, and done this evil in thy sight, that thou mightst be justified when thou speakest, and clear when thou judgest.[233] The same feeling is expressed by Ezra, O Lord God of Israel thou art righteous. . . . behold we are before thee in our trespasses, for we cannot stand before thee because of this.[234] And Nehemiah uses language to the same effect; Thou art just in all that is brought upon us; for thou hast done right, but we have done wickedly.[235] There can, therefore, be no true repentance without this contrite spirit of self-condemnation and abasement.

The confession of sin, on which the Scriptures lay so much stress, is the outward expression of this inward sense of ill-desert. It is not enough that we should secretly condemn ourselves. God requires a full and ingenuous confession of our sins. And this our own hearts will prompt us to make. As there is no desire in the penitent to extenuate his guilt, so there is no disposition to conceal it. On the contrary, the soul is anxious to acknowledge every thing; to take shame to itself, and to justify God. We accordingly find

---

232. Is. lvii. 15.
233. Ps. li. 4.
234. Ezra ix. 15.
235. Neh. ix. 33.

that a large part of the penitential portions of the Scriptures is taken up in recording the confessions of the people of God. When I kept silence, said the Psalmist, my bones waxed old through my roaring all the day long. For day and night thy hand was heavy upon me; my moisture was turned into the drought of summer. I acknowledged my sin unto thee, and mine iniquity have I not hid. I said I will confess my transgressions unto the Lord; and thou forgavest the iniquity of my sin.[236] So long as he attempted to conceal his guilt, he found no relief; the hand of God continued to press heavily upon him; but when he acknowledged his transgressions he obtained forgiveness. The wise man therefore says, He that covereth his sins shall not prosper; but whoso confesseth and forsaketh them, shall find mercy.[237] The New Testament is equally explicit as to this part of our duty. If we say that we have no sin, we deceive ourselves, and the truth is not in us. If we confess our sins, he is faithful and just to forgive us our sins, and to cleanse us from all unrighteousness.[238]

This confession must be made to the person against whom we have sinned. If we have sinned against our fellow men, we must confess to them. If we have sinned against the church, we must confess to the church; and if we have sinned against God, our confession must be made to God. The Old Testament, in commanding restitution in case of injury done to our neighbour, thereby commanded acknowledgement to be made to the injured party. And in the New Testament we are required to confess our faults one to another.[239] As, however, the great majority of our sins are committed against God, it is to him that our confessions are to be principally made. And even in those cases in which we sin against men, we, in a still higher sense, sin against God. Our sense of guilt in his sight, therefore, will prevail over the sense of our injustice to those whom we have offended. Thus David, though he had, in the most grievous manner, sinned against his neighbour, was so affected with the enormity of his sin as committed against God, that he said, Against thee, thee

---

236. Ps. xxxii. 3.
237. Prov. xxviii. 13.
238. 1 John i. 8, 9.
239. James v. 16.

only have I sinned and done this evil in thy sight.[240] In the inspired records of penitential sorrow, we accordingly find that confession is constantly made to God. Let thine ear now, said Nehemiah, be attentive and thine eyes open, that thou mayest hear the prayer of thy servant which I pray before thee, now day and night, for the children of Israel thy servants, and confess the sins of the children of Israel which we have sinned against thee; both I and my father's house have sinned, and have dealt very corruptly against thee, have not kept the commandments or the statutes, nor the judgments which thou commandest thy servant Moses. Indeed the greater portion of the remarkable prayers of Daniel, Ezra, and Nehemiah, which form the most authentic record of the exercises of genuine repentance, is taken up with confessions of sin; which shows how essential such confession is to the proper discharge of this duty. No man, therefore, whose heart does not lead him freely, fully and humbly to acknowledge his sin before God, can have any satisfactory evidence that he truly repents.

There is indeed a confession which remorse extorts from the lips of those whose hearts know nothing of that godly sorrow which is unto life. Thus Judas went to his accomplices in treachery and said, I have sinned in that I have betrayed the innocent blood; and then went and hung himself. This, however, is very different from that ingenuous acknowledgment of sin which flows from a broken spirit, and which is the more full and free, the stronger the assurance of forgiveness.

Though the Scriptures plainly teach that in all true repentance there is a sense of sin, self-loathing, self-condemnation, sorrow and confession, yet such is the poverty of human language, that these very terms may be, nay, must be, employed to express the exercises of those who do not truly repent. It is said of Judas that he repented; and we cannot doubt that his repentance included a conviction of guilt, sorrow, self-abhorrence and confession. Yet all this was nothing more than the operation of the impenitent remorse which often drives men to despair, and which serves to feed the fire that never shall be quenched. Although we are forced

---

240. Ps. li. 4.

to describe the exercises which attend the sorrow of the world, and those which accompany the sorrow which is of God, by the same terms, they are nevertheless essentially different in their nature. There is a gleam of hope and a glow of love pervading the exercises of the true penitent, which impart to all his exercises a peculiarity of character, and cause them to produce effects specifically different from those which flow from despairing remorse, or the agitations of an awakened conscience. His views of the justice and holiness of God produce, not only a conviction of sin and sorrow for having committed it; but also an earnest desire to be delivered from it as the greatest of all evils, and an anxious longing after conformity to the image of God, as the greatest of all blessings. The repentance of the ungodly consists of the operations of conscience combined with fear; the repentance of the godly, of the operations of conscience combined with love. The one is the sorrow of the malefactor; the other the sorrow of a child. The one tends to despair and opposition to God; the other to hope and a desire after his favour. Both may lead to obedience; but the obedience in the one case is slavish; in the other, filial. In the one case it is mere penance; in the other it is repentance.

The circumstance which, perhaps, most perceptibly distinguishes true repentance from mere conviction and remorse, is, that the former flows from the apprehension of the mercy of God. There is no hope in the repentance of the ungodly. They may see by the light of conscience and of the divine law, that their sins are exceedingly great. They may be filled with terror from the apprehension of divine justice, and even humbled and confounded under a view of the infinite holiness of God and of their own vileness, but there is no sense of forgiving mercy, no apprehension of the divine favour. Instead, therefore, of turning towards God, they turn from him. After the example of Adam, they would gladly hide themselves from his presence. And so terrible, at times, is that presence, that they madly seek a refuge from it in the darkness of the grave, or call upon the rocks and the mountains to cover them. This is the sorrow which worketh death. But in every case of real turning unto God, there is more or less distinct apprehension of his mercy. This may be so feeble as only to enable the soul to say, Though he slay me, yet I will trust in him; or, Who knoweth if he will return and repent and leave a blessing behind him;[241] or, to adopt the language of David, If I shall find favour in the eyes of the Lord, he will bring me again. But if he thus say, I have no pleasure in him; behold here am I, let him do to me as seemeth good unto him.[242] This, however, is sufficient to turn fear into hope and rebellion into submission.

It may be that the hope which saves the soul from sinking into despair and which prevents it from turning from God in aggravated opposition, is at times, nothing more than a conviction that he is merciful, without any distinct apprehension of the way in which his mercy can be exercised, or any confident persuasion of our own acceptance. Still the soul believes that he is the Lord, the Lord God, merciful and gracious, long suffering and abundant in goodness and truth.[243] It has courage to adopt the language of the Psalmist: Thou God are good and ready to forgive; and plenteous in mercy to all those that call upon thee.[244] In all the records of penitence, therefore, contained in the Scriptures, we find the recognition of the divine goodness as the great operative principle in turning the soul unto God. Thus Nehemiah says, Thou art a God ready to pardon, gracious and merciful, slow to anger, and of great kindness.[245] And the prophet presents this consideration as the great motive to those whom he calls to repentance; Rend your hearts and not your garments, and turn unto the Lord your God; for he is gracious and repenteth him of evil.[246]

But inasmuch as there can be no confidence of forgiving mercy, which is not founded on the revelation of the purpose of God; and as there is no revelation of a purpose to pardon except through the mediation of Jesus Christ, so however indistinct may be, at times, the view which the soul takes of the plan of salvation, there must still be a reference to the Saviour in all authorized expectations of mercy. The penitent may not know how God can be just and yet the justifier of sinners, and yet be persuaded not only that he is merciful, but that he has found a ransom and can consistently save us from going down

---

241. Joel ii. 14.
242. 2 Sam. xv. 25, 26.
243. Ex. xxxiv. 6.
244. Ps. lxxxvi. 5.
245. Neh. ix. 17.
246. Joel ii. 13.

into the pit. Doubtless, however, under the light of the gospel, it is far more common that the soul sees all that it discovers of the mercy of God and of the possibility of pardon in the face of Jesus Christ. It is in him that God has revealed himself as reconciled unto the world, not imputing unto men their trespasses. It is because he was made for us, that we can be made the righteousness of God in him. All evangelical hope rests on the assurance that though we have sinned we have an advocate with the Father, Jesus Christ the righteous, who is the propitiation for our sins. This is the hope which is effectual in winning the soul back to God. It is the discovery of the love of God in giving his own Son that whosoever believes on him, should not perish but have eternal life. It is this that breaks the hard heart, revealing to it the exceeding turpitude of its sins, and at the same time disclosing the readiness of God freely to forgive those who come to him through Christ. It is therefore not so much the threatenings of the law, as the apprehension of the love of God, which turns the sinner from his rebellion, and draws him back to submission and obedience. All repentance without this is legal and slavish. It is such as that of Pharoah, or Judas, or of the thousands whom an awakened conscience and fear of wrath drive from their former sins, and force to walk in clanking chains along a mistaken road in search of heaven. This is the only repentance which conscience and the apprehension of divine justice can produce. A soul cannot approach an unreconciled God, any more than it can embrace a consuming fire. A sense of the favour of God, or a hope in his mercy, is essential to our returning to him with confidence and love.

There is indeed a belief in the mercy of God which, instead of leading men to repentance, encourages them to continue in sin. This is a belief which arises out of ignorance. It is founded on the misapprehension of the character of God. It is easy for those who know nothing of the divine holiness and justice and who look upon sin as a misfortune or a trifle, to believe that God will not be severe to mark iniquity. To such persons the mercy of God seems a matter of course; restricting its offers to no class of men, but covering with its mantle the sins of the penitent and of the reprobate. As they see no reason why God should not forgive, they easily hope in his mercy. But when their eyes are opened to his immaculate purity which forbids his looking on sin with allowance; to his justice which forbids him to spare the guilty; to the strictness of his law and to the fearfulness of its penalty; when conscience is aroused and adds its sanction to the judgment of God, in a voice whose authority and power can neither be questioned nor evaded, then these hopes of mercy are seen to be as the spider's web. They are swept away in a moment, and the difficulty now is, to believe that pardon, once thought so certain, is even possible. Hence the assurances that God is plenteous in mercy and ready to forgive are so numerous and earnest in the Scriptures. Hence the way in which mercy can be exercised, consistently with those attributes which are seen to enter into the essential excellence of God, is so clearly set forth. Hence the invitations, the promises, yea, even the oath of God, are given to beget hope in the mind of the convinced and humbled sinner. It is not the whole, but the sick, who need the physician; and it is not for the careless, who feel no need of pardon, but for the anxious, who fear that there is scarcely room for mercy, that these assurances are given.

It is not, therefore, that hope of mercy which springs from ignorance and indifference, which is operative in the work of repentance, but that which is founded upon the promises of God embraced by faith. It is an enlightened hope. The soul in entertaining it, knows something of the difficulties in the way of pardon, and something of the method in which mercy can be consistently exercised. Such a hope is not a matter of course; nor is it an easy attainment. The sense of sin, the testimony of conscience, the holiness of God, the honour of his law, are all apparently opposed to any reasonable expectation of forgiveness. And, therefore, although the declarations of Scripture are so explicit on the subject, it often happens that the awakened sinner feels that though these declarations may be true in reference to others, they cannot be true as it regards himself. And when the goodness of God is revealed to him; when he sees the divine love surmounting all difficulties, no shipwrecked mariner surrounded by darkness and tossed by tempests, hails with greater joy the break of day than does such a soul the revelation of divine mercy. It is not joy merely; it is wonder, gratitude and love that take possession of his soul and fill him with the purpose of living devoted to God his Redeemer. It is this hope which gives new life to the soul, and accomplishes its return from the service of sin to the service of God.

Hope in the mercy of God being thus important, it is the great design of the Bible to reveal the love of God to sinners, in order to bring them back from their apostacy. The sacred volume is full of instruction on this important subject. Every command to repent, implies a readiness on the part of God to forgive. Every institution of divine worship implies that God is willing to receive those who return to him. Every instance of pardon mentioned in the Bible is left on record to show that there is forgiveness with God that he may be feared. With the same view he has given those declarations of his mercy, long-suffering and love, with which the Scriptures abound. And above all, for this purpose has he set forth his Son as a propitiation for our sins, that we may see not only that he is merciful, but how he can be merciful and yet just. These offers of mercy are made to all who hear the gospel, even to those whose sins are as scarlet, or red like crimson; and none lose the benefit of them who do not voluntarily and wickedly reject them; either carelessly supposing that they need no forgiveness, or unbelievingly refusing to accept of pardon on the only terms on which it can be granted.

That repentance, therefore, which is unto life, is a turning; not a being driven away from sin by fear and stress of conscience, but a forsaking it as evil and hateful, with sincere sorrow, humility and confession; and a returning unto God, because he is good and willing to forgive, with a determination to live in obedience to his commandments.

There are but two ways in which we can judge of the genuineness of this change. The one is the comparison of our inward experience with the word of God; the other with the observation of its effects. As every man is conscious of his own feelings, attention and comparison will generally enable him to ascertain their character. He may tell whether he has had such views of the justice and holiness of God as to produce a conviction of his own sinfulness and ill-desert; whether he has been forced to give up his self-complacency and to feel that disapprobation of his character and conduct, which leads the soul to confess with shame and sorrow its guilt and pollution in the sight of God. He may tell whether he has had such apprehensions of the mercy of God in Jesus Christ as to induce him to return to his heavenly Father, with a strong desire after his favour, and with a firm determination to live to his glory. These are the exercises which constitute repentance, and he who is conscious of them may know that he is turned from death unto life.

As, however, true self-knowledge is the most difficult of all attainments; and as the feelings, unless unusually strong, are hard to be detected in their true nature, the surest test of the character of any supposed change of heart is to be found in its permanent effects. By their fruits ye shall know them, is a declaration as applicable to the right method of judging ourselves as of others. Whatever, therefore, may have been our inward experience; whatever joy or sorrow we may have felt, unless we bring forth fruits meet for repentance, our experience will profit us nothing. Our repentance needs to be repented of, unless it leads us to confession and restitution in cases of private injury; unless it causes us to forsake not merely outward sins, which attract the notice of others, but those which lie concealed in the heart; unless it makes us choose the service of God, as that which is right and congenial, and causes us to live not for ourselves but for him who loved us and gave himself for us.

There is no duty the necessity of which is either more obvious in itself, or more frequently asserted in the word of God, than that of repentance. Nature itself teaches us that when we have done wrong, we should be sorry for it, and turn away from the evil. Every man feels that this is a reasonable expectation in regard to those who have offended him. Every parent especially looks with anxiety for the repentance of a disobedient child; and he considers nothing worthy of the name, but sincere sorrow and a return to affectionate obedience. No man need wonder, therefore, that God who requires nothing but what is right and who can require nothing less, commands all men every where to repent. The salvation offered in the gospel, though it be a salvation of sinners, is also a salvation from sin. The heaven which it promises is a heaven of holiness. The rivers of pleasure which flow from the right hand of God, are filled with the pure waters of life. No man, therefore, can be saved, who does not, by repentance, forsake his sins. This is itself a great part of salvation. The inward change of heart from the love and service of sin, to the love and service of God, is the great end of the death of Christ, who gave himself for his church, that he might sanctify and cleanse it with the washing of water, by the word, that he might present it to himself a glorious church, not having spot, or wrinkle, or any such thing; but that it should be holy and without blemish. A salvation for sinners, therefore, without repentance, is a contradiction.

Hence it is that repentance is the burden of evangelical preaching. Our Saviour himself when he began to preach, said, Repent, for the kingdom of God is at hand.[247] And when he came into Galilee preaching the gospel, he said, The time is fulfilled, and the kingdom of God is at hand, repent ye and believe the gospel.[248] The commission which he gave his apostles was, That repentance and remission of sins should be preached in his name among all nations.[249] In the execution of this commission his disciples went forth and preached, Repent ye and be converted, that your sins may be blotted out, when the times of refreshing come from the presence of the Lord.[250] Paul, in the account which he gave Agrippa of his preaching, said that he showed first unto them in Damascus, and at Jerusalem, and throughout all the coasts of Judea, and then unto the Gentiles, that they should repent and turn unto God, and do works meet for repentance.[251] And he called upon the elders at Ephesus to bear witness that he had taught publicly and from house to house, testifying both to the Jews and to the Greeks, repentance towards God and faith towards our Lord Jesus Christ.[252]

Repentance then is the great, immediate and pressing duty of all who hear the gospel. They are called upon to forsake their sins and to return unto God through Jesus Christ. The neglect of this duty, is the rejection of salvation. For, as we have seen, unless we repent we must perish. It is because repentance is thus indispensably necessary, that God reveals so clearly not only the evil of sin, and the terms of his law, but his infinite compassion and love; that he calls upon us to turn unto him and live, assuring us that he is the Lord, the Lord God merciful and gracious, longsuffering, and abundant in goodness and truth. This call to repentance commonly follows men from the cradle to the grave. It is one of the first sounds which wakes the infant's ear; it is one of the last which falls on the failing senses of the dying sinner. Every thing in this world is vocal with the voice of mercy. All joy and all sorrow are calls to return unto God with whom are the issues of life. Every opening grave, every church,

---

247. Matt. iv. 17.
248. Mark i. 15.
249. Luke xxiv. 47.
250. Acts iii. 19.
251. Acts xxvi. 20.
252. Acts xx. 21.

every page of the Bible, is an admonition or an invitation. Every serious thought or anxious foreboding is the voice of God, saying, Turn ye, for why will ye die? It is through all these admonitions that men force their way to death. They perish, because they deliberately reject salvation.

It is one of the mysteries of redemption, that under the economy of mercy, all duties are graces. Though repentance is our duty, it is not less the gift of God. Those who wrest the Scriptures to their own destruction, gladly seize on such truths either as an excuse for delay, under pretence of waiting God's time, or as a palliation of the guilt of a hard and impenitent heart. But those who feel the greatness of the work required of them, rejoice in the truth, and rouse themselves with new energy to their duty, no longer a hopeless task, and with all earnestness work out their own salvation, because it is God that worketh in them to will and to do, according to his own pleasure.

Chapter VIII.

Profession of Religion.

SECTION I.	*The nature and necessity of a public profession of religion.*

Religion consists in a great measure in the secret intercourse of the soul with God; in those acts of adoration, gratitude, confidence and submission which the eye of man cannot see, and with which the stranger cannot intermeddle. These secret exercises by controlling the external conduct, and by supplying the motives for the humble demeanor and benevolent actions of the Christian, cannot indeed fail to manifest their existence; but all unnecessary parading them upon the notice of others borders on the offence which our Saviour condemned in the ancient Pharisees. Agreeably to his directions, our alms are to be given in secret; when we pray we should pray in secret, and when we fast, we should not appear unto men to fast, but unto our Father, who seeth in secret. In these words Christ does more than condemn hypocrisy; he not only forbids the performance of religious duties with the design of being seen of men, but he teaches that true religion is unobtrusive and retiring. It avoids the glare of day. It is holy, solemn, secret, rejoicing in being unobserved. It is directly opposed to the ostentatious display of religious feelings in which those delight, who seem to make religion consist in talking about it.

Although religion is thus retiring in its character, and although it consists in a great measure in the secret intercourse of the soul with God, it nevertheless has its social and public relations, which render it impossible that a true Christian should desire to keep the fact of his being a Christian a secret from the world. This is indeed often attempted, for a time, by those whose faith is weak, and who dread the reproach with which a profession of religion is, under many circumstances, attended. The temptation to such concealment cannot well be appreciated by those who have always lived in the bosom of a religious society, where the profession of religious sentiments is a passport to confidence and respect. Such persons little know the trial to which those of their brethren are exposed whose parents or associates will view all experimental religion with hatred or contempt, and who visit every manifestation of pious feeling with the chastisement of cruel mockings. To a greater or less degree, a large portion of the people of God, are called upon to endure this trial; and they are often tempted to ask whether they cannot be religious without letting it be known. If religion is a secret thing, why may it not be kept a secret? To this question the answer is simple and decisive. The confession of Christ before men is declared in Scripture to be essential to salvation. Whosoever, said our Saviour, confesseth me before men, him will I confess before my father which is in heaven; but whosoever denieth me before men, him will I also deny before my Father which is in heaven.[253] Again, whosoever shall be ashamed of me and of my words in this adulterous generation; of him also shall the Son of Man be ashamed, when he cometh in the glory of his Father and with the holy angels.[254] Paul also in writing to Timothy says, Be not ashamed of the testimony of the Lord, nor of me his prisoner, but be thou partaker of the afflictions of the gospel according to the power of God.[255] If we suffer, we shall also reign with him; if we deny him, he also will deny us.[256] And still more explicitly, when

---

253. Mark x. 32.
254. Mark viii. 38.
255. 2 Tim. i. 8.
256. 2 Tim. ii. 12.

teaching the condition of salvation, he says, If thou shalt confess with thy mouth the Lord Jesus, and shall believe in thy heart that God hath raised him from the dead, thou shalt be saved. For with the heart man believeth unto righteousness, and with the mouth confession is made unto salvation.[257] The same truth is taught in all those passages which assert the necessity of baptism, because baptism involves a public profession of the gospel. Thus our Saviour in his commission to the apostles said, He that believeth and is baptized shall be saved.[258] And on the day of Pentecost, when the people were convinced of the sin of having rejected Christ, and asked what they should do, Peter answered, Repent and be baptized, every one of you, in the name of the Lord Jesus.[259] It was not enough that they should retire to their houses and repent before God; they must publicly acknowledge Christ and their allegiance to him. There is, therefore, no condition of discipleship more clearly laid down than this. If we do not acknowledge him as our Saviour, he will not acknowledge us as his disciples. If we are not willing to share with him in the reproach and contradiction of sinners, we cannot share in the glory which he has received from the Father.

The relation in which we stand to Christ as our king renders a public acknowledgment of his authority necessary. In the kingdoms of this world, no one is admitted to the privileges of citizenship without a profession of allegiance. And in the kingdom of Christ those who do not acknowledge his authority, reject him. By refusing to confess him as Lord they declare that they are not his people.

The church is also often compared in Scripture to a family. Can a child live in his father's house without acknowledging his parent? May he receive the blessings of a mother's love, and not acknowledge her to be his mother? May he pass her in the street without recognition, and then steal, under cover of the night, to be fed at her table and to be protected by her care? As every one feels that no child, without proper filial feelings, could hesitate to acknowledge his parents, so we may be assured that we are not the children of God,

---

257. Rom. x. 9, 10.
258. Mark xvi. 16.
259. Acts ii. 38.

if we are afraid or ashamed to acknowledge him as our Father, and our obligations to honour and obey him.

It is still further to be considered that Christians are the worshippers of Christ. The apostle salutes the Corinthians as those who call upon the name of the Lord Jesus; and from the beginning, in Jerusalem and at Damascus, Christians were designated as those who called on the name of Christ.[260] But what kind of worshipper is he who is ashamed or afraid to acknowledge his God? All the relations, therefore, in which a Christian stands to Christ, as his king, as the head of the family of God and as the object of divine worship, involve the necessity of confessing him before men; and we practically reject him in all these relations by neglecting or refusing this public profession of him and his religion.

A moment's consideration of the nature of the religion of Jesus Christ must convince us of the impossibility of being a secret Christian. Not the heart only, but the whole external deportment must be regulated by that religion. It forbids many things which the world allows; it enjoins many things which the world forbids. Obedience to its precepts of necessity includes a public profession; because such obedience draws a line of distinction between its disciples and the people of the world. This is one of the reasons why the people of God are called saints. They are distinguished, separated from others and consecrated to God. When they cease to be thus distinguished from those around them, they cease to be saints. If their inward temper and outward conduct do not mark them out as a peculiar people, they are not Christians. A city set on an hill cannot be hid. It cannot be that those who deny themselves and take up their cross and daily follow Christ; whose affections are set upon things above; who walk by faith and not by sight; who live unto God and keep themselves unspotted from the world, should not visibly differ from those whose spirit, principles and objects are all worldly. Nor is it possible that this difference should exist, without an avowal, on the part of the Christian, of the cause of it. He must appeal to the authority of Christ as the justification of his conduct, and, therefore, cannot live as a Christian without confessing Christ.

---

260. Acts ix. 14, 21.

Besides the general temper and deportment required by the gospel, there are many specific duties enjoined by Christ which imply a public profession of his religion. The organization of his church as a visible society, supposes the separation of a people recognizing his authority, and professing to act in obedience to his laws. The commission which he gave to his disciples was, that they should go into all the world, preaching his gospel, making disciples, baptizing them in his name, gathering them into distinct societies and appointing officers over them for conducting public worship and for the exercise of discipline. All this supposes that his followers should constitute a body publicly acknowledging him as their head, and confessing him as their Lord and Saviour before the world. How can a man keep the fact of his being a Christian a secret, when Christianity is, by its author, made to assume this visible, organized form? It is specially enjoined upon every believer to associate himself with the church, to assemble with his fellow Christians for public worship, and to unite with them in celebrating the Saviour's death? If a Christian is one who obeys Christ, and if obedience includes those external acts which involve this public acknowledgment of him, then no man can be a Christian who does not make this acknowledgment.

There are few duties (and those founded on positive precepts) commanded in the word of God, which right feelings do not, of themselves, urge us to discharge. If we are required to forsake sin, to serve God, to love the brethren, to live for others rather than ourselves, to be instant in prayer, to join in the public and social worship of God; these are things in which the renewed heart instinctively delights. The external command guides and sanctions the performance; but the motive to obedience is not mere regard to authority. In like manner, while the public confession of Christ is enjoined in Scripture as a necessary duty, it is, at the same time, the spontaneous tribute of every Christian heart. If no subject requires to be urged to acknowledge a sovereign whom he loves; if no child needs to be commanded to confess a parent whom he reveres, much less does the believer need to be forced to confess the Saviour whom he regards as the brightness of the Father's glory; to whom he feels indebted for redemption, and whom he hopes to worship and serve with saints and angels in heaven. It is not meant to be asserted that no believer is ever ashamed of Jesus, nor that under circumstances of peculiar trial he may not fear to acknowledge his truth or to assume his name.

Peter once denied his master. But it is certainly true that no man can have right views of Christ and right feelings towards him, without habitually, openly and gladly acknowledging him as his God and Saviour. He will esteem the reproach of Christ greater riches than the treasures of Egypt, and choose rather to suffer affliction with the people of God than to enjoy the pleasures of sin for a season.

It is not difficult to understand the nature of the duty now under consideration. To confess Christ is to recognise his character and claims. It is to acknowledge that Jesus is the Christ. It is to admit the truth of the doctrines which he taught. It is to profess our allegiance to him as our Lord and Saviour. This confession must be public; it must be made before men; it must be made with the mouth, and not left to be inferred from the conduct. It should be remembered that this includes more than the mere assumption of the name Christian, in distinction from Pagan or Mahommedan. If men misconceive or misrepresent the character of Christ, a profession of such erroneous views is not the confession which he requires. To acknowledge Christ as a good man, or an inspired teacher, is in fact to deny him in his true Saviour as the Son of God, as the propitiation for sin, as the only mediator and the sovereign Lord of the living and the dead. And to acknowledge the gospel merely as a code of morals, is to reject it as the revelation of the grace of God. The confession which is required is the public acknowledgment of Christ in his true character, and of his gospel in its real nature. It will not do to strip the gospel of every thing offensive to human pride and to acknowledge the rest. The very thing to be done is to take the shame of professing what is a scandal to the Jews and foolishness to the Greeks. It is to acknowledge our faith and confidence in a Saviour despised and rejected of men, and in doctrines which human reason can neither discover nor comprehend.

There are several ways in which this public confession is to be made. As already remarked there is a confession included in the obedience rendered to the commands of Christ. Obedience, therefore, is one form of confession, and can never be rendered without distinguishing those who yield it as the followers of Christ. Again, occasions frequently occur in which Christians are called upon to avow the truth, to defend it against gainsayers, to urge it upon those over whom they have influence or authority, or to give a reason of the hope that is in them, with meekness and fear. But the chief and most important mode of confession is attendance upon the ordinances of Baptism and the Lord's Supper. So much prominence is given to these institutions, in the word of God, that every Christian should have clear ideas of their nature and of his own duty in regard to them.

SECTION II. *Baptism and the Lord's Supper. The nature, design and efficacy of these ordinances.*

That Baptism and the Lord's supper, whatever other important ends they may be intended to serve, were appointed as a mode of publicly professing our faith in the gospel, is clearly taught in the Bible. The public participation of the rites of any religion is, in its nature, a profession of that religion. It is on this ground the apostle charges with idolatry the Corinthians who, within the precincts of the heathen temples, partook of the sacrifices offered to idols. I speak as to wise men, judge ye what I say. The participation of a Christian ordinance, is it not an act of Christian worship? The participation of a Jewish sacrifice, is it not an act of Jewish worship? and by parity of reasoning, is not the participation of a heathen ordinance an act of heathen worship? This is the purport of the apostle's argument in 1 Cor. x. 15–21, and it is obviously founded on the admitted truth, that joining in the celebration of the ordinances of the gospel, is, from the nature of the act, a profession of the religion of Christ. The recipient thereby places himself in communion with the object of worship and with all his fellow worshippers. For we being many are one bread and one body; for we are all partakers of one bread. Hence the apostle adds, Ye cannot drink of the cup of the Lord and of the cup of devils; ye cannot be partakers of the Lord's table and the table of devils. It is impossible to be in communion with Christ and Satan at the same time, and, therefore, it is the grossest inconsistency to partake at the same time of the ordinances of Christ and of the sacrifices of devils. All this supposes that a participation of Christian ordinances is a profession of the Christian religion. When Christ commanded the apostles to make disciples, baptizing them, he obviously intended that baptism should be a badge of discipleship, or that by that rite his followers should acknowledge their relation to him. This, indeed, is the prominent idea in the formula, To baptize in the name of any one. And hence Paul reminded the Corinthians that they were not his disciples or followers, by asking them, Were ye baptized in the name of Paul? It is, however, unnecessary to dwell upon this point, as it is universally conceded that the participation of the ordinances of the gospel is the appointed mode of confessing Christ before the world.

As it is the duty of every Christian to confess Christ, and to confess him in this particular way, it is necessary to inquire more particularly into the nature and design of these ordinances. It has long been customary in the church to call these institutions sacraments. Little light, however, can be derived from the use of this term, because it is not a scriptural word, and because it is employed by ancient writers in a very comprehensive sense. As it comes from the word meaning to consecrate, any thing sacred was called a sacrament. The Romans applied the term to a sum of money deposited in the hands of the High Priest to abide the decision of a suit. They also called the oath by which soldiers consecrate themselves to the military service a sacrament; and in the Latin church, (whence we have borrowed the word), it was used as synonymous with mystery, not only as applied to things which had a hidden meaning, but in its wider sense as signifying what was undiscoverable by human reason. In this sense the Gospel itself, the calling of the Gentiles, the future conversion of the Jews are sacraments. It is not from a word of such latitude of meaning that the nature of the Christian ordinances can be learned; but, on the contrary, the Christian sense of the word must be determined from what the Scriptures teach concerning the ordinances to which the word is now applied.

They are, in the first place, rites of divine appointment, and not of human institution. When Christ was about to ascend into heaven, he said, Go ye, therefore, and teach all nations, baptizing them in the name of the Father, of the Son, and of the Holy Ghost; teaching them to observe all things whatsoever I have commanded you; and, lo, I am with you always, even unto the end of the world. The rite of baptism was, therefore, instituted by Christ, and is to be continued as long as there are disciples to be made, even unto the end of the world. And on the night in which he was betrayed, he instituted the Lord's supper, saying, This do in remembrance of me, with the command that it should be observed until he comes. The New Testament furnishes abundant evidence that the apostles enjoined, both by precept and example, the observance of these ordinances, agreeably to the Saviour's directions. No rite, therefore, is a sacrament in the

Christian sense of the term, which is not a matter of divine appointment, and of perpetual obligation.

In the second place, the Bible teaches us that the sacraments are the signs of spiritual blessings. They are designed by outward, significant actions, to represent inward, spiritual gifts. The great blessing offered in the Gospel is union with Christ, and the consequent participation of his merits and spirit, by which we are freed from condemnation and pollution of sin. And this is the blessing which baptism and the Lord's supper are designed to represent. Hence it is said, As many as have been baptized into Christ, have put on Christ; which implies union with him.[261] Believers are said to be baptized into one body.[262] That is, by baptism they are constituted one body; but they are one body only in virtue of their union with their common head. Know ye not, asks the apostle, that so many of us were baptized into Jesus Christ, were baptized into his death, i.e. so as to be united with him in his death.[263] As union with Christ is the great blessing signified by baptism, and as pardon and sanctification are the consequences of that union, this ordinance is also represented as symbolizing these two great blessings of the covenant of grace. Thus on the day of Pentecost, Peter said to the people, Repent, and be baptized every one of you, in the name of Jesus Christ, for the remission of sins.[264] And Ananias said to Paul, Arise and be baptized, and wash away thy sins, calling on the name of the Lord.[265] In many similar passages the reference of baptism to pardon is very clearly expressed.

No less clear is its intended significancy of sanctification. This is plainly taught in the passages from the epistles to the Galatians and Romans, quoted above, in which baptism is declared to represent our union with Christ, and our death to sin and our living unto God. And in the epistle to Titus,[266] it is called "the washing of regeneration;" and in the epistle to the Ephesians,[267] Christ is said to sanctify his

---

261. Gal. iii. 27.
262. 1 Cor. xii. 13.
263. Rom. vi. 2.
264. Acts ii. 38.
265. Acts xxii. 16.
266. Titus iii. 5
267. Eph. v. 26.

church, "with the washing of water by the word." It need hardly be remarked that the ordinance is appropriately significant of these great truths. Water is the common means of purification. Both the guilt and pollution of sin, are represented in Scripture as a defilement, and hence they are said to be washed away by the blood and Spirit of Christ. It is this two-fold purification that is so appropriately represented by the ordinance in question.

The same truths, under a different aspect, are exhibited in the Lord's supper. That the bread represents the body of Christ, and the wine his blood, is expressly declared by our Saviour when he said, "This is my body, this is my blood." And by our participation of the bread and wine, our participation of that of which they are the symbols, is clearly represented. The cup of blessing which we bless, is it not the communion of the blood of Christ? The bread which we break, is it not the communion of the body of Christ. For we being many are one bread, and one body, for we are all partakers of that one bread.[268] Here, as in the passage quoted above in reference to baptism, believers are declared to be one body, because by partaking of the Lord's supper their communion with the Lord Jesus is expressed. These ordinances, therefore, though in different ways, set forth the same great truth. They are both divinely appointed symbols of our union with Christ, and of our participation of the benefits which flow from his mediation and death.

We should greatly err, however, if we supposed they were merely signs. We are taught that they are seals; that they were appointed by Christ to certify to believers their interest in the blessings of the covenant of grace. Among men a seal is used for the purpose of authentication and confirmation. It is intended to assure the party concerned that the document to which it is attached, is genuine and binding. In condescension to our weakness, God has been pleased not only to promise pardon and purity to believers, but to appoint these ordinances as seals of his promises. The simple assurance given to Noah that the earth should not a second time be destroyed by a deluge, might have been a sufficient foundation for confidence; but God saw fit to appoint the rainbow to be a perpetual confirmation of his covenant; and throughout all generations when that bow ap-

---

268. 1 Cor. x. 16, 17.

pears, men feel that it is not merely a sign of the returning sun, but a divinely appointed pledge of the promise of God. In like manner God willing more abundantly to show unto his people the immutability of his promise, has confirmed it by these seals, which are designed to assure the believer that as certainly as he receives the signs of the blessings of the covenant, he shall receive the blessings themselves.

That these ordinances were really intended to confirm the promises of God, is plain from the fact that Paul says that circumcision was the seal of the righteousness of faith; that is, it was designed to assure Abraham and his descendants that God would regard and treat as righteous all who believed his words. And that the apostle regarded baptism in the same light is obvious from Col. ii. 11, where baptism and circumcision are spoken of as of similar import. And in reference to the Lord's supper, the Saviour said, This cup is the New Testament in my blood; that is, the new covenant was ratified by his blood. Of that blood the cup is the appointed memorial, and it is, therefore, at the same time, the memorial and confirmation of the covenant itself; it is the assurance to us that God has promised the blessings of that covenant to all believers. Baptism and the Lord's supper are, therefore, visible pledges or confirmations of the fact that Christ has died, that his death has been accepted as a propitiation for sin, and God, for his sake, will grant pardon, sanctification and eternal life to all them that believe.

If, however, the sacraments are seals on the part of God, the reception of them implies a voluntary engagement on the part of the Christian to devote himself to the service of Christ. The gospel is represented under the form of a covenant. It is so called by Christ himself. But a covenant implies mutual stipulations. God promises to his people pardon and salvation; in his strength, they promise faith and obedience. The sacraments are the seals of this covenant. God, in their appointment, binds himself to the performance of his promise; his people, by receiving them, bind themselves to trust and serve him. This idea is included in the representation given in Romans vi. 3, 4, where believers are said to have been buried with Christ in baptism, that as he rose from the dead, they also should walk in newness of life. It is included also in the very formula of baptism; for to be baptized in the name of the Father, Son and Holy Ghost, implies a voluntary dedication of ourselves to God, as our Father, Redeemer and Sanctifier. The same thing is taught in all the passages in which a participation of Christian ordinances, is said to include a profession of the gospel; for the gospel imposes duties as well as promises blessings.

It is probably in this view of these ordinances that the name, sacraments, was so generally applied to them. For as the oath by which the soldier consecrated himself to the military service, was called a sacrament, so the ordinances in which the believer binds himself to the service of Christ, was appropriately designated by the same term. The phrase sacramental host is, therefore, not inaptly applied to the people of God, considered as a great multitude, who have solemnly bound themselves by sacraments to live to his glory.

Baptism and the Lord's supper being ordinances of divine appointment and perpetual obligation, designed to distinguish the followers of Christ from the world; to exhibit the truths of the gospel; to seal to believers the divine promises, and to bring them into covenant with God, the interesting question arises, What good do they do? What benefits are we authorized to expect from them? The answer commonly given to this question by the great body of evangelical Christians is, that the sacraments are efficacious means of grace, not merely exhibiting to, but actually conferring upon those who worthily receive them, the benefits which they represent. As they are divinely appointed to set forth Christ and his benefits, and to assure the believer of his interest therein, they have, even as moral means, a powerful influence to confirm his faith, to excite his gratitude and love, and to open the fountains both of penitence and joy. But as the word of God has not only its own moral influence, as truth, in the sanctification of the soul, but also, when attended by the demonstration of the Spirit, a divine and effectual power; so the sacraments have not only the influence due to the lively exhibition of truth, but as means of God's appointment, and attended by his Spirit, they become efficacious signs of grace, communicating what they signify. Nothing less than this can satisfy the strong language of the Scriptures on this subject, or the experience of God's people. When the Christian, in the exercise of faith, sees in the water of baptism the lively emblem of the purifying influence of the blood and Spirit of Christ, and in the bread and wine the memorials of the Saviour's death, and knows that they are appointed to be a pledge of salvation of all believers, he receives Christ, in receiving the appointed symbols of his grace; he receives anew the forgiveness of his sins; he enters into fellowship with God, and his soul is filled with the Holy Ghost. Hence it is that believers so often find their strength renewed, their faith confirmed, their purposes invigorated, their hearts filled with joy and love, while attending on these ordinances.

As the efficacy of the sacraments is a subject of great practical importance, it is necessary to examine more particularly what the Scriptures teach on this subject. Baptism is called the washing of regeneration; it is said to unite us to Christ,[269] to make us partakers of his death and life,[270] to wash away our sins,[271] to save the soul.[272] The bread and wine, in the Lord's supper, are said to be the body and blood of Christ; to partake of these emblems, is said to secure union with Christ and a participation of the merits of his death.[273] These and similar passages must be understood either with or without limitation. If they are to be limited, the limitation must not be arbitrarily imposed, but supplied by the Scriptures themselves. We have no right to say that the sacraments confer these benefits in every case in which no moral impediment is interposed, because no such limitation is expressed in the passages themselves, nor elsewhere taught in the Scriptures. The limitation which the Scriptures do impose on these passages is the necessity of faith. They teach that the sacraments are thus efficacious, not to every recipient, but to the believer; to those who already have the grace which these ordinances represent. If it be asked how they can be said to confer the grace which is already possessed? Let it be remembered that he who has been sprinkled with the blood of Christ, needs the application to be often repeated; he who has received the Holy Spirit needs to receive him again; he who has received Christ needs to receive him day by day that he may live upon him. That the Scriptures teach that the passages in question are to be understood with the qualification just stated, is clear because otherwise they would teach that every one who is baptized is a child of God, renewed by the Holy Spirit, united to Christ

---

269. Gal. iii. 27.
270. Rom. vi. 4, 5.
271. Acts xxii. 16.
272. 1 Pet. iii. 21.
273. 1 Cor. x. 16, 17.

and made a partaker of the saving benefits of his death. But this cannot be true, first, because the Bible abundantly teaches that those who are renewed and receive the Holy Spirit, have the fruits of the spirit, love, gentleness, goodness, and faith. Where these are not, there the Spirit is not. But these fruits do not uniformly, nor even generally attend the reception of the outward ordinance. We know that although Simon Magus was baptized, he remained in the gall of bitterness and in the bond of iniquity. We know, from Paul's epistles, that many of the baptized Galatians and Corinthians were the enemies of the cross of Christ. We know from our own daily observation that multitudes of those who are baptized and received to the Lord's supper, do not differ in temper or life from the world around them. God, therefore, in the actual administration of his kingdom, contradicts that interpretation of his word which makes it teach that the sacraments always confer the benefits which they represent. It is to degrade the renewing of the heart and the gift of the Holy Ghost, into things of no account, to represent them as the portion of the unholy multitudes who in every age and church have been admitted to baptism and the Lord's supper.

In the second place this interpretation is opposed to what the Scriptures elsewhere teach of the nature of sacraments. The opinion that such ordinances uniformly convey grace and introduce the recipient into favour with God, was one of those false doctrines of the Jews which Paul so earnestly combatted. Great is the virtue of circumcision for no circumcised person enters hell, was the confident and destructive persuasion of the formalists of that age. In opposition to this doctrine, the apostle assured them that circumcision would, indeed, profit them, if they kept the law; but if they broke the law, their circumcision became uncircumcision. For he is not a Jew who is one outwardly, neither is that circumcision which is outward in the flesh; but he is a Jew who is one inwardly; and circumcision is that of the heart, in the spirit, and not in the letter.[274] We have here a very explicit statement of the nature and efficacy of a sacrament. It has no efficacy in itself considered; its value depends on the presence or performance of the condition of the covenant to which it is attached. If the Jews kept the law, their circumcision secured to them all the

---

274. Rom. ii. 25–29.

blessings of the covenant under which they lived. But if they broke the law, their circumcision was of no avail. It was, therefore, not external circumcision that made a man a Jew; but the circumcision of the heart, of which the external rite was the sign. In like manner it is not external baptism that makes a man a Christian, but the baptism of the Spirit, of which the washing with water is the appointed symbol. The two are not necessarily connected, and where the latter is wanting, the former can be of no avail. And, lest it should be supposed that we have no right to apply what is said of the sacraments of the old dispensation to those of the new, the very same doctrine is taught in reference to the New Testament sacraments themselves. The apostle Peter says, We are saved by water; not ordinary water, but by baptism; not mere external baptism, however, but by the sincere turning of the hearts to God, that is, by the inward change of which baptism is the outward sign.[275] This passage, in its doctrinal import, is precisely parallel to that referring to circumcision just quoted. Neither rite, therefore, necessarily conveyed the grace of which they were the signs, and to neither is any value ascribed apart from the spiritual change which they are appointed to represent. In like manner, in reference to the Lord's supper, the apostle teaches that, so far from the mere external act being necessarily connected with the reception of the benefits of Christ's death, those who ate and drank unworthily, ate and drank judgment to themselves. Nothing, indeed, can be more opposed to the whole spirit of the religion of the Bible, than the doctrine that external rites are necessarily connected with spiritual blessings; that the favour of God is to be obtained by mere unresisting submission to religious ceremonies. A man may be baptized, or circumcised on the eighth day, he may belong to the purest and most apostolic church, he may be blameless as touching all the external prescriptions of the Gospel, and still be destitute of the grace of God and unprepared for his presence. It is not by works of righteousness, much less by ceremonial observances, that we are to be saved, but by the righteousness of Christ and the renewing of the Holy Ghost. He is not a Christian who is one outwardly, nor is that baptism which is outward in the flesh; but he

---

275. 1 Pet. iii. 21.

is a Christian who is one inwardly, and the baptism which is unto salvation, is of the heart, in the spirit and not in the letter.

In the third place, that the sacraments are not designed to convey grace to those who have it not, is plain because the Scriptures require those who are admitted to these ordinances to make a profession of their faith and repentance. When the apostles began to preach, we are told that, Those that gladly received the word were baptized.[276] When the eunuch desired to be baptized, Philip said to him, if thou believest with all thy heart, thou mayest.[277] Cornelius did not receive the Holy Spirit, in the first instance by baptism, but when Peter had evidence that he had already received the Spirit, he asked, Can any man forbid water, that these should not be baptized, which have received the Holy Ghost as well as we?[278] Paul was a penitent believer before his baptism; and thus in all other cases when men were baptized, they professed to be Christians. They were not made Christians by their admission to the sacraments; but their Christian character or standing was thereby acknowledged. It has accordingly been the custom in all ages to require a profession of faith on the part of those who are received to sealing ordinances. But faith is an exercise of a renewed heart; and if faith supposes regeneration, and baptism supposes faith, then by the voice of the church as well as of Scripture, baptism also supposes the renovation of the heart.

Finally, God bears his testimony against the doctrine which teaches an inseparable connexion between these ordinances and spiritual blessings, by granting these blessings to those who have not received any sacramental rite. Abraham was justified before he was circumcised; Cornelius was a just man, and accepted of God, and a recipient of the Holy Ghost, before he was baptized; the penitent thief was assured of his admission into paradise though he was never born of water. If then the Scriptures require the evidence of regeneration in those who would acceptably attend upon the sacraments; if they teach that many who receive the outward sign do not receive the inward grace; and on the other hand, that many receive the in-

---

276. Act. ii. 41.
277. Acts viii. 37.
278. Acts x, 47.

ward grace, who have not received the outward sign, then do they also teach that these ordinances are not appointed to convey, in the first instance, pardon and sanctification, but to be signs and seals of those blessings to the penitent believer, and that to him, and to him only are they efficacious means of grace.

It is, therefore, obvious that those passages in Scripture which refer our salvation to baptism and the Lord's supper cannot, consistently with the plain teaching of the Bible, be understood strictly according to the letter. At the same time it must not be supposed that they are to be perverted, or taken in any other than their natural sense; that is, in any other sense than that which the universally received rules of interpretation justify and require. It is agreeable to the common language of men and to the usage of the Scriptures, that when any declaration or service is the appointed means of professing faith and obedience, making such declaration or performing such service is said to secure the blessings which are promised to the faith thereby professed. It is said, whosoever confesseth that Jesus Christ is come in the flesh is born of God; and again, with the mouth confession is made into salvation. This is said because confession implies faith; and no one supposes that an insincere, careless, heartless confession will secure the salvation of any man. Thus also we are said to be saved by calling on the Lord, because invocation implies trust. In like manner we are said to be saved by baptism, because baptism implies faith. If this faith be wanting, baptism can do us no more good than a heartless confession. There is no more difficulty in understanding why the Scriptures should connect salvation with the use of the sacraments, than in understanding why they should connect the same blessing with invocation or confession. There is no difficulty in either case, if we allow the Scriptures to explain themselves, and interpret them as we explain all other writings.

Again, it is according to scriptural usage to ascribe to a sign the name and attributes of the thing signified. Thus circumcision is called the covenant of God, because it was the sign of that covenant. Christ called the cup the new covenant; the wine he called his blood and the bread his body. Those who partake of the wine are, therefore, said to receive his blood, and of course the benefits which it purchased.

It is to be remembered, also, that the sacraments are seals, and that it is common to attribute to any ceremony, by which an engagement is ratified, the efficacy which belongs not to the ceremony, but to the engagement itself. The ceremonial of inauguration is said to induct a man into the office, the right to which it merely publicly declares and confirms. Even in the strict language of the law, a deed, with its signature and seal, is said to convey a right of property, although it is simply the evidence of the purpose of the original possessor. It is that purpose which conveys the right, and if it can be shown that the man who holds the deed was not the man intended by the grantor, the deed would be regarded as worthless. If a man deeds an estate to A, on the assumption that he is the son of B, should it be proved that A was not the son of B, the deed would convey to him no valid title. But the blessings of the Gospel are declared to be intended for penitent believers; the sacraments are the external means of recognising the conveyance of these blessings; to those who are really what they profess to be, they do in fact convey and secure these blessings; to others they confer no such benefits. When an unbeliever receives these ordinances, he no more obtains a title to the blessings which they represent, than a man obtains a title to an estate by falsely assuming the name of the person for whom it is intended.

There is nothing, therefore, in the language of the Scriptures on this subject which is not perfectly consistent with the common protestant doctrine that the sacraments have no inherent efficacy of their own, but become efficacious means of grace to those who believe; the Holy Spirit thereby communicating to believers the blessings of which those ordinances are the significant representations.

SECTION III. *Obligation to attend upon the Sacraments. Qualifications for the proper discharge of the duty.*

The obligation which rests upon all Christians to attend upon the ordinances of Baptism and the Lord's supper, arises clearly from what has been shown to be their nature and design. We have seen that they are institutions appointed by Christ himself. He has commanded all his followers to be baptized and to commemorate his death, in a prescribed manner. As obedience to Christ is necessary, so is participation of these ordinances. As, however, it is a necessity arising out of a positive command, it is a qualified necessity, since such commands are not binding under all circumstances. It is impossible that a sinner should be saved without faith and repentance; but it is not impossible that he should be saved without the sacraments. As we are bound to keep the sabbath as part of our obedience to God, and yet may innocently labour on that day when necessity or mercy requires it; so although bound to present ourselves at the table of the Lord as an act of obedience, we may be innocently absent, whenever that absence is not the effect of a wilful or disobedient spirit. As, however, the command of Christ on this subject is express, the obligation which it imposes is of the strongest character.

In the second place, it has been shown that to confess Christ before men is an indispensable duty, and that the sacraments are the appointed means for making this confession; it follows, therefore, that attendance on the sacraments is also an indispensable duty. When in human governments the laws prescribe a particular mode in which we are to acknowledge allegiance to our country, it is not competent for us to neglect that mode; nor have we a right to adopt a different method of acknowledgment, or to suffer our allegiance to be inferred from our conduct. If we wish to be recognised as citizens, we must in the prescribed form acknowledge ourselves such. And if Christ has prescribed a particular way in which he will be acknowledged by his followers, intelligently and wilfully to refuse obedience to his command, is to renounce our allegiance to him and to forfeit the benefits of his kingdom.

Again, as the sacraments are the seals of the covenant of grace, to reject these seals is to reject the covenant itself. It is not meant that they are in such a sense indispensable that if a man perform the conditions of the covenant, he will be excluded from its benefits, for the want of the seals. Among men, indeed, we often see that the want of the prescribed number of witnesses to a signature, the want of a seal, or even a clerical error in a document, is sufficient to set aside a solemn engagement. Nothing of this kind can occur under the government of God, where justice is never embarrassed by technical formalities. The apostle expressly teaches that as circumcision becomes uncircumcision, if the law be broken, so, on the other hand, if a man keep the law, his uncircumcision shall be counted for circumcision. It is admitted, therefore, that if a man has the faith, repentance and obedience required by the gospel, his salvation is secure. But no man has a right to assume that he has this faith and repentance, who neglects to obey the commands of Christ. The essential conditions of salvation have been the same under every dispensation. If any man, under the old economy, had the faith of Abraham, he was entitled to the blessings promised to Abraham. Nevertheless, as circumcision was the appointed means of expressing that faith, and of accepting the covenant of which it was the condition, it was expressly declared, that the uncircumcised man-child, whose flesh of his foreskin is not circumcised, that soul shall be cut off from the people; he hath broken my covenant.[279] Is it not equally true that those who intelligibly and wilfully neglect baptism and the Lord's supper, break the covenant under which the church is now placed? It will not do for us to say, if we have the substance, the form is of little account. We all know that if an ancient Israelite had repentance toward God and faith in the promised Messiah, his sins were forgiven; and yet unless he expressed his faith by bringing the appointed sacrifice to the altar, he was not forgiven. God saw fit that the mode of pardon should be thus exhibited and recognised. In like manner he now requires that the method of salvation should be publicly acknowledged and set forth in the ordinances of baptism and the Lord's supper. We do, therefore, as really reject the covenant of God by neglecting these ordinances, as did the Israelites who rejected circumcision or the offering of sacrifices.

Another illustration of this subject may be borrowed from the marriage contract. The essence of the covenant is the mutual consent of parties. But in all civilized countries some public manifestation of that consent is essential to the validity of the engagement. Thus, also, the essence of our covenant with God is repentance and faith; but baptism and the Lord's supper being the divinely appointed means of signifying and ratifying the engagement, they can no more be neglected than the public recognition of the marriage covenant.

It was a fatal perversion when the Jews imagined that circumcision and sacrifices without faith and obedience, were effectual to salvation, and it is no less a fatal delusion to imagine that baptism and the Lord's supper without those inward graces can secure the favour of God. But in avoiding one extreme, we must not run into the opposite. Though the ancient sacrifices without faith were an abomination to the Lord; the sacrifices were still, by divine appoint-

---

279. Gen. xvii. 14.

ment, necessary; and although the Christian ordinances, without the grace which they represent, are empty forms, they too by divine appointment are obligatory and, in their place, essential.

No Christian, however, needs to be forced by stress of authority to yield obedience to the commands of Christ. It is enough for him that it is the will of his Saviour that the truths and blessings of the Gospel should be exhibited and commemorated by the perpetual observance of the ordinances of baptism and the Lord's supper. Though he were unable to see any fitness in such observance, or though experience taught him nothing of its value, yet would he cheerfully obey. Much more may he be expected to yield a ready obedience, when he knows both from Scripture and experience, that these ordinances are made to the believer the channels of divine blessings; that they are means of grace and sources of the purest spiritual enjoyments; that they bring him into communion with Christ and unite him in holy fellowship with all his brethren. He knows that to neglect these divine institutions is not only to violate a command of God and to break his covenant; it is to refuse to be fed at his table and to reject the provision which he has made for the life of our souls.

If the sacraments are such important means of grace, and if attendance upon them is a duty so plainly enjoined in the word of God, it is important to enquire what are the proper qualifications for the acceptable discharge of this duty.

In considering this subject we must not confound the qualifications which the church has a right to demand of those who present themselves as candidates for Christian communion, with those which such candidates are bound to seek in themselves. The church cannot judge the heart; she can only require a credible profession. It is her duty to explain the nature of the gospel, with its promises and commands, and to state clearly what is the nature of the service in which those engage, who profess to embrace the offers of salvation. Those who, when thus instructed, declare that they accept the offers of divine mercy, and purpose to live in obedience to the divine commands, she receives into communion, unless there be some tangible evidence of the insincerity of their professions. This she does, not because she judges them to be true Christians, but because they possess the qualifications which alone she has a right to demand. No priest under the old dispensation ever ventured to debar a man from the altar, because in his own mind, he might judge him to be destitute of the faith and penitence implied in the act of presenting a sacrifice. If the offerer had the external qualifications prescribed by the law, he was admitted. To Him who searches the heart, it was left to decide upon his spiritual state. Thus also, under the gospel dispensation, we find the apostles baptizing and admitting to the Lord's supper all who made the requisite profession and against whom no visible evidence of insincerity could be produced. Whatever was considered a sufficient reason for excommunicating a church member, was of course regarded as sufficient to exclude an applicant for admission. It is of importance to remember that the church does not profess to believe all those to be true Christians, whom she admits to her communion. Of their inward sincerity she cannot judge; to their own master they must stand or fall. Many are no doubt confirmed in a false judgment of themselves, because they consider their admission to the church to be an expression of the judgment of their pastor, or brethren, that they are what they profess to be. It is natural for them to think well of themselves, when they consider experienced Christians as pronouncing a favourable judgment of their spiritual state. But they should remember that it is not the prerogative of the church to judge the heart; she must receive all who have the external qualifications which the Scriptures require.

But though the church is obliged to confine her demands to a credible profession of faith and repentance, it is the duty of those who seek admission to her communion, to see that they have all the qualifications which the nature of the service demands. These qualifications may all be reduced to knowledge and piety.

Did the Scriptures teach that the sacraments had an inherent efficacy of their own; that the water of baptism had power to wash away sin, and the bread and wine a virtue to sustain spiritual life, then indeed they might be administered to the ignorant, the insensible, or the dying. But if we are taught that the efficacy both of the word and ordinances depends not on them, nor on those who administer them, but on the Holy Spirit, revealing and applying the truth thereby exhibited, then it is plain that they must be understood in order to be beneficial. It is one of the most important doctrines of the Bible that God sanctifies his people through the truth. But truth is not truth to him who does not understand it. If you repeat to an ignorant man a mathematical formula, although it may contain a proposition of the highest value, to him it is nothing. It communicates no idea to his mind, and can produce no effect upon it. Or if you tell him that God has set forth his Son to be a propitiation for our sins through faith in his blood; if he does not understand the meaning of the words, it is as though he never heard them. We, therefore, do not preach in an unknown tongue; nor do we send Hebrew Bibles to the Hindoos, or the Greek Scriptures to the Hottentots. Unless the truth is understood, it is not present to the mind, and cannot operate upon it. In like manner, unless the sacraments are understood by those who receive them, they are, for them, an unmeaning ceremony. They either exhibit nothing, or they excite erroneous views and apprehensions. We degrade the Scriptures into formulas of incantation, and the sacraments into magical rites, if we suppose a knowledge of their meaning to be unnecessary. God is a Spirit, and they who worship him must worship him in spirit—intelligently as well as sincerely and inwardly. It is, therefore, essential to a proper attendance on the sacraments that we should know what they are designed to represent, what benefits they confer and what obligations they impose. When they are thus understood; when the believer sees in them the clear exhibition of the truths and promises of the gospel, and knows that they were appointed to be the means of his confessing Christ before men, and to ratify the gracious covenant of God with his soul, he then really receives the spiritual blessings of which the sacraments are outward signs.

The knowledge requisite to a proper understanding of the sacraments includes a knowledge of all the essential doctrines of the Gospel. When a man is baptized in the name of the Father, of the Son and of the Holy Ghost, unless these sacred names represent to his mind some definite idea; unless he knows them to be the names of the persons of the Godhead, he cannot know what he does in submitting to be baptized. He does not acknowledge Jehovah; nor does he receive him as his covenant God, Redeemer and Sanctifier. As baptism is designed to signify and seal our union with Christ, and our deliverance through him from the guilt and dominion of sin, unless we know ourselves to be sinners, and know that it is necessary for us to be united to Christ, and by his blood and Spirit, to be pardoned and renewed, the ordinance for us loses all its significancy. Thus a knowledge of the truth concerning God, concerning sin, atonement and regeneration is essential to a proper participation of this ordinance. And as the Lord's supper is intended to be a memorial of the death of Christ, unless we know who he was, why he died and what benefits his death secures, we are incapable of profitably joining in this service. All the affections must have an appropriate object. If we love, we love something, if we fear, we fear something; if we desire, we desire something. There can be neither faith, nor love, nor penitence, nor hope, nor gratitude, but as objects suited to these exercises are presented to the mind; and the nature of these exercises depends upon the nature of the objects which call them forth. If they are excited by the truth, they are right and good; and just in proportion to the clearness with which the truth is spiritually discerned, will be the purity and strength of the religious emotions. Knowledge, therefore, is essential to religion.

We must not suppose, however, that knowledge and learning are synonymous terms, or that all knowledge is derived from without, through the medium of the understanding. Very far from it. A large part of our knowledge is derived from our own consciousness or inward experience. The same extenal revelation may be presented to two equally intelligent men; if the one is made, by the Spirit of God, to feel in accordance with the truth, and the other is destitute of such feelings, the former will possess a knowledge of which the latter has no conception. He will have an insight into the nature of the things revealed, and into their truth and value, which is due entirely to what passes within his own bosom. These men, although they may be equal in learning, will differ greatly in knowledge. We accordingly find that the ignorant, among God's people, have often far more knowledge of religious truth, than many learned men. They have more correct views of its nature; and the words by which it is expressed excite in their minds far more definite conceptions of the real objects of the religious affections. As, however, God does not reveal new truths, but sanctifies his people by his word, there must be external instruction in order to this inward spiritual knowledge; hence ignorance of the truths revealed in the Scriptures, as it is inconsistent with the existence of right religious feeling, or in other words, with religion itself, so it is inconsistent with the proper participation of those ordinances by which those truths are set forth and confirmed.

The other qualifications for an acceptable participation of the sacraments are naturally suggested by the view given of their nature. As they are the appointed means for making a public profession of religion, it is of course requisite that we should be and believe what we therein profess. The substance of this profession is that we are Christian; that we believe in Christ as the Redeemer of sinners; that we accept of the terms of salvation proposed in the Gospel and purpose to live in obedience to its commands. If we have not this faith; if we do not thus purpose to renounce our sins and live unto God, then we do make a false profession, and our service must be unacceptable to God.

Viewing the sacraments as seals of the covenant of grace, it is plain that they require the qualifications just mentioned in those who receive them. That covenant relates to deliverance from sin. God therein engages to grant us salvation; and we engage to accept of his mercy on the terms on which it is offered. If he promises to be our God; we promise to be his people. But how can those who love sin and are determined not to forsake it, enter into this solemn engagement with God? How can those who have no sense of their need of pardon, no desire for holiness, no sorrow for past transgressions, thus covenant with God for forgiveness, sanctification and eternal life?

With regard to the Lord's supper we are taught that it was specially designed to be a memorial of Christ's death. If we join in celebrating his death, we profess to believe not only that he died, but that he was all that he claimed to be; that his death secures the benefits which the Scriptures attribute to it; and that we are bound to aid in keeping this great event in perpetual remembrance. The proper discharge of this duty requires that we should have a due sense of our obligations to Christ for having loved us and given himself for us. It requires that we should reverence and love him in some measure in proportion to his excellence and the value of the blessings which we receive from him. It requires that we should be prepared to own him, who by wicked hands was crucified and slain, as our Lord and Saviour, and as such to obey and trust him.

In whatever light, therefore, the sacraments are viewed, whether as the means of publicly confessing Christ, or as signs and seals of spiritual blessings, or as commemorative of the work of redemption, no man can profitably, or acceptably attend upon them, without adequate knowledge of their nature, without faith in the truths which they represent and confirm, or without the penitence, gratitude and love which those truths, when really believed, necessarily produce. Where this knowledge, faith and love are found, there are the requisite qualifications for acceptable attendance on the sacraments; where they are wanting, such attendance must include false professions and insincere promises.

We must not, however, suppose that the want of these qualifications frees us from the obligation to obey the command of Christ to be baptized and to commemorate his death. We are certainly bound to worship God though destitute of the reverence, faith and love which such worship requires; and the plea of unfitness for the service cannot justify us in absenting ourselves from the ordinances which Christ has appointed. If we fear to assume the responsibility of a public profession of religion, we should remember that we make such profession every time we join in the public worship of the sanctuary. If we say we should offend God by approaching his table, without due preparation, let us remember that we offend him every time we pray, or hear the gospel without faith, penitence and obedience. It is in vain to attempt to introduce consistency into a half religious life. If men will renounce all claim to be of the number of God's people, and reject his service entirely, they may so far be consistent. But they cannot choose one part of his service and reject another; they cannot profess to be penitent and believing by joining in the worship of God, and declare themselves impenitent and unbelieving by absenting themselves from the sacraments. They do not place themselves on neutral grounds by such inconsistency. Their only safe and proper course is to repent and believe. Then will they be acceptable worshippers and acceptable communicants. If they frequent the temple of God with a sincere desire to do his will, and seek his favour, let them, in the same state of mind, obey all his commands. If they come to the Lord's table to please Christ, to obey his will, to express their gratitude for his death, let them come. As their day is, so shall their strength be.

From the review of this whole subject, it is clear that the public confession of Christ is an indispensable condition of discipleship; that this confession must be made by attending on the ordinances which he has appointed; that these ordinances are not only the signs and seals of spiritual blessings, but are made, by the Holy Spirit, to the believer, effectual means of grace; that attendance upon them is, therefore, an indispensable duty; requiring no other qualifications than such as are necessary for the acceptable worship of God; and, consequently, that it is incumbent on all those who sincerely desire to serve and honour Christ, and to partake of his salvation, to receive the sacraments, in obedience to his will.

Chapter IX.

Holy Living.

SECTION I.   *The nature of true religion.*

It is natural that those who have experienced the agitations which frequently attend upon conversion, and have felt the peace which flows from a hope of acceptance with God, to imagine that the conflict is over; the victory won, and the work of religion accomplished. This imagination is soon dissipated. Birth is not the whole of life; neither is conversion the whole of religion. A young mother may, in the fulness of her joy, forget for a moment the great duties of her vocation that lie before her; but when she looks upon her infant, so wonderful in its organization and instinct with an immortal spirit, she feels that it is entirely dependent. An hour's neglect might prove its ruin. Thus the young Christian, although at first disposed to think that his work is finished, soon finds that the feeble principle of spiritual life needs to be watched and nourished with ceaseless care. If abandoned at its birth, it must perish as certainly and as speedily as an exposed infant.

Another mistake on this subject is made by those who suppose that religion is a fitful sort of life; an alternation of excitement and insensibility. Those who labour under this delusion, are religious only on certain occasions. They live contentedly for months in unconcern, and then, if they can be moved to tenderness or joy, they are satisfied with the prospect of another period of collapse. No form of life is thus intermittent. Neither plants nor animals thus live. Men do not, when in health, pass from convulsions to fainting, and from fainting to convulsions; nor does religion, when genuine, ever assume this form. It has, indeed, its alternations, as there are periods of health and sickness, of vigour and lassitude in the animal frame; but just so far as it deserves in the name of religion, it is steady, active and progressive; and not a series of spasms.

It is a still more common error to suppose that religion is rather an external than an internal service. There are multitudes who consider themselves to be religious, because they attend upon religious services; who suppose that a regular attendance upon public worship, and the outward forms of religion is enough to entitle them to the character of Christians.

The Scriptures teach us that religion is a new, spiritual life. Its commencement is, therefore, called a new birth, a creation, a spiritual resurrection. It is, as to its principle or source, mysterious. No man can tell what life is. He sees its different forms in vegetables, animals, and in the rational soul; but he cannot detect the secret spring of these different kinds of activity. The nature of spiritual life is not less inscrutable. The wind bloweth where it listeth; ye hear the sound thereof, but ye cannot tell whence it cometh, nor whither it goeth. So is every one that is born of the Spirit. A new kind of activity manifests itself in the soul that is born of God; but whence that activity springs, and how it is maintained, are among the secret things of God. We cannot doubt, however, that there is some permanent cause of those new exercises. We know that the life of the body does not consist in the acts of seeing, hearing, tasting, &c.; nor does the soul consist of thought and volition; neither does spiritual life consist in the acts which manifest its existence. There is in regeneration a change effected in the state of the soul which accounts for its perceptions, purposes and feelings being different from what they were before, and for their so continuing. The cause of this difference is sometimes called a new heart, a grace, or the spirit, or the new man, or the renewal of the inner man. All these terms are used to designate the principle of spiritual life, which manifests itself in the fruits of holiness. It is called life because it is thus permanent, or abiding. Those who for a time manifest a degree of ardour and activity in relation to religion and then lose all interest in the subject, are like dead bodies on which electricity may for a while produce some of the appearances of animation, but which soon become insensible to all means of excitement. In such cases there is no principle of life. Where religion is genuine, it has its root in a new heart and is, therefore, permanent.

It is moreover characteristic of the life of sentient and rational creatures, to be spontaneous in its exercises. There are certain acts to which it prompts and in which it delights. It is not by constraint that animals eat, or drink, or sport in the consciousness of strength;

neither is it by compulsion that men exercise their minds in the reception and communication of ideas and the reciprocation of feeling. To be so isolated from their fellow-beings as to be prevented from giving vent to the force of intellectual and social life, is the severest of all condemnations. In like manner reverence, gratitude, love, submission, are the spontaneous exercises of the renewed heart. They are the free, unbidden, unconstrained effusions of the soul. That religion which is reluctant, or forced, whether by fear or stress of conscience, is spurious. Filial obedience, if rendered from a dread of punishment, or from mere regard to appearances, is very different from that which flows from respect and love; and unless the service which we render to God flows unbidden from the heart, it is no evidence that we are his children. The Bible represents the people of God as delighting in the things of God. His word, his ordinances, his sanctuary, his presence are their chief joy. When a man is ill, he takes little pleasure in the ordinary sources of enjoyment, and when the Christian is in a declining state, he knows little of the joy which belongs to religion. Still whatever there is of spiritual life in any soul, will manifest itself in spontaneous exercises of piety.

Again, life, in all the forms in which we are acquainted with it, is progressive; feeble at the beginning, it advances gradually to maturity, It is thus in plants, in animals, and in the rational soul; and it is thus also in the spiritual life. There is a joy which attends the beginning of a religious life, which very often declines; a fact which may lead even the true Christian to think that religion itself is declining in his heart. Such joy, however, is a very uncertain criterion of the progress or decline of the spiritual life. The gambols of young animals show an exuberance of joy, which those that have reached maturity no longer experience. But how imperfect is the organization of these playful creatures, how small is their power of endurance, how little their serviceable strength, in comparison with that of those who know not half their joys. It is not unnatural, therefore, that young Christians should feel a glow of happiness from the exercise of feelings, delightful from their novelty as well as from their nature, which those mere advanced may have ceased to experience, and in whom feeling has ripened into principle, and more joyful emotions settled into a peace which passes all understanding.

Though joy is not the proper criterion of progress in the divine life, it is as essential to its nature to be progressive, as it is to the life of the body to increase in stature as it advances from childhood to maturity, or to that of the mind to gather strength in its progress from infancy to manhood. A man with the mind of an infant is an idiot; he is destitute of what belongs to a rational being. And a Christian, who makes no progress in holiness, must be essentially defective. The surest evidence of such progress is increase of strength; strength of faith; strength of purpose; strength of principle; strength to do right, to resist evil, and to endure suffering. The people of God go from strength to strength, perfecting holiness in the fear of the Lord.

True religion, then, is not an external service; nor is it a mere excitement of fear and sorrow succeeded by peace and joy; nor is it a fitful alternation of such exercises. It is a permanent principle of action, spontaneous in its exercises and progressive in its nature. These attributes, are essential to its genuineness, but they do not constitute its whole character. It is a participation of the divine nature,[280] or the conformity of the soul to God. It is described as the putting off the old man with his deeds and putting on the new man, which is renewed in knowledge after the image of him that created him;[281] or a being renewed in the spirit of our mind, that we may put on the new man, which after God is created in righteousness and true holiness.[282] These two passages express the same truth. To be renewed in knowledge, or rather, unto knowledge, means to be renewed so as to know; and knowledge includes the perception, recognition and approbation of what is true and good. This comprehensive sense of the word is not unusual in the Scriptures; and hence it is said, that to know God and Jesus Christ is eternal life. Such knowledge is the life of the soul; it is conformity to God in the perception and approbation of truth. No higher conception of moral excellence can be formed than that which resolves it into the harmony of the soul with God in judgment and will. This is what in the parallel passage, the apostle calls righteousness and holiness of truth, (that is, founded upon, or arising from truth.) The same idea of sanctification is presented in Rom. xii. 2, when it is said, Be ye transformed by the renewing of your mind, that ye may prove (or, approve) what is that good, and

---

280. 2 Pet. i. 4.
281. Col. iii. 10.
282. Eph. iv. 24.

acceptable and perfect will of God. This is true religion, to approve what God approves, to hate what he hates, and to delight in what delights him.

It is obvious from this representation that the whole man is the subject of this change. There are new perceptions, new purposes and new feelings. The mind becomes more and more enlightened, the will more submissive to the rule of right, and the affections more thoroughly purified. The apostle in his epistle to the Thessalonians says, The God of peace sanctify you wholly; and I pray God your whole spirit, and soul and body be preserved blameless unto the coming of our Lord Jesus Christ.[283] The body is the subject of sanctification in various ways. It is the temple of the Holy Ghost,[284] and is, therefore, holy as consecrated to the service, and hallowed by the presence of God. Our bodies are also members of Jesus Christ, and in virtue of this union, they partake of the benefits of redemption, and are hereafter to be fashioned like unto his glorious body. And still further, the influence of the body upon the soul is so manifold, for good or evil, and, in our fallen state, so predominantly for evil, that no small part of the work of sanctification consists in counteracting that influence. Paul says of himself, I keep under my body, and bring it into subjection; lest by any means, when I have preached to others, I myself should be a castaway.[285] And he declares it to be one of the conditions of life, that believers should, through the Spirit, mortify the deeds of the body.[286] The body, therefore, is sanctified not only by redeeming it from the service of sin and consecrating it to the service of God, but also by restraining its power over the soul, making it temperate in its demands and submissive to the will of the renewed man.

As the work of sanctification extends to all our faculties, so the image of God which it is designed to impress upon the soul, includes all moral excellence. The different graces, such as love, faith, meekness, kindness, &c., are but different manifestations of one and the same principle of goodness. Not that justice and benevolence are the

---

283. 1 Thess. v. 23.
284. 1 Cor. vi. 19.
285. 1 Cor. ix. 27.
286. Rom. viii. 13.

same sentiment or disposition, for they are distinct; but the same principle which makes a man just, will make him benevolent. Religion, or the principle of divine life, prompts to all kinds of excel-, lence; and, in itself, as much to one as to another; just as the principle of life, in plants and animals and in the rational soul, leads to a harmonious development of the whole in all its parts. The root increases as the branches enlarge; the body grows as the several members increase in size; and judgment and memory gain strength as the other powers of the mind increase in vigour. Every thing depends upon this harmonious progress. If the arms retained their infantile proportions, while the rest of the body advanced to maturity, deformity and helplessness would be the result. Or if judgment and feeling gained their full force, while memory and conscience remained as in infancy, the mind would be completely deranged. The same law of symmetrical development is impressed upon the life of the soul. If it exists at all, it manifests itself in all the forms of goodness. There may be some kinds of excellence, where others are absent; but then such excellence has not its source in the divine life; or in a new heart; for that, in its very nature, includes all moral excellence. We feel it to be a contradiction to say that he is a good man, who though just, is unkind; because goodness includes both justice and benevolence. And it is no less a contradiction to say that a man is religious who is not honest, because religion includes honesty as well as piety. It is not simply intended that the word religion comprehends and expresses all forms of moral excellence, but that the thing meant by religion, or the new man, the principle of grace or of divine life in the heart, includes within itself all kinds of goodness. Reverence, love, submission, justice, benevolence, are but different exercises of one and the same principle of holiness. There can be no holiness without benevolence, none without reverence, none without justice. The man, therefore, who is renewed in the spirit of his mind after the image of God, is one who has that moral excellence which expresses itself, according to its different objects and occasions, in all the various graces of the Spirit.

The Scriptures give especial prominence to the love of God as the most comprehensive and important of all the manifestations of this inward spiritual life. We are so constituted as to take delight in objects suited to our nature; and the perception of qualities adapted to our constitution, in external objects, produces complacency and desire. The soul rests in them as a good to be loved for its own sake; and the higher these qualities, the more pure and elevated are the affections which they excite. It is the effect of regeneration to enable us to perceive and love the infinite and absolute perfection of God, as comprehending all kinds of excellence, and as suited to the highest powers and most enlarged capacities of our nature. As soon, therefore, as the heart is renewed it turns to God, and rests in his excellence as the supreme object of complacency and desire.

Love to God, however, is not mere complacency in moral excellence. It is the love of a personal being, who stands in the most intimate relations to ourselves, as the author of our existence, as our preserver and ruler, as our father, who with conscious love watches over us, protects us, supplies all our wants, holds communion with us, manifesting himself unto us as he does not unto the world. The feelings of dependance, obligation and relationship, enter largely into that comprehensive affection called the love of God. This affection is still further modified by the apprehension of the infinite wisdom and power of its object. These attributes are the proper object of admiration; and, when infinite in degree and united with infinite goodness, they excite that wonder, admiration, reverence and complacency which constitute adoration, and which find in prostration and worship their only adequate expression. There is no attribute of religion more essential to its nature than this reverence for God. Whenever heaven has been opened to the view of men, its inhabitants have been seen with their faces veiled and bowing before the throne of God. And all acceptable worship upon earth, proceeds from the humble and contrite who tremble at his word.

The exercise of these feelings of reverence and love is either, (so to speak,) casual, as the thoughts of God pass and repass through the soul during the busy hours of the day; or it is more prolonged, when the soul withdraws from the world, and sets itself in the presence of God, to adore his excellence, to thank him for his goodness, and to supplicate his blessing. The spirit of devotion which so pre-eminently distinguished the Redeemer, dwells in all his people. They are all devout; they all walk with God; they all feel him to be near and rejoice in his presence; and they all have communion with him in acts of private and public worship. There is no religion without this intercourse of the soul with God, as there is no life without warmth and motion in the body. And as the body rapidly decays when dead; so the soul perishes when not in communion with God.

This love of God will manifest itself into submission and obedience. The former is an humble acquiescence in the will of God, including the perception and acknowledgment that the commands of God concerning all things are right, and that his dispensations are all wise, merciful and just. Even when clouds and darkness are round about him, religion forces upon us the conviction that justice and judgment are the habitation of his throne. The renewed soul filled with the assurance of the wisdom, power and goodness of God, resigns itself into his hands, saying, Thy will be done. When under the influence of this spirit, it is free from the discontent and misgivings which destroy the peace and aggravate the guilt of those who have no such confidence that the judge of all the earth will do right.

Love to God must produce obedience, because it supposes a conformity of the soul to God in the perception and love of what is true and right; and obedience is only the expression or outward manifestation of this conformity; just as disobedience is the evidence of a contrariety between our will and the will of God. Wherever there is reconciliation to God, or the restoration of the divine image, there must be conformity of heart and life to the will of God. It is a contradiction to say that a man is like God, or is a partaker of his nature, who does not love what God loves, and avoid what he hates. Obedience is but love in action. It is but the voice, and look, and carriage which affection, of necessity, assumes. For the love of God is not, as already said, mere love to excellence; it is the love of a heavenly Father; and therefore, it secures obedience, not only because it supposes a congeniality of mind, if we may so speak, between the people of God and God himself, but also because it is his will that we should be obedient; it is what is pleasing to him; and love is no longer love if it does not lead to the purpose and endeavour to give pleasure to its object. He that hath my commandments and keepeth them, said our Saviour, he it is that loveth me. Obedience is not so much the evidence of love, as it is love itself made visible, or expressed. The habitual tenor of a man's life gives a more faithful exhibition of his state of heart, than any occasional ebullition of feeling, or any mere verbal professions; and where the tenor of the life is not in conformity with the will of God, there the heart must be in opposition to that will; and on the other hand, whever there is love, there must be obedience.

It would be out of analogy with the order of things as established by God, if the exercises of the spiritual life were not attended by peace and joy. Happiness is so intimately associated with these exercises that the apostle says, To be spiritually minded is life and peace. Excellence and enjoyment are blended in inseparable union; so that all right emotions and affections are pleasurable. And this pleasure is, in kind if not in degree, proportionable to the dignity of the powers from whose exercise they flow. The senses afford the lowest kind of happiness; then, in an ascending scale, the social affections; then the intellectual powers; then the moral emotions, and then the religious affections. The kind of enjoyment which attend these latter is felt to be more pure and elevated, more satisfying and better suited to our nature, than that which flows from any other source. Hence the Scriptures ascribe to communion with God a joy that is unspeakable and full of glory, and a peace which passes all understanding. Joy, therefore, is one of the fruits of the Spirit; it is one of the accompaniments and evidences of spiritual life; it is a healthful affusion; it is the oil of gladness, which the Spirit pours over the renewed soul, to invigorate its exercises, to brighten its visage, and to make it active in the service and praise of God.

As the image of God, after which the soul is renewed, consists in moral excellence, and as moral excellence means that state of mind, which causes a man to feel and act right under all circumstances, it is impossible that those who have correct views and feelings in regard to God, should not feel and act correctly in regard to their fellow-men. Those whom the Bible designates as good men are benevolent and just no less than devout. The comprehensive statement of our duty towards our fellowmen, is found in the command, Thou shalt love thy neighbour as thyself. The love here intended is that disposition which leads us to regard our neighbour with respect and kindness, and to seek to do him good. This love is long-suffering and kind; it does not envy the happiness of others but rejoices in their welfare. It is not proud, nor does it behave itself unseemly. It seeketh not its own. It rejoices not in iniquity, but rejoices in the truth. It beareth all things, believeth all things, hopeth all things. Without this love, all professions of piety, all gifts, all outward acts of self-denial or charity, are worthless. It belongs essentially to the Christian character; for as self-love, prompting us to the pursuit of our own happiness, belongs to our nature as men, so benevolence, prompting us to seek the happiness of others, belongs to the nature of the new man. A new man means a good man, one who is like God, holy, just, benevolent and merciful.

This meek, kind, trustful temper, which religion never fails to produce, is, of course, variously modified by the various characters of individuals, and by the relations of life. It is no part of the teaching of the Bible that we must regard all men with the same feelings. While it inculcates benevolence towards all men, it makes provision for the peculiar and closer relations in which men stand to each other, as members of one family, or one society. And the same principle of religion which produces this general benevolence, secures the exercise of all the affections which belong to the various relations of life. It causes us to render obedience to whom obedience is due, fear to whom fear, honor to whom honor. It makes men in their intercourse with their equals respectful, considerate and amiable; in their conduct to their inferiors condescending, just and kind.

It cannot be too well considered that these social virtues are essential to true religion. The people of God are those who are like God; but God, as we have seen, is just, merciful, long-suffering, abundant in goodness and truth. Those, therefore, who are dishonest, unkind, proud, revengeful, or deceitful, are not his people; they do not bear the heavenly image, and have never been renewed in the spirit of their minds. Let no man deceive himself with the hope that though a bad parent, child, or neighbour, he may be a good Christian. A Christian is like Christ.

Another form in which a renewed heart cannot fail to manifest itself is in self-denial. If any man will come after me, said the Saviour, let him deny himself, and take up his cross and follow me. The necessity of self-denial arises partly from the fact that the gratification of our own wishes is often inconsistent with the good of others; and partly from the fact that so many of our desires and passions are inordinate or evil. The rule prescribed by the gospel is, that we are not to please ourselves, but every one must please his neighbour, for good to edification, even as Christ pleased not himself, but though he was rich, yet for our sakes he became poor, that we, through his poverty, might be rich.

The daily intercourse of life furnishes constant occasion for the exercise of this kind of self-denial. He who has the same mind that was in Christ, instead of being selfish, is ready to defer his own advantage to that of others, to give up his own gratification, and even his own rights for the good of others. If meat causes his brother to offend, he will not eat meat while the world lasts. To the Jews, he becomes a Jew, that he may gain the Jews. To the weak, he becomes weak, that he may gain the weak. He does not live for himself. His own interest is not the main end of his pursuit. As a disinterested regard for the good of others pre-eminently distinguished the Redeemer, it characterises all his followers; for God has predestinated them to be conformed to the image of his Son.

The call for self-denial arising from the corruption of our nature, is still more frequent. In consequence of the fall, the senses have attained an undue influence over the soul; they are incessant in their demands, and become more importunate the more they are indulged. It is inconsistent with reason to yield ourselves to the power of these lower principles of our nature; for reason itself teaches us that if a man is governed by his body, he is the servant of a slave. But if even a rational man feels bound to subject the body to the mind, the religious man cannot be sensual. They that are Christians have mortified the flesh with its affections and lusts; they keep their bodies in subjection.

What belongs to the body is, in a certain sense, external; the evil dispositions of the heart are in more intimate connection with the soul. Pride, vanity, envy, malice, the love of self are more formidable foes than mere bodily appetites. They are stronger, more enduring, and more capable of deceit. As these dispositions are deeply seated in our nature, the putting off the old man, which is corrupt, or the destruction of these unholy principles, is the most difficult of all Christian duties, and renders the believer's life a perpetual conflict. The flesh lusteth against the spirit and the spirit against the flesh, so that he cannot do those things that he would. In this conflict, however, the better principle is habitually, though not uniformly, victorious; for the children of God walk not after the flesh, but after the spirit.

It appears, then, even from this short survey, that true Christians are renewed after the image of God so as to be holy; they love God, they rest with complacency on his perfections, they acquiesce in his will, and rejoice in their relation to him as his creatures and children. They are habitually devout and have fellowship with the Father of their spirits and with Jesus Christ his Son. They are obedient children, not fashioning themselves according to their former lusts, but as he that called them is holy, so are they holy in all manner of conversation. As they bear the image of a just and merciful God, they are honest and benevolent towards their fellow-men, not seeking their own, but the good of others. And as this victory over themselves and this conformity to the image of God cannot be obtained without conflict and self-denial, they keep up a constant opposition to the more subtle evils of the heart.

Some may be ready to say that if this is religion, then no man is religious. It is certainly true that many are called, and few chosen. Strait is the gate and narrow is the way, which leadeth unto life, and few there be that find it. We must take our idea of religion from the Bible, and not from the lives of professors. It cannot be denied that the Bible makes religion to consist in love to God and man; nor can it be questioned that the love of God will manifest itself in reverence, devotion and obedience, and the love of men in benevolence and justice. And our own conscience tells us that no external forms, no outward professions, no assiduity in religious services, can entitle us to the character of Christians, unless we are thus devout and obedient towards God, thus just and benevolent towards our fellow-men, and thus pure and self-denying as regards ourselves. But while it is certain that these traits are all essential to the Christian character, it is not asserted that all Christians are alike. There is as great diversity in their characters as Christians, as in their bodily appearance, their mental powers, or social dispositions. But as all men, in the midst of this endless variety, have the same features, the same mental faculties, and the same social affections, so all Christians, however they may differ in the strength or combination of the Christian graces, are all led by the Spirit and all produce the fruits of the Spirit.

Having given this brief outline of the nature of true religion, it is proper to say a few words as to its necessity. It should be ever borne in mind that the necessity of holiness is absolute. With regard to other things, some, though desirable, are not essential, and others, though essential under ordinary circumstances, are not universally and absolutely necessary. But holiness is necessary in such a sense that salvation, without it, is impossible, because salvation principally consists in this very transformation of the heart. Jesus is a Saviour because he saves his people from their sins. Those, therefore, who are not sanctified, are not saved. The doctrine that a man may live in sin, and still be in a state of salvation, is as much a contradiction, as to say that a man may be ill, when in health. A state of salvation is a state of holiness. The two things are inseparable; because salvation is not mere redemption from the penalty of sin, but deliverance from its power. It is freedom from bondage to the appetites of the body and the evil passions of the heart; it is an introduction into the favour and fellowship of God; the restoration of the divine image to the soul, so that it loves God and delights in his service. Salvation, therefore, is always begun on earth. Verily, verily, I say unto you, he that believeth in me hath eternal life. This is the language of our Saviour. To be spiritually minded is life; to be carnally minded is death. There is no delusion more inexcusable, because none is more directly opposed to every doctrine of the Bible, than the idea that a state of grace is consistent with a life of sin. Without holiness no man can see God. Whatever our ecclesiastical connexions may be, whatever our privileges or professions, if we are not holy in heart and life; if we are not habitually governed by a regard to the will of God; if we do not delight in communion with him, and desire conformity to his image; if we are not led by the Spirit and do not exhibit the love, joy, peace, long-suffering, gentleness, goodness, faith, meekness and temperance which that Spirit always produces—then we are not religious men, nor are we in a state of salvation.

The Bible knows nothing of proud, selfish, covetous, impure Christians. Christians are partakers of a holy calling, they are washed, and sanctified and justified in the name of the Lord Jesus, and by the Spirit of our God; they are saints, the sanctified in Christ Jesus; they mind spiritual things; they have crucified the flesh with its affections and lusts; they are poor in spirit, meek, pure in heart, merciful; they hunger and thirst after righteousness. Not that they have already apprehended, or are already perfect; but they follow after, if that they may apprehend that for which they are also apprehended of Christ Jesus; forgetting the things that are behind, and reaching forth unto those things which are before, they press toward the mark for the prize of the high calling of God in Christ Jesus. Their conversation is in heaven; from whence also they look for the Saviour, the Lord Jesus Christ, who shall change our vile body, that it may be fashioned like unto his glorious body, according to the working whereby he is able to subdue all things unto himself.

Again, as God is holy, it is necessary that his people should be holy. There can be no communion without concord, or congeniality. If one loves what another hates, approves what another condemns, desires what another rejects, there can be no fellowship between them. What concord hath Christ with Belial; or what fellowship hath light with darkness? So long, therefore, as we are what God disapproves; so long as we do not love what he loves, there can be no fellowship between him and us. Hence Christ says, Marvel not that I said unto you, ye must be born again. That which is born of the flesh, is flesh; and that which is born of the Spirit, is spirit. The carnal mind is enmity against God, and so long as this prevails it is impossible that we should enjoy his presence. As God is the only adequate portion of the soul; as his favour and fellowship are essential to our happiness; as heaven consists of seeing, loving and serving God, it is plain that unless we are sanctified we cannot be saved; we cannot enjoy the society, the employments, or the pleasures of the people of God above, if we take no delight in them here. The necessity of holiness, therefore, arises out of the very nature of God, and is consequently absolute and unchangeable.

We know also that holiness is the end of redemption. Christ gave himself for his church that he might sanctify and cleanse it, and that it should be holy and just without blemish. He died the just for the unjust that he might bring us unto God. The object of redemption is not attained in the case of those who remain in sin; in other words, they are not redeemed. It is, therefore, to subvert the whole Gospel, and to make the death of Christ of none effect, to suppose that redemption and continuance in sin are compatible. The whole design and purpose of the mission and sufferings of the Saviour would be frustrated if his people were not made partakers of his holiness; for the glory of God is promoted in them and by them only so far as they are made holy, and the recompense of the Redeemer is his bringing his people into conformity to his own image, that he may be the firstborn among many brethren. Every child of God feels that the charm and glory of redemption is deliverance from sin and conformity to God. This is the crown of righteousness, the prize of the high calling of God, the exaltation and blessedness for which he longs, and suffers and prays. To tell him that he may be saved without being made holy, is to confound all his ideas of salvation, and to crush all his hopes. The nature of salvation, the character of God, the declarations of his word, the design of redemption, all concur to prove that holiness is absolutely and indispensably necessary, so that whatever we may be, or whatever we may have, if we are not holy, we are not the children of God nor the heirs of his kingdom.

SECTION II. *The means of sanctification.*

The attainment of holiness is often treated, even by Christian writers, as a mere question of morals, or at most of natural religion. Men are directed to control, by the force of reason, their vicious propensities; to set in array before the mind the motives of virtuous living, and to strengthen the will by acts of self-restraint. Conscience is summoned to sanction the dictates of reason, or to warn the sinner of the consequences of transgression. The doctrines of the presence and providence of God, and the future retribution, are more or less relied upon to prevent the indulgence of sin, and to stimulate to the practice of virtue. Special directions are given how to cultivate virtuous habits, or to correct those which are evil.

As we are rational beings and were meant to be governed by reason in opposition to appetite and passion, there is much that is true and important in such disquisitions on the practice of virtue. But as we are depraved beings, destitute of any recuperative power in ourselves, such rules and the efforts to which they lead, must, by themselves, be ineffectual. God has endowed the body with a restorative energy, which enables it to throw off what is noxious to the system, and to heal the wounds, which accident or malice may have inflicted. But when the system itself is deranged, instead of correcting what is amiss, it aggravates what would, otherwise, be a mere temporary disorder. And if by external means the evil is checked in one part, it re-appears in another. Though you amputate a decaying limb, the remaining portion may soon exhibit symptoms of mortification. So long as the system is deranged such means are mere palliatives, concealing or diverting the evil, but leaving the source of it untouched. It is no less true that so long as the heart is unrenewed, all that reason and conscience can do is of little avail. They may obstruct the stream, or divert it into secret channels, but they cannot reach the fountain. As we retain since the fall, reason, the power of choice, conscience, the social affections, a sense of justice, fear, shame, &c., much may be done, by a skilful management of these principles of action, towards producing propriety of conduct and even great amiability and worth of character. But it is impossible, by these means, to call into existence right views and feelings towards God and our neighbour, or to eradicate the selfishness, pride and other forms of evil by which our nature is corrupted. A man may be brought, by reason and conscience, to change his conduct, but not to change his heart. A sense of duty may force him to give alms to a man he hates, but it cannot change hatred into love. The desire of happiness may induce him to engage externally in the service of God, but it cannot make that service a delight. The affections do not obey the dictates of reason, nor the commands of conscience. They may be measurably restrained in their manifestations, but cannot be changed in their nature. They follow their own law. They delight in what is suited to the disposition of him who exercises them. Holding up to them what they ought to delight in, cannot secure their devotion.

It is not meant to depreciate reason and conscience, but it is necessary that their true province should be known, that we may not rely upon inadequate means in our efforts to become holy. Though Scripture and experience teach us that our own unaided powers are insufficient to bring us to the knowledge and love of God, the rules which reason suggests for the culture of moral excellence, are, for the renewed man, far from being destitute of value. It is no doubt of importance that we should be acquainted with the counsels of the wise on this subject, and that we should habituate ourselves to the vigilant use of all these subordinate means of improvement; remembering, however, that it is not by the strength of our own purposes, nor by the force of moral considerations, nor by any rules of discipline, that the life of God in the soul can be either produced or sustained.

While one class of men place their chief reliance for moral improvement upon reason and conscience, another, and perhaps a larger class, rely upon means which, though they have no tendency in themselves to produce holiness, are falsely assumed to have, in virtue of the appointment of God, an inherent efficacy for that purpose. Such are not only the ablutions, pilgrimages and penances of the heathen, but the multiplied rites of corrupt Christian churches.

Sprinkling the body with consecrated water, the repetition of forms of prayer, attendance upon religious services not understood, anointing with oil, the imposition of hands, receiving, though without faith, the holy sacraments, are supposed to convey grace to the soul. Great reliance is placed on retirement from the world; on praying at particular times or places, or in a particular posture, and on the whole routine of ascetic discipline. With what laborious and unavailing diligence these means of destroying sin have been employed, the history of the church gives melancholy evidence. Even in the days of the apostles disposition to rely on such means for attaining holiness had begun to manifest itself. There were even then men who commanded to abstain from meats, who forbade marriage, who said, taste not, touch not, handle not; which things, says the apostle, have indeed a show of wisdom in will-worship and humility, and in neglecting and dishonouring the body, and yet only served to satisfy the flesh.[287]

The Scriptures teach us a different doctrine. They teach that believers are so united to Christ, that they are not only partakers of the merit of his death, but also of his Holy Spirit, which dwells in them as a principle of life, bringing them more and more into conformity with the image of God, and working in them both to will and to do, according to his own good pleasure. They teach that so long as men are under the law, that is, are bound to satisfy its demands as the ground of their acceptance with God and are governed by a legal spirit, or a mere sense of duty and fear of punishment, they are in the condition of slaves; incapable of right feelings towards God, or of producing the fruits of holiness. But when, by the death of Christ, they are freed from the law, in the sense above stated, their whole relation to God is changed. They are no longer slaves, but children. Being united to Christ in his death, they are partakers of his life, and in virtue of this union they bring forth fruit unto God. They are henceforth led by the Spirit which dwells in them; and this Spirit is a source of life not only to the soul but also to the body; for if the Spirit of him that raised Christ from the dead, dwell in us, he that raised up Christ from the dead shall also quicken our bodies, by his

---

287. Col. ii. 21–23.

Spirit that dwelleth in us. The doctrine of sanctification, therefore, as taught in the Bible is, that we are made holy not by the force of conscience, nor of moral motives, nor by acts of discipline, but by being united to Christ so as to become reconciled to God, and partakers of the Holy Ghost. Christ is made unto us sanctification as well as justification. He not only frees from the penalty of the law, but he makes holy. There is, therefore, according to the gospel, no such thing as sanctification, without or before justification. Those who are out of Christ are under the power, as well as under the condemnation of sin. And those who are in Christ are not only free from condemnation, but are also delivered from the dominion of sin.

The nature of the union between Christ and his people, on which so much depends, is confessedly mysterious. Paul having said, We are members of his body, of his flesh, and of his bones, immediately adds, This is a great mystery.[288] It is in vain, therefore, to attempt to bring this subject down to the level of our comprehension. The mode in which God is present and operates throughout the universe, is to us an impenetrable secret. We cannot even understand how our own souls are present and operate in the bodies which they occupy. We need not, then, expect to comprehend the mode in which Christ dwells by his Spirit in the hearts of his people. The fact that such union exists is clearly revealed; its effects are explicitly stated, and its nature is set forth as far as it can be made known by the most striking illustrations. In his intercessory prayer, our Saviour said, I pray—that they all may be one, as thou Father art in me and I in thee, that they also may be one in us.—I in them, and thou in me, that they may be made perfect in one.[289] He that keepeth his commandments, says the apostle, dwelleth in him, and he in him; and hereby we know that he abideth in us, by the Spirit, which he hath given us.[290] If any man have not the Spirit of Christ, he is none of his, but if Christ be in you, the body, (adds the apostle,) may die, but the soul shall live.[291] Know ye not, asks Paul, that your body is the temple of the

---

288. Eph. v. 32.
289. John xvii. 21–23.
290. 1 John iii. 24.
291. Rom. viii. 9–11.

Holy Ghost, which is in you, which ye have of God, and ye are not your own.[292] And to the same effect, Know ye not that ye are the temple of God, and that the Spirit of God dwelleth in you.[293]

The Scriptures are filled with this doctrine. The great promise of the Old Testament in connection with the advent of the Messiah was, that the Holy Spirit should then be abundantly communicated to men. Christ is said to have redeemed us in order that we might receive this promised Spirit.[294] And the only evidence of a participation of the benefits of redemption, recognized by the apostles, was the participation of the Holy Ghost, manifesting itself either in the extraordinary powers which he then communicated, or in those lovely fruits of holiness which never fail to mark his presence.

The effects ascribed to this union, as already stated, are an interest in the merits of Christ, in order to our justification, and the indwelling of his Spirit in order to our sanctification. Its nature is variously illustrated. It is compared to that union which subsists between a representative and those for whom he acts. In this view Adam is said to be like Christ and Christ is said to be the second Adam; for as in Adam all die, so in Christ shall all be made alive. This idea is also presented whenever Christ is said to have died for his sheep, or in their place; or when they are said to have died with him, his death being virtually their death, satisfying in their behalf the demands of justice and redeeming them from the curse of the law. It is compared to the union between the head and members of the same body. The meaning of this illustration is by no means exhausted by saying that Christ governs his people, or that there is a community of feeling and interest between them. The main idea is that there is a community of life; that the same Spirit dwells in him and in them. As the body is every where animated by one soul, which makes it one and communicates a common life to all its parts; so the Holy Ghost, who dwells in Christ, is by him communicated to all his people, and makes them in a peculiar sense, one with him and one among themselves, and imparts to all, that life which has its seat and source in him. As the body is one, and hath many members, and all

---

292. 1 Cor. vi. 19.
293. 1 Cor. iii. 16.
294. Gal. iii. 13, 14.

the members of that one body, being many are one body; so also is Christ, for by one Spirit are we all baptized into one body—and have all been made to drink into one Spirit.[295] Another illustration, but of the same import, is employed by Christ, when he says, I am the vine, ye are the branches; he that abided in me and I in him, the same bringeth forth much fruit; for without me ye can do nothing. As the branches are so united to the vine as to partake of its life and to be absolutely dependent upon it, so believers are so united to Christ as to partake of his life and to be absolutely dependent on him. The Holy Spirit communicated by him to them, is, in them, the principle of life and fruitfulness.

Christ and his people are one. He is the foundation, they are the building. He is the vine, they are the branches. He is the head, they are the body. Because he lives, they shall live also; for it is not they that live, but Christ that liveth in them. The Holy Spirit, concerning which he said to his disciples, He dwelleth with you and shall be in you, is to them not only the source of spiritual life, but of all its manifestations. They are baptized by the Spirit;[296] they are born of the Spirit;[297] they are called spiritual, because the Spirit of God dwells in them,[298] whereas, the unregenerate are called natural, or sensual, "not having the Spirit."[299] Believers are sanctified by the Spirit;[300] they are led by the Spirit;[301] they live in the Spirit;[302] they are strengthened by the Spirit;[303] they are filled with the Spirit.[304] By the Spirit they mortify sin,[305] through the Spirit, they wait for the hope of righteousness;[306] they have access to God by the Spirit,[307] they

---

295. 1 Cor. xii. 12, 13.
296. Luke iii. 16.
297. John iii. 5.
298. 1 Cor. iii. 16.
299. Jude 19.
300. 1 Cor. vi. 11.
301. Rom. viii. 14.
302. Gal. v. 25.
303. Eph. iii. 16.
304. Eph. v. 18.
305. Rom. viii. 13.
306. Gal. v. 5.
307. Eph. ii. 18.

pray and sing, in the Spirit.[308] The Spirit is to them a source of knowledge,[309] of joy,[310] of love, long-suffering, goodness, faith, meekness, temperance.[311] This doctrine of the indwelling of the Holy Spirit is so wrought into the texture of the Gospel as to be absolutely essential to it. It ceases to be the Gospel if we abstract from it the great truth, that the Spirit of God, as the purchase and gift of Christ, is ever present with his people, guiding their inward exercises and outward conduct, and bringing them at last, without spot or blemish, to the purity and blessedness of heaven.

The secret of the holy living lies in this doctrine of the union of the believer with Christ. This is not only the ground of his hope of pardon, but the source of the strength whereby he dies unto sin and lives unto righteousness. It is by being rooted and grounded in Christ that he is strengthened with might by his Spirit in the inner man, and is enabled to comprehend the breadth, the length, and depth and heighth of the mystery of redemption and to know the love of Christ which passes knowledge and is filled with all the fulness of God. It is this doctrine which sustains him under all his trials, and enables him to triumph over all his enemies, for it is not he that lives, but Christ that lives in him, giving him grace sufficient for his day, and purifying him unto himself, as one of his peculiar people zealous of good works.

As union with Christ is the source of spiritual life, the means by which that life is to be maintained and promoted are all related to this doctrine and derive from it all their efficacy. Thus we are said to be purified by faith,[312] to be sanctified by faith,[313] to live by faith,[314] to be saved by faith.[315] Faith has this important agency because it is the bond of our union with Christ. It not only gives us the right to plead his merits for our justification, but it makes us partakers of his Holy Spirit. Christ has promised that all who come to him

---

308. 1 Cor. xiv. 15.
309. Eph. i. 17.
310. 1 Thess. 1. 6.
311. Gal. v. 22.
312. Acts xv. 9.
313. Acts xxvi. 18.
314. Gal. ii. 20.
315. Eph. ii. 8.

shall receive the water of life, by which the apostle tells us is meant the Holy Spirit. It is by faith, and in the persuasion of our consequent union with Christ, that we have confidence to draw near to God and to open our souls to the sanctifying influence of his love. It is by faith that we receive of his fulness and grace for grace. It is by faith that we look to him for strength to overcome temptations and to discharge our duties. It is by faith that we receive those exceeding great and precious promises, whereby we are made partakers of the divine nature.

All Christians know from experience that faith in Christ is the source of their holiness and peace. When beset with temptations to despondency or sin, if they look to him for support, they are conscious of a strength to resist, or to endure, which no effort of will and no influence of motives ever could impart. When they draw near to God as the members of Christ, they have freedom of access and experience a joy which is unspeakable and full of glory. When pressed down by afflictions if they remember that they are one with him who suffered for them, leaving them an example, they rejoice in their tribulations, knowing that if they suffer they shall also reign with him.

Moreover, as in virtue of union with Christ we receive the Holy Spirit as the source of spiritual life, to maintain that life we must avoid every thing which may provoke the Spirit to withdraw from us. The Bible teaches that the Spirit may be grieved; that his influences may be quenched; that God, in judgment, often withdraws them from those who thus offend. Evil thoughts, unholy tempers, acts of transgression are to be avoided not merely as sins, but as offences against the Holy Spirit. We must remember that to defile the soul with sin, or the body by intemperance or impurity, is sacrilege, because we are the members of Christ and our bodies the temples of the Holy Ghost. On the other hand, right thoughts, just purposes, holy desires are to be cherished, not only as right in themselves, but as proceeding from that heavenly agent on whom we are dependent for sanctification.

This is a very different thing from opposing sin and cultivating right feelings on mere moral considerations, and in dependence on our own strength. This may be what the world calls morality, but it is not what the Bible calls religion. Such considerations ought to have and ever will have, with the Christian, their due weight; but they are not his dependence in his efforts to become holy, nor is his reliance upon his own resources. The life which he leads is by faith in Jesus Christ; and it is by constant reference to the Holy Spirit, and dependence on him that that life is maintained. For it is as inconsistent with the religion of the Gospel, to suppose that we can make ourselves holy by our own strength, as that we can be justified by our own works.

It is principally through the efficacy of prayer that we receive the communications of the Holy Spirit. Prayer is not a mere instinct of a dependent nature, seeking help from the author of its being; nor is it to be viewed simply as a natural expression of faith and desire, or as a mode of communion with the Father of our spirits; but it is also to be regarded as the appointed means of obtaining the Holy Ghost. If ye being evil, know how to give good gifts unto your children; how much more shall your heavenly Father give the Holy Spirit to them that ask him. Hence we are urged to be constant and importunate in prayer, praying especially for those communications of divine influence by which the life of God in the soul is maintained and promoted.

The doctrine that the Holy Spirit works in the people of God both to will and to do according to his own pleasure, is not inconsistent with the diligent use of all rational and scriptural means, on our part, to grow in grace and in the knowledge of God. For though the mode of the Spirit's influence is inscrutable, it is still the influence of a rational being on a rational subject. It is described as an enlightening, teaching, persuading process, all which terms suppose a rational subject rationally affected. The in-dwelling of the Spirit, therefore, in the people of God, does not supersede their own agency. He acts by leading them to act. Thus we are commanded to do, and in fact must do, what he is said to do for us. We believe, though faith is of the operation of God; we repent, though repentance is the gift of Christ; we love, though love, gentleness, goodness and all other graces are the fruits of the Spirit. The work of sanctification is carried on by our being thus led under this divine influence to exercise right dispositions and feelings. For the law of our nature, which connects an increase of strength with the repeated exercise of any of our powers, is not suspended with regard to the holy disposition of the renewed soul. Philosophers say that the vibrations imparted to the atmosphere by the utterance of a word never cease.

However this may be, it is certain every pious emotion strengthens the principle of piety, and leaves the soul permanently better. The good derived from that influence, or from those services which call our love, faith, or gratitude into exercise, is not transient as the exercises themselves. Far from it. One hour's communion with God produces an impression never to be effaced; it renders the soul for ever less susceptible of evil and more susceptible of good. And as the Holy Spirit is ever exciting the soul to the exercise of holiness, and bringing it into communion with God, he thus renders it more and more holy, and better fitted for the unchanging and perfect holiness of heaven.

It is principally by the contemplation of the truth, the worship of God, and the discharge of duty that these holy exercises are called into being. All thought and affection suppose an object on which they terminate, and which, when presented, tends to call them forth. We cannot fear God unless his holiness and power be present to the mind; we cannot love him except in view of his excellence and goodness; we cannot believe, except in contemplation of his word, nor hope, unless in view of his promises. As those affections suppose their appropriate objects, so these objects tend to excite the affections. Were it not for our depravity, they never could be brought into view without the corresponding affection rising to meet them. And notwithstanding our depravity, their tendency, resulting from their inherent nature, remains, and as that depravity is corrected or removed by the Holy Spirit, these objects exert on the soul their appropriate influence. We are, therefore, said to be sanctified by the truth;[316] to be made clean through the word of Christ;[317] to be born again by the word of truth;[318] to be changed into the image of God by beholding his glory.[319]

It is most unreasonable to expect to be conformed to the image of God, unless the truth concerning God be made to operate often and continuously upon the mind. How can a heart that is filled with the thoughts and cares of the world, and especially one which is often

---

316. John xvii. 19.
317. John xv. 3.
318. James i. 18.
319. 2 Cor. iii. 18.

moved to evil by the thoughts or sight of sin, expect that the affections which answer to the holiness, goodness or greatness of God should gather strength within it? How can the love of Christ increase in the bosoms of those who hardly ever think of him or of his work? This cannot be without a change in the very nature of things, and, therefore, we cannot make progress in holiness unless we devote much time to the reading, hearing, meditating upon the word of God, which is the truth whereby we are sanctified. The more this truth is brought before the mind; the more we commune with it, entering into its import, applying it to our own case, appropriating its principles, appreciating its motives, rejoicing in its promises, trembling at its threatenings, rising by its influence from what is seen and temporal to what is unseen and eternal; the more may we expect to be transformed by the renewing of our mind so as to approve and love whatever is holy, just and good. Men distinguished for their piety have ever been men of meditation as well as men of prayer; men accustomed to withdraw the mind from the influence of the world with its thousand joys and sorrows, and to bring it under the influence of the doctrines, precepts and promises of the word of God.

Besides the contemplation of the truth, the worship of God is an important means of growing in grace. It not only includes the exercise and expression of all pious feelings, which are necessarily strengthened by the exercise, but it is the appointed means of holding communion with God and receiving the communications of his grace. They that wait on the Lord shall renew their strength; they shall mount up with wings as eagles,they shall walk and not be weary, they shall run and not faint. Blessed are they that dwell in thy house; they shall be still praising thee. They shall go from strength to strength, till they appear before God in Zion. This is a matter of experience as well as revelation. The people of God have ever found in the private, social and public worship of the Father of their spirits, the chief means of renewing their spiritual strength. The sanctuary is the temple of God on earth whose services are preparatory to those of the temple not made with hands eternal in the heavens. It is here too that the sacraments, as means of grace, have their appropriate place. They are to us what the sacrifices and rites of the old dispensation were to the Israelites. They exhibit and seal the truth and promises of God, and convey to those who worthily receive them the blessings which they represent. The Christian, therefore, who is desirous of increasing in the knowledge and love of God, will be a faithful attendant on all the appointed forms and occasions of divine worship. He will be much in his closet, he will be punctual in the sanctuary and at the table of the Lord. He will seek opportunities of fellowship with God, as a friend seeks intercourse with his friend; and the more he can enjoy of this communion, the better will he be prepared for that perfect fellowship with the Father of lights which constitutes the blessedness of heaven.

Finally, to be good, we must do good. It has been falsely said that action is the whole of oratory, and as falsely supposed that action is the whole of religion. There is no eloquence in action except as it is expressive of thought and feeling, and there is no religion in outward acts except as they are informed and guided by a pious spirit. It is only by maintaining such a spirit that external works can have any significance or value. It is perhaps one of the evil tendencies of our age, to push religion out of doors; to allow her no home but the street or public assembly; to withhold from her all food except the excitement of loud professions and external manifestations. This is to destroy her power. It is to cut her off from the source of her strength, and to transform the meek and holy visiter from heaven, into the noisy and bustling inhabitant of the earth. It is so much easier to be religious outwardly than inwardly; to be active in church duties, than to keep the heart with all diligence, that we are in danger of preferring the form of religion to its power. The same love of excitement and desire to be busy which makes men active in worldly pursuits may, without changing their character, make them active in religious exercises. But if there is danger on this side, there is quite as much on the other. Although religion does not consist in outward acts, it always produces them. Whosoever hath this world's good, and seeth his brother have need, and shutteth up his bowels of compassion from him, how dwelleth the love of God in him?[320] The love of God can no more fail to produce obedience to his commands, than a mother's love can fail to produce watchfulness and care for her infant. That man's religion, therefore, is vain which expends itself in exercises that relate exclusively to his own salvation. And doubtless many Christians go halting all their days, because they confine

---

320. 1 John iii. 17.

their attention too much to themselves. It is only by the harmonious exercise of all the graces, of faith and love towards God, and of justice and benevolence towards men, that the health of the soul can be maintained or promoted. It is not merely because the exercise of benevolence strengthens the principle of benevolence that doing good tends to make men better, but God has ordained that he that watereth shall be watered also himself. He distils his grace on those who labour for the temporal and spiritual benefit of their fellow men, and who follow the example of the blessed Redeemer, walking with God while they go about doing good.

True religion as we find it described in the Bible is neither an external show, nor a fitful ebullition of feeling. It is a permanent, spontaneous and progressive principle of spiritual life, influencing the whole man and producing all the fruits of righteousness. It is not any one good disposition, but the root and spring of all right feelings and actions, manifesting itself in love and obedience towards God, in justice and benevolence towards man, and in the proper government of ourselves. This divine life can neither be obtained nor continued by any mere efforts of reason or conscience, or by any superstitious observances, but flows from our union with Christ, who causes his Holy Spirit to dwell in all his members. In order to promote this divine life it is our business to avoid every thing which has a tendency to grieve the Spirit of all grace, and to do every thing by which his sacred influence on the heart may be cherished. It is by this influence that we are sanctified, for it leads us to exercise all holy dispositions in the contemplation of the truth, in the worship of God and in the discharge of all our relative duties.

This unpretending volume, designed for the use of educated youth, was written with the view of impressing on its readers those great truths of revelation which are immediately connected with practical religion. It is designed to convince them that all scepticism as to the divine authority of the Scriptures is inexcusable, inasmuch as the Bible brings with it its own credentials. It makes such a revelation of the character of God, of the rule of duty and of the plan of salvation as challenges immediate assent and submission to their truth and goodness. It sets forth the Redeemer as the Son of God and the Saviour of sinners, in whom the glory of God is so revealed that those who refuse to recognise him as their God and Saviour refuse, to infinite excellence, their confidence and obedience. In order that every mouth may be stopped, the Bible, thus replete with evidence of its divine origin, is confirmed by all kinds of adequate proofs from miracles, prophecy and history, that it is, indeed, the word of God.

The divine authority of the Scriptures being established, the great question to be decided by every one by whom they are known, is, What do they teach as to the plan of salvation and the rule of duty? It has been our design to aid the reader in answering this question for himself; to show him that the Bible teaches that we are all sinners, and that, being sinners, we have lost the favour of God and are unable to effect our own redemption. When we feel that this is true with regard to ourselves, we are convinced of sin, and are irresistibly led to ask what we must do to be saved? In answer to this question the Scriptures set forth Jesus Christ as born of a woman, made under the law, satisfying its demands, dying the just for the unjust, rising again from the dead, and ascending up on high, where he ever liveth to make intercession for us. They teach us that it is not for any thing done or experienced by us, but solely for what Christ has done for us, that we are justified in the sight of God; and that in order to our being saved through Christ, we must accept him as our Saviour, not going about to establish our own righteousness, but submitting to the righteousness of God. Those who thus believe, do, at the same time repent; that is, they turn from sin unto God, through Jesus Christ. They are now his followers, and declare themselves to be such by confessing him before the world and by devoutly attending upon those ordinances which he has appointed to be means of acknowledging our allegiance to him, and of communicating his grace to us. The Scriptures further teach that our work is but begun when we have thus renounced the world and joined ourselves unto the Lord. The spiritual life commenced in regeneration is carried on by the Holy Spirit, who dwells in all the people of God, by teaching them to look to Jesus Christ, as their living head, for all those supplies of grace and all that protection which their circumstances require. They are thus washed, sanctified and justified in the name of the Lord Jesus, and by the Spirit of our God, and being made meet for the inheritance of the saints in light, they will be at last admitted into God's blissful presence and enjoy the full communications of his grace and love for ever and ever.

II

COMMENTARY ON THE BOOK OF ROMANS,
Romans 6:1–11

From his first years as Professor of Oriental and Biblical Literature, Charles Hodge lectured regularly on the Pauline epistles, an assignment which he continued even after assuming the chair of theology. From these lectures came the first major publication of his career at Princeton, a commentary on the Book of Romans published in 1835.[1] This work reflects Hodge's learning in Europe, for it includes citations and discussions of some of the most recent German work on this important book of the New Testament. Even more, however, the commentary hoisted a flag for Princeton against doctrinal innovations in America. Early in the 1830s the Congregationalist Moses Stuart and the New School Presbyterian Albert Barnes published commentaries on Romans which questioned the "forensic unity" of both Adam and humanity and Christ and the Christian. They suggested, that is, that the bond between the individual and the race (or Christ) was more ethical than essential, more a figure of speech than a fundamental reality. Such views were anathema to Hodge and Alexander. And so in the pages of the *Princeton Review* and in his own commentary, Hodge upheld the view that the guilt of Adam's sin was imputed to all humanity, just as the imputation of Christ's righteousness was the foundation of every Christian's life.[2]

---

1. *Life*, pp. 271–79.
2. Hodge, "Stuart on the Romans," *BRPR* 5 (Apr. 1833); "Barnes on the Epistle to the Romans," *BRPR* 7 (Apr. 1835).

The commentary, with its reflection of continental scholarship, its theological rigor, and its warm evangelical spirit, was a mature piece of work. Even so, as one recent historian has noted, Hodge's arguments could be eclectic in the extreme—"Philological, logical, historical, philosophical, and theological factors were lined up indiscriminately, with apparently equal weight: no relative values were assigned. His strategy seems to have been to amass the largest possible body of evidence in support of the case for imputation."[3] For its importance in antebellum theological debates, the commentary nonetheless remains a significant work for historians.

For the purposes of this book, Hodge's commentary is also important for other reasons. In it Hodge put into practice principles he would later articulate in *The Way of Life*, especially the injunction to learn from the Scriptures how to live as a Christian. The selection which follows is Hodge's commentary on Romans 6:1–11, a passage where Paul tells Christians why, though they be saved by grace, they should not continue sinning in order to enjoy a greater measure of God's mercy. It is a passage, like much of *The Way of Life*, in which Hodge's careful study of the Bible broadens out into a fulsome exercise of devotion.

Hodge wrote the commentary under unusual circumstances while laid up in bed with the ailment in his leg. As A. A. Hodge reported, the book was composed "during the darkest days of his confinement, the winter of 1834 and '35, while stretched horizontally on a couch, and his right limb often bound in a steel-splint."[4] In spite of the impropitious circumstances under which it was written, the commentary was immediately recognized as an important work, and its second edition, which Hodge prepared in 1864, remains in print.[5]

The text below is from an abridged and simplified edition published in 1836 for the use of lay Bible students. In its day, it actually

3. Stephen J. Stein, "Stuart and Hodge on Romans 5:12–21: An Exegetical Controversy About Original Sin," *Journal of Presbyterian History* 47 (Dec. 1969): 348. This is a helpful article on the general issues in this controversy.

4. *Life*, p. 271.

5. The 1864 edition of the Romans commentary is currently available from Eerdmans (Grand Rapids) and Banner of Truth (London).

circulated more widely than the longer edition.[6] The abridgement, however, is substantially the same as the original in the sections entitled "contents," "analysis," "doctrines," and "remarks." Only the "commentary" itself is changed, with discussions of technical matters and the Greek text omitted. The following is pp. 138–147 from the sixteenth printing of *A Commentary on the Epistle to the Romans. By Charles Hodge, Professor of Biblical Literature in the Theological Seminary at Princeton. For the Use of Sunday-Schools and Bible-Classes* (Philadelphia: William S. & Alfred Martien, 1858).

CONTENTS.

As the gospel reveals the only effectual method of justification, so also it alone can secure the sanctification of men. To exhibit this truth is the object of this and the following chapter. The sixth is partly argumentative, and partly exhortatory. In verses 1–11 the apostle shows how unfounded is the objection, that gratuitous justification leads to the indulgence of sin. In vs. 12–23 he exhorts Christians to live agreeably to the nature and design of the gospel; and presents various considerations adapted to secure their obedience to this exhortation.

CHAP. 6: 1–11.

[1]What shall we say then? Shall we continue in sin, that grace may abound? [2]God forbid. How shall we, that are dead to sin, live any longer therein? [3]Know ye not, that so many of us as were baptized into Jesus Christ were baptized into his death? [4]Therefore we are buried with him by baptism into death: that like as Christ was raised up from the dead by the glory of the Father, even so we also should walk in newness of life. [5]For if we have been planted together in the likeness of his death, we shall be also *in the likeness* of *his* resurrection: [6]knowing this, that our old man is crucified with *him,*

---

6. On the restricted circulation of the 1835 edition, see *The British and Foreign Evangelical Review* 14 (1865): 657.

that the body of sin might be destroyed, and that henceforth we should not serve sin. [7]For he that is dead is freed from sin. [8]Now if we be dead with Christ, we believe that we shall also live with him: [9]knowing that Christ being raised from the dead dieth no more; death hath no more dominion over him. [10]For in that he died, he died unto sin once: but in that he liveth, he liveth unto God. [11]Likewise reckon ye also yourselves to be dead indeed unto sin, but alive unto God through Jesus Christ our Lord.

ANALYSIS.

The most common, the most plausible, and yet the most unfounded objection to the doctrine of justification by faith, is, that it allows men to live in sin that grace may abound. This objection arises from ignorance of the doctrine in question, and of the nature and means of sanctification. It is so preposterous in the eyes of an enlightened believer, that Paul deals with it rather by exclamations at its absurdity, than with logical arguments. The main idea of this section is, that such is the nature of the believer's union with Christ, that his living in sin is not merely an inconsistency, but a contradiction in terms, as much so as speaking of a live dead man, or a good bad one. Union with Christ, being the only source of holiness, cannot be the source of sin. In v. 1 the apostle presents the objection. In v. 2 he declares it to be unfounded, and exclaims at its absurdity. In vs. 3, 4 he exhibits the true nature and design of Christianity, as adapted and intended to produce newness of life. In vs. 5–7 he shows that such is the nature of union with Christ, that it is impossible for any one to share the benefits of his death without being conformed to his life. Such being the case, he shows, vs. 8–11, that as Christ's death on account of sin was for once, never to be repeated; and his life a life devoted to God; so our separation from sin is final, and our life a life consecrated to God.

COMMENTARY.

(1) *What shall we say then?* What inference is to be drawn from the doctrine of the gratuitous acceptance of sinners, or justification without works by faith in the righteousness of Christ?

Shall we continue in sin that grace may abound? i.e. be more conspicuously displayed. The form in which the objection to the apostle's doctrine is here presented, is evidently borrowed from the close of the preceding chapter. Paul had there spoken of the grace of the gospel being more conspicuous and abundant in proportion to the evils which it removes. It is no fair inference from the fact that God has brought so much good out of the fall and sinfulness of men, that they may continue in sin. Neither can it be inferred from the fact that he accepts of sinners, on the ground of the merit of Christ, instead of their own (which is the way in which grace abounds), that they may sin without restraint.

(2) *God forbid*, in the Greek, *let it not be*. Paul's usual mode of expressing denial and abhorrence. Such an inference is not to be thought of. *How shall we, that are dead to sin, live any longer therein?* How can good men be bad men? or, how can the dead be alive? It is a contradiction and an absurdity, that those who are dead to sin should live in it. There are two points to be here considered. The first is the sense in which Christians are said to be dead to sin; and the second, the proof (vs. 3, 4) that such is really the case with all true believers. The words rendered *we that are dead to sin* (we that have died to die), may mean have died on account of sin, or in respect to sin. The latter is more consistent with the usual force of the expression, as in the phrases, "dead to the law;" "dead to sins," &c, &c., which mean *free from, delivered from the influence of.* In this case probably the apostle intended to express the general idea that our connexion with sin had been effectually broken off. This is effected, as he immediately teaches, by the death of Christ. His meaning, therefore, is, 'How can those who, in virtue of their union with Christ, have been effectually freed from the dominion of sin, live any longer therein?' It enters into the very idea of a Christian that he should be thus dead to sin, and his living in it consequently involves a contradiction.

(3) *Know ye not that so many of us were baptized into Jesus Christ, were baptized into his death?* In this and the following verse we have something more in the form of argument in answer to the objection in question. The apostle reminds his readers that the very design of Christianity was to deliver men from sin; that everyone who embraced it, embraced it for this very object; and, therefore, it was a contradiction in terms to suppose that any should come to

Christ to be delivered from sin in order that they might live in it. And, besides this, it is clearly intimated that such is not only the design of the gospel, and the object for which it is embraced by all who cordially receive it, but also that the result or necessary effect of union with Christ is a participation of the benefits of his death.

Were baptized into Jesus Christ. In the phrase *to be baptized into any one,* the word rendered *into* has its usual force as indicating the object, design, or result for which any thing is done. To be baptized into Jesus Christ, or unto Moses, or Paul, therefore, means to be baptized in order to be united to Christ, or Moses, or Paul, as their followers, the recipients of their doctrines, and expectants of the blessings which they have to bestow; see Matt. 28:19. 1 Cor. 10:2. 1 Cor. 1:13. In like manner, in the expression *baptized into his death,* the preposition expresses the design and the result. The meaning, therefore, is, 'we were baptized in order that we should die with him,' i.e. that we should be united to him in his death, and partakers of its benefits. Thus "baptism unto repentance," Matt. 3:11, is baptism in order to repentance; "baptism unto the remission of sins," Mark 1:4, that remission of sins may be obtained; "baptized into one body," 1 Cor. 12:13, i.e. that we might become one body, &c. The idea of the whole verse, therefore, is, 'That as many as have been baptized unto Jesus Christ, have become intimately united with him, so that they are united with him in his death, conformed to its object, and participate in the blessings for which he died.' Much to the same effect the apostle says, Gal. 3:27, "As many as have been baptized into Christ, have put on Christ," i.e. have become intimately united to him. Paul uses the expression *baptized into Christ,* not for the mere external or formal profession of the religion of the gospel, but for the cordial reception of it, of which submission to the rite of baptism was the public and appointed expression. The meaning, therefore, is, that those who have sincerely embraced Jesus Christ, have done it so as to be united with him, conformed to his image and the design for which he died. Christ died in order that he might destroy the works of the devil, 1 John 3:8; to save his people from their sins, and to purify to himself a peculiar people, zealous of good works, Tit. 2:14.

(4) *Therefore we are buried by baptism into his death, that like as Christ was raised up,* &c. 'Such being the nature and design of the gospel, if we accept of Christ at all, it is that we should die with

him; i.e. that we should attain the object for which he died, viz. deliverance from sin;' or, to use the apostle's figurative expression,
that as Christ was raised from the dead, we also might walk in newness of life.

The words *into death* are evidently to be connected with the
word *baptism;* it is *by a baptism unto death* that we are united to
Christ, as stated in the preceding verse. We are said to be *buried with
Christ;* i.e. we are effectually united to him in his death. The same
idea is expressed in v. 8, by saying "we are dead with him;" and in
v. 5, by saying we are "planted together in the likeness of his
death." It does not seem necessary to suppose that there is any allusion to the mode of baptism, as though that rite was compared to
a burial. No such allusion can be supposed in the next verse, where
we are said *to be planted* with him. Baptism is, throughout this passage, as in Gal. 3:27, taken for the reception of Christ, of which it
is the appointed acknowledgment. The point of the comparison is not
between our baptism and the burial and resurrection of Christ; but
between our death to sin and rising to holiness; and the death and
resurrection of the Redeemer. As Paul had expressed, in v. 2, the
idea of the freedom of believers from sin, by the figurative phrase
"dead to sin," he carries the figure consistently through; and says,
that by our reception of Christ we became united to him in such a
way as to die as he died, and to rise as he rose. As he died unto sin
(for its destruction), so do we; and as he rose unto newness of life,
so do we.

Christ is said to have been raised up *by the glory of the Father.*
Some would render these words *on account of the glory,* &c. But
this is inconsistent with usage. They either are equivalent to *glorious
Father,* see ch. 1:23, 25; or the word rendered *glory* may be used for
power or *might,* as in the Septuagint, Isa. 12:2. 45:24. Compare Col.
1:11. *Even so we also should walk in newness of life.* These words
express the design for which we receive Christ or were baptized unto
him; it is that we should exhibit that new life which we receive from
him, and which is analogous to his own, inasmuch as it is unending
and devoted unto God; see vs. 9, 10, where this idea is more fully
expressed.

(5) *For if we have been planted together in the likeness of his
death,* &c. As the preceding verse had declared the object of our
union with Christ to be newness of life; this verse exhibits the nec-

essary connexion between the means and the end, by showing that we cannot be united to Christ in his death, without being united to him also in his resurrection.

For if we have been planted together. The original word here used means properly *connate, born together;* but it is applied variously to things intimately united, as things growing together, to branches of the same tree, limbs of the same body, &c. &c. The idea, therefore, here expressed by it, is an intimate and vital union with Christ, such as exists between a vine and its branches. Compare John 15:1–8.

In the likeness of his death; i.e. in a death similar to his. We die as he died. This results from the fact of our intimate union with him. Hence, in v. 6, we are said "to be crucified with him;" and, in v. 8, "to be dead with him." If we are so united to Christ as to die with him (i.e. to obtain the benefits of his death), we also die as he died. This accounts for the introduction of the word *likeness,* expressive of a comparison between our death to sin and the death of Christ. But we experience this similar or spiritual death only because of the union with Christ, in virtue of which his death was, in the sight of God, equivalent to our death.

We shall be also in the likeness of his resurrection. The future tense, *shall,* does not here express obligation merely, but also and mainly the certainty of the result. 'If united to Christ in his death, we shall be also in his resurrection. That is, we shall experience a resurrection similar to his, viz, an entrance on a new, glorious, and perpetual life.' That a spiritual resurrection is here principally intended, seems very plain, both from the preceding and succeeding context. And yet the idea of the future resurrection of the body is not to be entirely excluded. Paul, in ch. 8:11, brings the resurrection of the body forward as a necessary consequence of our union with Christ, or of our having the Spirit of life dwelling in us. The meaning probably is, that if we are true Christians, baptized in the death of Christ, united and conformed to him in this respect, the necessary result will be that the life of Christ will be manifested in us by a holy and devoted life here, by a life of glorious immortality, and by the resurrection of the body hereafter. All this is included in the *life* consequent on our union with Christ.

(6) *Knowing this, that our old man was crucified with him, &c.* This verse is either an amplification or confirmation of the preced-

ing. 'If united with the Lord Jesus,' says the apostle, 'in his death, we shall be in his life, for we know that we are crucified with him for this very reason, viz. that the body of sin might be destroyed.' In this view of the passage it is little more than an amplification of v. 5. But it may also be viewed thus, 'We are sure we shall be conformed to the life of Christ, because we know that our old corruptions have been destroyed by his death, in order that we should no longer serve them.' This verse then assigns the reason for the assertion contained in the last clause of the fifth.

The phrase *old man* generally means the natural corruption, or unholy affections of men. See Eph. 4:22, "Put ye off the old man which is corrupt," Col. 3:9, "Lie not to one another, seeing ye have put off the old man with his deeds, and have put on the new man." The apostle then says, that Christians know that the effect of union with Christ is the destruction of the power of sin. There is probably no allusion in the use of the word *crucified,* either to the slowness or painfulness of that particular mode of death, as though the apostle meant to intimate that the destruction of sin was a gradual and painful process. This indeed is true, but is not here expressed. The simple expression "dead with him," is substituted for this word in v. 8, and in Gal. 2:20, "I am crucifed with Christ," contains no such allusion. It is more probable, as Calvin remarks, that the word is used to intimate that it is solely in virtue of our participation in the death of Christ that we are delivered from the power of sin.

That the body of sin might be destroyed. The expression *body of sin* is probably a mere paraphrase for sin itself, see Col. 2:11; yet it is no doubt used with design, as sin is spoken of as a person that dies, whose members we are to mortify, and whom we are no longer to serve. The destruction of sin results from the death of Christ, inasmuch as we are thereby reconciled to God, and brought under the influence of all the considerations which flow from the doctrine of redemption, see v. 14; and because his death secures for us the Holy Spirit, who is the source of all holiness, ch. 8:3, 4, 9.

That henceforth we should not serve sin, i.e. be slaves to it. This clause expresses at once the result and design of the destruction of the power of sin. Paul's whole argument then in these two verses is, 'Such is the nature of our union with Christ, that if we partake of the benefits of his death, and are conformed to him in this respect, we shall certainly be conformed to his life; because by his death the power of sin is destroyed.'

(7) *For he that is dead is free from sin.* The meaning of this verse is somewhat doubtful. It may be considered as merely a statement of a general truth, designed for the illustration and confirmation of what Paul had just said. 'Death puts a final stop to all activity in this world. He that dies is entirely separated from all former pursuits and objects; they have lost all power over him, and he all interest in them. To be dead to sin, therefore, expresses a full and final separation from it.' Or the meaning may be this, 'What has just been said is true, for he that is dead with Christ is judicially free from sin; its power and authority are destroyed, as effectually as the authority of a husband over his wife (ch. 7:3, 4), or of a master over his slave (v. 18), is destroyed by death.' There are three ways, therefore, in which this verse may be explained. 1. As expressing a mere general truth. 2. By supplying, after the word *dead* the words *to sin,* 'He that is dead to sin, is free from it.' 3. By supplying the words *with Christ*, 'He that is dead with Christ is free from sin.' This last method seems the preferable one, on account of the relation of this verse to vs. 6, 8, "He that is dead (with Christ) is free from sin, for if we be dead with Christ, we believe we shall also live with him."

Is free from sin, literally, *is justified from sin. Is justified from sin* means, is pardoned, is freed from the guilt and punishment of sin by justification. This verse then assigns a very important reason for the truth which the apostle had so frequently stated, viz. that the believer could not live in sin. 'For he that is dead with Christ is thereby justified, and freed from the punishment of sin; he is thus reconciled to God; and as reconciliation and communion with God are the true sources of holiness, he is also freed from sin.' This interpretation is confirmed by the next verse, in which our dying with Christ is represented as securing our living with him. See Gal. 2:19, 20. 6:14. Col. 2:6. 3:3;. 1 Pet. 4:1. In all these passages, with more or less distinctness, the death of Christ, and believers dying with him, are represented as the ground and cause of their living unto God.

Verses 8–11. These verses contain the application of the truth taught in the preceding passages. 'If we are dead with Christ, we shall share in his life. If he lives, we shall live also. As his life is perpetual, it secures the continued supplies of life to all his members.

Death has no more dominion over him. Having died unto, or on account of sin once, he now ever lives to, and with God. His people, therefore, must be conformed to him; dead indeed unto sin, but alive unto God.' This passage does not contain a mere comparison between the literal death and resurrection of Christ, and the spiritual death and resurrection of believers, but it exhibits the connexion between the death and life of the Redeemer and the sanctification of his people.

(8) *Now if we be dead with Christ,* &c. If the truth stated in the preceding verses is admitted, viz, that our union with Christ is such that his death secures our deliverance from the penalty and power of sin, *we believe we shall also live with him.* That is, we are sure that the consequences of his death are not merely negative, i.e. not simply deliverance from evil, moral and physical, but also a participation in his life. *To live with Christ,* therefore, includes two ideas, association with him, and similarity to him. We partake of his life, and consequently our life is like his. In like manner, since we die *with* him, we die *as* he died. So, too, when we are said *to reign with him, to be glorified together,* both these ideas, are included; see ch. 8:17, and many similar passages. The life here spoken of is that "eternal life" which believers are said to possess even in this world; see John 3:36. 5:24; and which is manifested here by devotion to God, and hereafter in the purity and blessedness of heaven. It includes, therefore, all the consequences of redemption.

(9) *Knowing that Christ, being raised from the dead, dieth no more.* The perpetuity of Christ's life is presented, 1. As the ground of assurance of the perpetuity of the life of believers. We shall partake of the life of Christ, i.e. of the spiritual and eternal blessings of redemption, because he ever lives to make intercession for us, and to grant us those supplies of grace which we need, see ch. 5:10. John 14:19. 1 Cor. 15:23, &c. &c. As death has no more dominion over him, there is no ground of apprehension that our supplies of life shall be cut off. This verse, therefore, is introduced as the ground of the declaration "we shall live with him," at the close of v. 8. 2. The perpetuity of the life of Christ is one of the points in which our life is to be conformed to his.

(10) *For in that he died, he died unto sin once,* &c. This verse is an amplification and explanation of the preceding. Christ's life is perpetual, inasmuch as his dying unto sin was for once only; but as

he lives, he lives for ever in the presence, and to the glory of God. It is evident that Christ's dying *unto sin* must be understood in a different sense from that in which we are said to die *unto sin*. The dative probably here, as so often elsewhere, expresses the ground or reason for which any thing is done; see on v. 2, 'He died on account of sin.' The phrase, therefore, is to be understood as those in Gal. 1:4. Rom. 4:25, &c. &c., where he is said to have died *for sin*, i.e. for its expiation and destruction. This sacrifice, unlike the impotent offerings under the law, was so efficacious that it never need be repeated; and therefore Christ, having once suffered death, is never again to be subject to its dominion, Heb. 9:28. 1 Pet. 3:18.

But in that he liveth, he liveth unto God. The structure of this sentence is antithetical, agreeably to Paul's manner, see ch. 5:10; and this accounts for the form of the expression *he liveth unto God,* which is opposed to the phrase *he died unto sin.* Christ lives to the glory of God and in communion with him. This is the second point in which our life is to be conformed to his. It is to be not only perpetual, i.e. without relapse into spiritual death, but also devoted to the service and enjoyment of God.

(11) This verse contains an inference from the preceding discussion, and an application of it to the case of Christians. If Christ has died for the destruction and expiation of sin, and if all who belong to him are united to him in his death so as to have their sins expiated and destroyed; and if, moreover, their head, in whom they live, has risen to a new and endless life of glory and holiness, then let Christians view their relation to Christ in its true light, and live accordingly.

Likewise reckon ye also yourselves as dead indeed, unto sin, &c. That is, regard yourselves as having died with Christ for deliverance from the guilt of sin, see vs. 5, 6, 8; and also for the destruction of its power, see vs. 6, 7. *But alive unto God.* Let believers consider themselves partakers not only of the death of Christ, but also of his life. As his life is perpetual and devoted unto God, so also must theirs be. *Through Jesus Christ our Lord.* It is through Christ that we die unto sin, and live unto God. It is not we that live, but Christ who liveth in us, Gal. 2:19. The words rendered *through Christ* may be more literally translated *in Christ,* i.e. it is in virtue of union with him that we die unto sin and live unto God.

DOCTRINES.

1. Truth cannot lead to unholiness. If a doctrine encourages sin it must be false, vs. 1, 2.

2. There can be no greater contradiction and absurdity than for one who lives in sin to claim to be a Christian, v. 2.

3. Antinomianism is not only an error, it is a falsehood and a slander. It pronounces valid the very objection against the gospel which Paul pronounces a contradiction and absurdity, and which he evidently regards as a fatal objection, were it well founded, vs. 2, 3, 4, &c.

4. Baptism includes a profession of the religion taught by him in whose name we are baptized, and an obligation to obey his laws, vs. 3, 4.

5. The grand design of Christianity is the destruction of sin. When sincerely embraced, therefore, it is with a view to this end, v. 3.

6. The source of the believer's holiness is his union with Christ, by which his reconciliation to God, and his participation of the influences of the Holy Spirit, are secured, vs. 4, 6.

7. The fact that Christ lives is sufficient security that his people shall live in holiness here, and in glory hereafter, v. 8.

8. The only proper evidence that we are the partakers of the benefits of the death and life of Christ, is our dying to sin and living to God, v. 11, and the whole section.

9. The gospel, which teaches the only true method of justification, is the only system which can secure the sanctification of men. This is not only the doctrine of this section, but it is the leading truth of this and the following chapter.

REMARKS.

1. As the most prominent doctrinal truth of this passage is, that the death of Christ secures the destruction of sin wherever it secures its pardon, so the most obvious practical inference is, that it is vain to hope for the latter benefit, unless we labour for the full attainment of the former, vs. 2–11.

2. For a professing Christian to live in sin, is not only to give

positive evidence that he is not a real Christian, but it is to misrepresent and slander the gospel of the grace of God, to the dishonour of religion and the injury of the souls of men, vs. 2–11.

3. Instead of holiness being in order to pardon, pardon is in order to holiness. This is the mystery of evangelical morals, v. 4, &c.

4. The only effectual method of gaining the victory over our sins, is to live in communion with Jesus Christ; to regard his death as securing the pardon of sin, as restoring us to the divine favour, and as procuring for us the influences of the Holy Spirit. It is those who thus look to Christ, not only for pardon but holiness, that are successful in subduing sin; while the *legalist* remains its slave, vs. 6, 8.

5. It is a consolation to the believer to know that, if he has the evidence of being *now* a Christian, he may be sure that he shall live with Christ. As long and as surely as the head lives, so long and so surely must all the members live, v. 8, &c.

6. To be in Christ is the source of the Christian's life; to be like Christ is the sum of his excellence; and to be with Christ is the fulness of his joy, vs. 2–11.

III

CONFERENCE PAPERS

One of the tasks which Charles Hodge inherited when he became the senior professor at Princeton Seminary was leadership of the Sunday afternoon "conference." From the beginning of the seminary's history, the faculty and students had gathered at that time for discussion of designated biblical passages with the aim of increasing not academic expertise, but personal piety. Students and faculty both contributed to these sessions, although as time went on and the faculty grew in size, the professors tended to dominate the meetings. Alexander's effectiveness in this kind of devotional exercise was legendary, but Hodge too gained a reputation as a searching prober of hearts. His son has left a full record of the meetings which Hodge led:

> As he sat in the Conference he spoke freely, without paper, in language and with illustration spontaneously suggested at the moment. To the hearer the entire exercise appeared extemporaneous. The *matter* presented was a clear analysis of the scriptural passage, or theme, doctrinal or practical, chosen for the occasion. . . . As to the *manner* the entire discourse was in the highest degree earnest, fervent and tender to tears; full of conviction and full of love. While the temporary impressions made upon most hearers was less remarkable than that produced by Dr. Alexander, in his happiest moods, all the students, and especially those who were diligent in taking notes, felt that they took

away with them from Dr. Hodge a far larger mass of coherent thought for permanent use.[1]

One of the reasons for Hodge's mastery of this form was revealed after his death when the family discovered a full sheaf of outlines which Hodge had prepared ahead of time for these sessions. He
apparently wrote a new outline for each Sunday, even where a passage or theme was being repeated. A. A. Hodge gathered up 249 of
these expanded outlines for publication in 1879. Like the presentations in *The Way of Life* and the more formal biblical commentaries,
these outlines reveal once more Hodge's commitment to the idea that
the finest spirituality emerged from the sincerest attention to the
Scriptures. The following outlines, which are among those speaking
most directly to Christian devotion, are taken from *Conference Papers* (New York: Charles Scribner's Sons, 1879), pp. 219–21, 25–
26, 298–99, 177–79, 61–62, 291–92, 58, 197–99, 152–53, 27–29,
242–43, 346–48, 356–58, 372–73. A. A. Hodge had presented these
outlines in thematic arrangement, but here they are ordered by date
of presentation.

THE LOVE OF CHRIST CONSTRAINETH US. 2 COR. 5: 14.

[*May 4th*, 1850.]
(Last conference of the session.)

Unity belongs to all the works of God. This is seen in our solar
system, and in the universe. It is also seen in the constitution of man.
Diversity is reduced to unity. so in character. No man becomes great
or successful, who has not one object, and one constraining motive.
So with the Christian. There is, and must be, something to give unity
to the character as Christian. This is the love of Christ as the constraining motive, and the glory of Christ as the one object. It is this
that gives simplicity, strength, and consistency to the Christian. It is
the want of this that leaves him driven about by every wave and
wind.

---

1. A. A. Hodge, ''Preface'' to Charles Hodge, *Conference Papers* (New
York: Charles Scribner's Sons, 1879), p. xi.

It is not enough to look forward to doing good, promoting knowledge, religion, and the happiness of men, and being governed by this and that motive. This leaves all vague, indefinite, and changing. We must have one definite object, and one constraining motive. Both are here presented.

I. *The love of Christ is the constraining influence.* The "love of Christ" is his love to us. (*a.*) Because this is the common sense. (*b.*) Because it is that love which is illustrated by his dying for us. (*c.*) Because he is so often spoken of as loving us.

"Constraineth us." The word means to restrain, to have in one's power. This is the sense here. The love of Christ takes possession of us, of all our faculties, of our thoughts, affections and powers. It masters and controls us. How inconceivable the blessedness of those thus possessed. It elevates them; it fills them with courage, patience and power. If we have this we need naught else for our happiness or usefulness.

This love of Christ is 1. The love of Jesus, of God manifested in the flesh. It is of great importance to have God thus brought near to us. 2. It is not general benevolence, nor is it philanthropy. It is the love of a person to particular persons. "He loved *me*," said the apostle. There is as much difference between general benevolence and personal love as between the diffused rays of the sun and those rays concentrated in a focus. 3. This love is sovereign, not founded on our merit. He loved us when enemies, when ungodly, when lying in our blood. 4. It is infinitely great. It led to the eternal Son of God dying for us. 5. This love is unchanging. A woman may forget her infant, but Christ's love never fails. 6. This love is tender, considerate, sympathizing, ἐχτρξφειν (to bring up), χαι θαλπειν (to foster), its objects. Go out under the conviction that you are the objects of this love. Let it exert its full influence upon you.

Why has it this power? Because, 1. His death is our death. His love constrains us, because we are convinced that when he died we all died. And the effect of this persuasion that we are the objects of his love, makes us conscious that his death is ours. There are two senses in which this is true. His death avails for all the ends which our death could have accomplished. It satisfies justice, frees from the penalty of the law, honors God, and promotes the good of the universe. Let a man feel this, and he will feel the effect of the love of Christ in dying for us. But, secondly, we died with Christ analogically. As he died to sin, so do we. We renounce it, become free from its power. This is the first reason of the power of the love of Christ, as dying for us, it secures our dying to sin.

2. The second is, that we live not for ourselves, but for him who died for us, and rose again. This, then, is the one object for which the Christian lives, (1.) Not for himself, not that he may be happy, not that he may promote the welfare of others, but,

(2.) That he may glorify Christ.

How is this to be done? 1. By making it the definite object of our lives. 2. By entire subjection to his will. 3. By adherence to his truth. 4. By devotion to his service, *i.e.,* by striving to bring men to know, to love, to worship, and to obey Christ. So far as we accomplish this end, we accomplish all other good ends. Two things you should carry with you everywhere, and to the end of life.

1. That the conviction of the love of Christ, the sense of his love, its greatness and freeness, should fill you and govern you. 2. That the single object of life is thus to cause him to be glorified. Do this and you will be blessed, and a blessing, go where you will, and suffer what you may.

THE ADVENT.

[*December 24th*, 1854.]

The redemption of the world by Jesus Christ is the middle point in the history, not of our race only, but of the universe.

Reasons for believing this.

1. The nature of the event.

2. The declaration of the Scriptures that through the Church is the glory of God to be especially manifested. Hence follows the obligation of regarding this event as of all others the most important to be remembered.

The reasons why we should thus remember it and cherish a fixed sentiment of gratitude for this manifestation of love, are

I. *The infinite condescension and love which it displays;* the exaltation of the Son of God; and the depth to which he humbled himself in becoming man.

II. *From the benefits which we derive from it;* first, as individuals, and second, as a race.

First. As individuals. Under this head are 1. Pardon,—a deliverance from hell. 2. Holiness, or a deliverance from sin. 3. Reconciliation to God, or the enjoyment of his favor. Communion with him who is the infinite source of all good. 4. Exaltation; first as to our persons, in glory, dignity and excellence; and second as to honor and authority.

Second. As a race. Peace on earth and good will to men. Our world is redeemed. It is not to continue under the dominion of sin. It is not to remain the kingdom of darkness. Christ is to reign over the earth. Holiness, peace, happiness are to prevail universally. And in our redeemed race, exalted by union with the Son of God, is to be made the most wonderful exhibition of the glory of God.

Third. This is the third great reason why we should thus gratefully bear in mind the coming of God in the flesh. God is thereby to be honored in the highest degree, to all beings and to all ages. He is to be adored as the God of Redemption, even more than as Creator and Governor.

The two great duties which press upon every man who hears the gospel are, 1. To accept of Christ as his own Saviour, and 2. To make him known to others as the Saviour of men.

MEDITATION AS A MEANS OF GRACE.

[*Oct. 28th,* 1855.]

I. *What is meditation?*

It is the serious, prolonged, devout contemplation of divine things. 1. This is distinguished from mere intellectual examination or consideration. It has a different object. The object of the one is to understand, of the other to experience the power. 2. It is distinguished from casual devout thought and aspiration.

II. *It is a means of grace.* By means of grace is meant a divinely appointed instrumentality for promoting holiness in the soul. That meditation is such a means is proved, 1. From its being frequently enjoined in Scripture for this end. 2. From the example of the saints as recorded in Scripture. 3. From the experience of the people of God in all ages.

III. *Why is it thus salutary?*

1. Because God has appointed his truth as the great means of sanctification.

2. Because the truth, to produce its effect, must be present to the mind. "God is not in all his thoughts," it is said of the wicked. "Estranged from God," is the description of the ungodly.

3. The intimate relation between knowledge and feeling, between the cognition and recognition, the γνῶσιζ (knowing), and the ξπίγνωσιζ (acknowledgment) of divine truth.

4. Because all unholy feelings are subdued in the presence of God, unsound principles are corrected in the light of divine truth. We become conformed to the things with which we are familiar.

IV. *Subjects on which we should meditate, are, God,—his law,—his Son,—the plan of salvation,—our own state as sinners,—heaven, etc.*

V. *Difficulties in the way of this duty.*

1. The difficulty of continuous thought. 2. Preoccupation with other things. 3. Indisposition to holding communion with God. 4. Want of method and purpose.

VI. *Directions for the performance of the duty.*

1. Form the purpose to be faithful in its discharge, from a sense of duty and conviction of its importance.

2. Have a time and place sacred to the duty.

3. Connect it with prayer, not only in the formal sense of the word, but also as meaning converse with God. 4. Connect it with the reading of Scriptures. Meditate on the word. Read it slowly, with self-application, and pondering its import. 5. Cultivate the habit of controlling your thoughts. Do not let them be governed by accident or fortuitous association. Keep the rudder always in your hand. 6. Do not be discouraged by frequent failure; and do not suppose that the excitement of feeling is the measure of advantage. There may be much learned, and much strength gained when there is little emotion. 7. Consecrate the hours especially of social and public worship to this work. Let the mind be filled with God while in his house.

SPIRITUAL CONSOLATION.

[Feb. 17th, 1856.]

Man is a child of sorrow. Though possessed of numerous sources of enjoyment and much happiness, there is no man who has not to drink of the cup of sorrow. The sources of sorrow are numerous. 1. Bodily pain and infirmity. 2. Pressure of external circumstances, poverty, disappointment, loss of reputation, and of confidence of friends. 3. Bereavements. 4. Sin in others, more or less nearly connected with us. 5. Sin in ourselves. Its power and its effects on the conscience. Its effect on faith and hope, and therefore despondency and fear of reprobation or final condemnation. From all these sources, man is certain to be more or less affected.

There are three sources of consolation. 1. The world. 2. Satan, who comforts his children with false hopes, with unbelief, and with sinful pleasures, as the drunkard drowns his sorrows in the bowl.

3. The Holy Ghost. He is set forth in the Scriptures as the Comforter.

II. *The Holy Ghost as Comforter.* The word παράκλητοζ (paraclete) means indeed more than Comforter, but it includes that idea. It was when speaking of the sorrow of his disciples that Christ promised to send them the Holy Ghost.

1. The need of a divine comforter arises, first, from the insufficiency of man for himself. He has no adequate resource in himself of knowledge, holiness or happiness. He must go out of himself for all these forms of good. Secondly, from the insufficiency of the creature. The world can never give the good we need. The soul of man, formed for God, can only be holy or happy in communion with God.

2. The way in which the Holy Ghost acts as our Comforter is, therefore, first, by bringing us to God, as the overflowing source of all good. Christ has opened the way, but we have access only through or by the Holy Spirit. This is the first great work of the Spirit.

Secondly, it is by taking the things of Christ and showing them unto us. That is, by revealing to us the glory of the Son of God. He thus fills the soul with a new affection, causes it to overflow with such admiration and delight, in view of Christ, that all our sorrows are lost in that sea of joy. This is a matter of daily experience. A man has been sadly afflicted by the sense of evil, when the accession of a far greater good has caused him to forget his sorrow in his joy.

Thirdly, by revealing and applying the truth to the heart and conscience, and giving us faith to embrace and appropriate it. Thus the convinced sinner is consoled by a view of Christ as a sacrifice and priest, and by having faith given to embrace him. Thus the soul, harassed and discouraged by the power of sin, is comforted by the promise, "My grace is sufficient for thee." Thus those who are weighed down by outward afflictions are comforted by the Spirit enabling them to see that these afflictions will work out for them a far more exceeding and eternal weight of glory. This is often carried so far that the believer glories in infirmities. It can be made so great that the stake itself has no terror.

Fourthly, by giving the soul such views of heaven as to render all earthly things inconsiderable.

Fifthly, by shedding abroad the love of God in the heart, and testifying with our spirit that we are the children of God. Christ by his Spirit nourishes and cherishes, ἐκτρέφει καὶ θάλπει, (ektrephei kai thalpei) his people as a tender mother her infant, Eph. v:29.

III. *How to enjoy these consolations.*

1. We must not seek consolation elsewhere. If we turn to the world, God will leave us to the world. It is only by looking to the Spirit, we can enjoy the consolations of the Spirit.

2. We must be careful not to grieve the Holy Ghost, by whom we are sealed unto the day of Redemption.

THE MEMORY OF CHRIST AND THE REASON
WHY IT SHOULD BE CHERISHED.

[March 9th, 1856. Communion Sunday.]

Distance, absence and the past, form a dark region into which the eye cannot penetrate. Where are the Patriarchs, Adam, Enoch, Methuselah, Noah, Abraham, Moses, Isaiah, and all the prophets? Not absolutely forgotten because they are historical, but thought of as shadows, shades only.

There are three classes of persons hidden in the past. 1. Those who have lived and died as the leaves of the forest, and left no trace.

Such are the vast mass of men. 2. Those whose names are insepar-
ably connected with the history, and who can never be forgotten as
long as history is cultivated. 3. Those who not only have accomplished great things in their generation, but the effects of whose lives
and acts continue and determine the condition of the present generation. To this class belong all men who are the authors of great rev-
olutions and of permanent institutions, or of systems of doctrine or
of philosophy which consciously determine the opinions or conditions of succeeding ages. Such were the men of our Revolution, Mohammed, Luther, Calvin.

Christ constitutes a class by himself. He is not only an historical
personage, as Sesostris or Numa. He is not only the author of a system of doctrine embraced by one-third of the human family; not only
the founder of the Church, which determines the form of modern civilization, and therefore, in that sense, cannot be forgotten, as his
name is mentioned many millions of times every day, and in every
part of the world. All this is true, but all this is too little.

To remember is not merely to recall the past, as the object of
present knowledge. It is also to estimate, appreciate and duly consider. When we remember God, we remember our obligations, our
privileges, and the promises which were made to us. There is recognition of the truth, and an appreciation of the effect which it ought
to produce, which is implied and intended.

To remember Christ is therefore not merely to call to mind the
facts of his life; nor to acknowledge our obligations to him as the
teacher of the gospel and the founder of the Church, as Mussulmans
may remember Mohammed; but besides all this, it is to consider and
appreciate our present relation to him. It is to cherish the lively consciousness that he is our life. 1. Our deliverer from death, the judicial
death to which we were exposed, and from which we are preserved
only by him. We are to remember the hand which holds us up from
Hell every moment. A man floating on the ocean might as well forget
the plank which sustains him; or the man suspended over an abyss,
forget the rope which holds him up, as we, to forget Christ.

2. We are to remember, *i.e.*, be always mindful of the fact that
it is not we that live, but Christ that liveth in us; that all right
thoughts, all just purposes, all holy affections, all good acts, are the
product of his continued agency in our hearts. Shall the branch forget
the vine? The earth the sun?

3. We are to remember that he is the author of all happiness, of peace of conscience; the source of God's favor, of our access to God, of communion with him, of all temporal and social blessings, of security from our spiritual enemies by whom we are surrounded, principalities and powers. Can a man forget the source of all his present joys? Can he forget his food, the air he breathes, the light of heaven, the all-sustaining power in which he lives and moves and has his being? Neither can the believer forget Christ.

4. We live not only in the past and in the present, but also in the future. We have an eternity before us. Christ is our life, not only in having delivered us and in now sustaining us, but in being to us, *a.* The principle of eternal life. *b.* In being its object, *i.e.,* to know him, to be with him, to be like him, to be engaged in his service, fills all our future with light and glory.

We cannot look back without seeing Christ. We cannot look beneath, above, or around us in the present, but he fills the whole horizon. We cannot look forward but he is the effulgence which sheds its glory on our eternal career. To remember Christ, therefore, is all our duty, for it is to live on him, to live for him, and to live with him.

PRAYER AS A MEANS OF GRACE.

[*September* 18*th,* 1859.]

I. *What is prayer?*

It is not simply petition, but converse with God, including, therefore, 1. The expression of our feelings in view of his greatness and glory, *i.e.,* adoration. 2. The expression of our feelings in view of his goodness, *i.e.,* thanksgiving. 3. The expression of our feelings in view of our sins and sinfulness, *i.e.,* confession. 4. The expression of our feelings in view of our wants, *i.e.,* supplication. Of course this converse with God may be,

1st. Solemn and formal, in the use of articulate words and on set occasions, in the closet, family, or sanctuary.

2d. Occasional and ejaculatory, and thus constant, as the bubbling of a spring of living water.

3d. Or in the uttered aspirations and longings of the soul after God, like the constant ascent of the flame towards heaven.

II. *Prayer, or this converse with God, is a means of grace.*

1. It is not merely a means of spiritual improvement, nor a means of securing divine blessings, but one of the appointed means of supernatural, divine communications to the soul from God.

2. This, therefore, is not due to a law of nature, according to which we are assimilated to those with whom we converse, but to the fact that in prayer God communicates himself, reveals his glory and his love to the soul.

3. The Holy Ghost is the Spirit of prayer, in the sense, (*a.*) That he reveals those objects which call forth spiritual affections, viz., the glory of God, his love, the glory and love of Christ, the inexhaustible riches of the divine promises, our own sinfulness and necessities. (*b.*) That he not only presents these objects, but also awakens the appropriate feelings. (*c.*) That he leads us to clothe those feelings, those adoring, penitential, grateful or craving feelings, in appropriate language, or in groanings which cannot be uttered. Thus he maketh intercession for us. Thus he is our παράκλητσζ, (advocate). Prayer thus inspired is not only always answered in some way, and that the best, but it is also a means of grace. It is the occasion and the channel of infusing new measures of divine life into the soul. It is not therefore prayer as the mere uttering of words, nor prayer as the uttering of natural desires of affection, as when one prays for his own life or the life of those dear to him; but it is prayer as the real intercourse of the soul with God, by the Holy Ghost, that is, the Holy Ghost revealing truth, exciting feeling, and giving appropriate utterance.

III. *Our duty in the premises is,*

1. To remember that this intercourse with God is optional. We can gain access to him only when he pleases to admit us.

2. That as it is the life of the soul, we should most earnestly desire and diligently seek it.

3. That we must seek it in his appointed way, that is, through Christ and the Spirit.

4. That we must seek it on the occasions on which he is wont to grant it, in the closet, the family, and the sanctuary.

5. That we must not wait for it, so as to pray only when we feel

the spirit of prayer. We must go to his courts, knock at his door, bow before the oracle, and expect him in the use of his appointed means.

CHRIST OUR PHYSICIAN.

[*January 27th*, 1861.]

I. *We are all laboring under the malady of sin.*—This malady is, 1. Universal. 2. It pervades our whole nature. 3. It is attended by great suffering, degradation and loss of power. 4. It will issue, if not arrested, in eternal death.

II. *No man can cure himself.*—This is proved, 1. By consciousness. 2. By experience. All efforts at self-cure result in failure or self-deception, or, at best in mitigation of the symptoms.

III. *No man, or set of men can cure others.*—This has been attempted, 1. By educators. 2. By philosophers. 3. By ascetics. 4. By ritualists. The world is filled with charlatans or quack pretenders to the power of healing the disease of the soul.

IV. *Christ is the only physician.*

1. He secures the right of applying the only effectual remedy by propitiating the justice of God, and securing liberty of access to the soul for the Holy Spirit.

2. He sends that Spirit as the Spirit of life and strength. As the constitution is radically affected, a radical cure is necessary, and this can only be effected by a life-giving spirit.

3. This cure is a long and painful process. The soul is not at once restored to a state of perfect health. It must pursue a protracted course of regimen. It must submit to self-denial, and to the use of the prescribed remedies.

4. But if we submit to his directions, the cure is certain and permanent. It results in immortal vigor, beauty and strength; to the restoration of our nature to a far higher state than its original condition.

5. Christ is not only the only physician, and one able to heal with certainty all our maladies, but he is accessible to every one and at all times. It is not any one form of spiritual disease, or any one degree of it, but all forms and all degrees. Any one in the last stage

of spiritual death may come to him with the certainty of being received and cured. He demands no conditions. He asks no terms. He requires no preparation, and will receive no recompense.

6. He is not only thus infallible and thus accessible, but he is tender, patient and forbearing. He has all the attributes of a good physician in infinite perfection.

Inferences.

1. The duty of every one to apply to him for cure.
2. The one reason why we or any are not cured must be in us, not in him.
3. The duty of making this physician known to others.

YE ARE CHRIST'S. I COR. 3:23.

[*March 10th, 1861.*]

The two ideas of dependence and possession are here expressed. "We are Christ's," means that we are dependent on him, and also that we belong to him. In the preceding verse the apostle had said, "All things are yours;" that is, all things are designed and overruled to promote your welfare, and all things are comprehended in that dominion or kingdom to which you are destined. Still you are nothing, you belong to Christ.

In this is involved, 1. The denial that we are our own. We do not belong to ourselves, in the sense that our own advantage can be the legitimate end of our pursuit, or that our own will can be the legitimate rule of our conduct.

2. The denial that we belong to the world, to parents, friends, country, mankind, in either of the above senses; that the good of parents, friends, &c., can be the legitimate end, or their will the legitimate rule.

3. Nor do we thus belong to the Church. This could not have entered the apostle's mind. But in after years it became a common form of apostacy from Christ, and still is. Men feel that they belong to the Church, live for and are governed by it, and know no higher end, or rule of duty.

4. Positively, the declaration includes, that we are Christ's in such a sense that his glory is the end, and his will the rule of our life. He, and he alone, has the right to us. To him, and to him alone, is this devotion and submission due.

II. *The proprietorship is founded,*

1. Not specially on creation, for as creatures we belong to God, the Triune God, but,

2. It is founded on gift. We were given to him in the counsels of eternity. From the countless orders of creatures, and from the countless millions of the race of man, the people of Christ were given to him as a possession, as a peculium, a specialty, in which he was to have a peculiar and exclusive right. This ground of proprietorship is supreme. God as sovereign of the universe can give what he pleases, and his will is the only real and stable ground of property or possession.

3. It is founded on purchase. This gives, (*a.*) The right of property as founded on justice. (*b.*) The purchase involving redemption from infinite evil gives the higher and tenderer obligation of gratitude, and (*c.*) The price paid being his own precious blood, it gives the highest of all obligations, that of love.

4. It is founded on the right of conquest. We were the captives of Satan. Christ has destroyed his power, and delivered us who were led captive by him at his will.

This general idea of possession is illustrated in various ways in the Scriptures. 1. We are the δοῦλοι (servants) of Christ, which expresses the relation as founded in justice. We are bound as his δοῦλοι to live for him, and to obey him. Any failure in this devotion or obedience is a violation of our relation to him as his servants or slaves.

2. We, *i.e.*, the Church, are his bride. This includes (*a.*) The idea of exclusive possession. (*b.*) Of preference and peculiar love. (*c.*) Of perfect community of interest.

3. We are his φίλοι, (friends) bound to him by the bond of mutual love and confidence.

4. We are his body, the members of his body. Nothing is so intimately a man's own as his body. It has a common life with him. It has a common consciousness with him. The pains and pleasures of the body are our own pains and pleasures. It has a common interest and destiny with him. So if we are Christ's body, we are bound to

him in all these ways. This is nearer and higher than δοῦλοι, φίλοι, νύμφη (bride).

III. *The blessedness resulting from this relationship.*

1. Security. If we belong to Christ as his δοῦλοι, φίλοι, νύμφη and σῶμα (body), we are secure, here and hereafter, for time and eternity.

2. Participation in Christ's excellence, both as to soul and body; in his happiness, in his glory and dominion.

IV. *Duties.*

1. That we should always act worthily of this relation; remember that we belong neither to ourselves nor to the world, but only to the Lord.

2. Contentment. We may well be satisfied if we are Christ's; for if we are his, all things are ours.

3. Not merely contentment, but joyful anticipation of Christ's coming and glory.

LIVING BY FAITH.

[*Feb. 16th, 1862.*]

I. *What is faith?* There are two senses of the term which it is at least convenient to distinguish; a principle or state of mind, and an act. When it is defined as the evidence of things not seen, etc., or when used as antithetical to sight, it is the former. When are commanded to believe, it is an act which we are required to put forth. These two things run into each other. When we trust, we perform an act, and we call into exercise an abiding principle. So when we believe in God or Christ, it is not merely a transient act, but an abiding principle which is called into exercise.

II. *Living by faith.*

Life includes all our activity as rational, moral and religious beings. Living by faith is to have our whole activity, inward and outward, permanently and characteristically determined by faith. It matters not whether we take this to mean by the objects of faith, or by the principle of faith. For the conscious exercise of the principle is on the objects.

All the things which call forth, regulate and determine our activity, our acts inward and outward, may be divided into two classes: objects of sight and objects of faith. The former includes all that we know of ourselves, *i.e.,* the knowledge of which we attain by the exercise of our own powers, and the conviction of the reality and truth of which rests on sense or reason; the latter includes all we know, only because it has been supernaturally revealed to us, and our conviction of whose truth and reality rests on the authority of God.

It is true that these two classes of objects are not entirely distinct. They overlap each other. There are some things which we know of ourselves which God has revealed. So that the same object may be an object of faith, and an object of knowledge. But, 1. This is true only of some of the objects of faith. 2. What is known is only imperfectly known, compared to what is revealed.

III. The real practical conviction which controls the life is not that which rests on knowledge, but that which rests on testimony.

Under the head of the objects of sight, therefore, fall, 1. All the objects of sense, all things material. 2. All the truths of science. 3. All the truths of philosophy. The negative fact with regard to Christians is, that their life is not determined and controlled by this class of objects. They are not the supreme objects of their attention, desire or pursuit. Under the head of objects of faith fall all those truths which have been supernaturally revealed. The are called in Scripture the things not seen, the things of God, the things of the Spirit. They embrace all the great truths of Theology, Anthropology, Soteriology, Eschatology, which are presented in the Scriptures, and our knowledge and conviction of which rests on the testimony of God. That testimony is not merely objective, not external as by human inspired lips, nor by miracles, but inwardly by the Spirit, which reveals the nature as well as the reality of these truths. Hence these things do and must control the life of the believer. They have a governing power over him. They command his attention, his affections, and they call forth his efforts.

This is the comprehensive sense of a life of faith. And we are commanded thus to live, and to do this we must, 1. Abstract ourselves from all undue, abnormal converse with the things of sight. We must not devote ourselves to them beyond what is necessary or what is due to their real, though subordinate importance. 2. We must keep our minds and hearts in contact with things unseen, the objects of faith, that they may exert their due influence on us. 3. Seek by prayer and the use of all appointed means the aid and fellowship of God's Spirit.

The Scriptures, however, speak of living by faith in another sense. We are said to live by faith of the Son of God. This means that our whole religious life is sustained, guided and controlled by faith in the Lord Jesus. That is, by believing what the Scriptures have revealed, 1. concerning his person; 2. concerning his relation to us; 3. concerning his work for us. This is the form under which, and the means by which the more general life of faith is maintained. It is vain to be religious in the general, to have faith in the general truths of Scripture, unless we have this specific life of faith in Christ. He is our life.

When a blind man is led by the hand, he walks by faith, not by sight. This is not a less safe mode of walking, not a less confident one, but it is a blind, dependent one. So a man is who is guided in a strange land. Thus the believer who is led by the hand of God into the knowledge of truth, the way of duty, the journey of life, and the path to heaven. He submits to be blindly led.

IMMANUEL.

[*Nov. 9th,* 1862.]

The names of persons in ancient times, and especially among the people of God, were significant. When given by the parents they were expressive of what they the parents designed either to symbolize or to commemorate. When given by God, they were a mode of revelation. God's giving of the Son of the virgin the name Immanuel, was a revelation of the fact that God was to be with us.

I. *The sense in which God is said to be with his people, or with man.* 1. It expresses the general sense of nearness. God is, of course, every where, but he is said to be where he especially manifests himself as present. He is not far from any one of us, for in him we live, and move, and have our being. This kind of nearness is common to all creatures, and especially to all rational creatures.

2. It expresses the general sense of favor and assistance. When we say, "The Lord be with you," we pray that he would aid and

sustain those whom we address. The Psalmist says of the Lord, "He is at my right hand, I shall not be moved," Ps. 10:8. This name of the Messiah was therefore a promise that God would be with us in the sense of showing us his favor. What the angels afterward announced, "Peace on earth and good will to men," was foretold in this prophetic designation.

All the ways and senses in which God for Christ's sake is said to be with us or favorable to us, it would be impossible to state. *a.* He is reconciled to us by the death of his Son. Christ has brought us to God. *b.* We are not only reconciled so far as his justice is concerned, but we are the objects of his love. *c.* He is everywhere present by his Spirit to aid, counsel and comfort. *d.* His providence is ever over us and watchful. The Lord is with us, at our right hand, around about us, near as a light, as protection, as strength, as consolation, as the infinite portion of the soul.

3. God with us, expresses that union which is effected by the incarnation; for it was because of the miraculous birth of this infant, more fully explained by the annunciation of the angel to the Virgin Mary, that the Holy Thing that was to be born of her was the Son of God. It was because the human and the divine natures were to be united in one person in that child that he was to be called Immanuel.

This union brought God and man into the most intimate fellowship in the person of Christ. But it did not stop there. It brought God into a relation to man such as he sustains to no other creature. *a.* It is such a relation that a divine person can say, we are one, *i.e.,* of one nature. *b.* That he can call us brethren. *c.* That he can sympathize with us. *d.* That what is done to us is done to him. *e.* That he lifts our nature above that of the angels. *f.* That he forever remains in this relation, filial, fraternal, conjugal, with his people.

4. God with us, means that he dwelleth with us and is in us; πὰρ ὑμῖν μένει καὶ ἐν ἐσται. Jn. xiv. 17. In virtue of the incarnation as a preliminary condition, and of the indwelling of the Spirit, Christ lives in his people. That is, he is the source of their spiritual life. The thoughts, feelings and actions which belong to that life are due to this peculiar relation between him and us. He is with us intimately, perpetually and everlastingly. It is a union nearer, dearer, and more lasting than any other.

Our great duty therefore is, 1. To live worthily of that union ourselves. 2. To endeavor to bring others to enjoy its blessings.

Consult the following passages and mediate upon them:—

"The Lord of hosts is with us." Ps. xlvi. 7.

"My faithfulness and my mercy shall be with him." Ps. lxxxix. 24.

"As I was with Moses, so I will be with thee." Josh. i.:5.

"Be not afraid, neither be thou dismayed; for the Lord thy God is with thee whithersoever thou goest." Josh. 1.:9.

"When thou passest through the waters I will be with thee." Isaiah xliii.2.

AND HE THAT TAKETH NOT HIS CROSS,
AND FOLLOWETH NOT AFTER ME,
IS NOT WORTHY OF ME. MATT. 10:38.

[Sept. 25th, 1864.]

There are two modes of presentation, as to the method and conditions of salvation, running through the Bible, the one representing the attainment of eternal life as easy, the other representing it as difficult. At one time we are told that "he that believeth and is baptized shall be saved;" and that whosoever confesses Christ before men, will also be confessed by him before his Father which is in heaven. We are not required to ascend to heaven, or go down to hell, but simply to believe with the heart and confess with the lips, that God has raised up Jesus from the dead. "Whosoever shall call on the name of the Lord, shall be saved." This is illustrated in many cases besides that of the dying thief. It is vastly important. We need a method of salvation, in which, in one sense, we have nothing to do. We cannot atone for our sins; we cannot merit eternal life; we cannot change our own heart. We have a Saviour who has done all things for us. All that is required, in this view of the case, is that we should be willing to be saved. We are the recipients and subjects, and not the agents of salvation. On the other hand, however, we are told that the righteous are scarcely saved. We are commanded to work out our salvation with fear and trembling; to strive to enter in at the strait gate; that many shall seek to enter in, and not be able. We are to crucify the flesh, to overcome the world, to resist the devices of Satan. We are laborers, soldiers, wrestlers, runners in a doubtful race.

These two modes of representation are of course consistent. The one regards the work of Christ, and its appropriation by us; the other concerns our acting consistently with the new relation into which we are brought to God. It may be easy to obtain adoption into a family, and difficult to live accordingly. It may be easy to have the eyes opened, the withered arm restored, but difficult to use those renovated members agreeably to the will of God. It is easy, in one sense, to believe; but to live a life of faith, to live so as to prove that our faith is genuine, may be a difficult task.

1. One of the conditions of salvation, that is, one of those things which we must do in order to prove that we truly believe, and belong to Christ, and which all who do believe will strive to do, is to live a holy life. That is, we are to avoid all sin, to exercise all right affections toward God and our fellow-men, and to be devoted to his glory and service.

2. Another thing is, to be willing to suffer for Christ. The cross is the emblem of suffering. To bear the cross is to endure suffering. The context shows that this is the meaning of the Lord in this place.

3. Another thing is, that we must love Christ more than any other object; more than our lives. And, therefore, if the sundering of all earthly ties be necessary to the service of Christ, we must be ready to submit to the sacrifice.

These are difficult conditions to fulfill; but, 1. They are essential. 2. They are reasonable. Nothing is required but what we ought to be gladly willing to perform. The difficulty arises not from the nature of the work so much as from our own state. If we were what we should be, if we were filled with faith and love, we should find all this easy. The early Christians did not find it hard to submit to the spoiling of their goods; they suffered it joyfully. Paul did not find it difficult to preach, to labor, to suffer. He rejoiced in all that he was called upon to do and to suffer in the cause of Christ.

Now this is illustrated and confirmed by the whole history of the Church, in its martyrs, confessors, missionaries, etc. They have been the happiest men on earth. We should bear in mind, then.

1. That we must be willing to suffer for Christ, and to renounce all things for him.

2. That those who do this are sustained in doing it. They receive in this world even a hundred-fold. Christ's heaviest burden is made light.

3. That these light afflictions are not worthy to be compared with the glory which shall be revealed in us.

4. That to refuse to suffer for Christ, to prefer father or mother, brothers or sisters, houses or land to him, involves the forfeiture of this life, and of the life that is to come.

His cross. Each man has his own cross. One has that form of trial referred to in the context; another, sickness, feebleness of body; another, poverty; another, want of success; another, reproach, another, insignificance. In any case we must bear our burden cheerfully, looking unto Christ as our example, our helper and our reward.

SO TEACH US TO NUMBER OUR DAYS
THAT WE MAY APPLY OUR HEARTS UNTO WISDOM.
PS. 90:12 (NO. 2.)

[*Jan. 12th,* 1868.]

There is a remarkable difference as to this verse in the versions. The Septuagint assumes a different reading: "Cause me to know thy right hand and those cordially, or in heart, instructed in wisdom." So the Vulgate. Luther's version: "Let us remember that we must die, in order that we may be wise." De Wette: "Teach us to number our days, that we may attain a wise heart." Young: "To number our days aright, let us know; and we bring the heart to wisdom." Alexander: "The number of our days let us know, and we will bring a heart of wisdom." Our version gives the true idea; a proper estimate of life tends to wisdom.

Life is short and uncertain. To act as though it were indefinitely long, or as though the possession of it was secure, is folly. This is a folly of which most men are guilty, and to which all men are exposed. We are ourselves sensible how little we lay to heart the brevity and uncertainty of life. How much we live as though we should live always. At twenty or thirty we live and feel as to life's continuance as we did at ten or fifteen. At fifty or seventy, it is all the same. We live in the present, and the present is as real at one age as at another. It requires an effort, therefore, to bring this truth home to our minds, so that it shall really affect and control our lives.

This is difficult from the nature of the case. Duration is equable.

There is nothing in time itself to mark the transition from one moment to another. The same is true of motion.

Nothing indicates the passage from one portion of space to another, but passing by some fixed object. Thus men feel in a balloon or on the ocean. Motion is noticed if the ship moves faster than the water; but not if it is only carried forward by a current. We are not sensible of the motion of the earth through space. Thus we are insensible to the flight of time. We have reason to pray that God would impress us with a sense of its rapidity, its brevity, its uncertainty. The reason in this matter must control the feelings.

There are two measures of time,—days, months and years being one, and events the other. A portion of time in which nothing specially important has occurred, may be as long as that which has determined the fate of an individual or of nations. What three years of the world's history can compare with those of our Lord's ministry? How far more important the first fifty years of the Church than the centuries that followed. How vast the consequences of the events of the Reformation period. How has the state of our country been changed by the four years of war just ended. How has the state of Europe been changed by the six weeks' campaign of the Prussian army.

So with the individual. If he is called upon to number his days he will estimate them not by hours, but by events. The years of his conversion, of his call to the ministry, of his ordination, of his entering into some special field of labor. One year may contain more to think of, more that moulds his destiny than all the other years of his life. The year a man yields to temptation may decide his fate for eternity.

The first lesson this teaches us is, the unspeakable value of time. In time we determine our eternal state. In time we do all we are ever to do for the good of others, or for our own advancement in good, or for the glory of God. This is our day for work. After this the night cometh when no man can work.

The second lesson is humility and penitential sorrow that our time has run so much to waste. What have we done? What progress in knowledge? Have we increased in piety? What have we accomplished for the Church or for the world? No man can make this review of life without being deeply sensible how greatly he has sinned; how he has wasted or allowed to lie unimproved this great talent of time which God has committed to our hearts. Regret is unavailing. Lost time and opportunity cannot be recalled.

The third lesson is that we should be brought to the solemn determination to make the most of the few days that remain. They must be few. They may be almost gone. Therefore let us apply our hearts unto wisdom. Let us be wise, wise in improving to the utmost our remaining days in living nearer to God, praying more, holding more constant intercourse with God our Saviour, in studying more, in laboring more for the good of others, for the progress of truth and holiness among men.

Fourth lesson: Gratitude to God for his forbearance and his abounding mercy to us, unprofitable servants.

O DEATH, WHERE IS THY STING?
O GRAVE, WHERE IS THY VICTORY?—I COR. 15:56.

[*April 11th, 1875.*]

Death is the king of terrors. The event of all others the most to be dreaded, and even to irrational animals an object of dread. As the love of life is natural and instinctive, so is the fear of death. It is, however, not only instinctive, it is rational. (*a.*) It is the end of the only kind of existence of which we have any consciousness or experience. To the eye of sense, it is annihilation. The dead, to all appearances, are as non-existent as the unborn. Where are the generations of the past?

(*b.*) It is the loss of all our possessions, of all sources of enjoyment to which we have been accustomed. It is the sundering of all social ties, a final separation of parents and children, &c.

(*c.*) Though to the eye of sense death is annihilation, it is not so to the eye of reason or of conscience. Such is the intellectual and moral nature of man, that all men have the apprehension or conviction of a state of conscious existence after death. But what that state is, human reason cannot tell. It is Hades. The torch of Science and the lamp of Philosophy are extinguished in the mephitic exhalations of the grave. The soul at death enters upon the unknown, the dark, the boundless, the endless.

(*d.*) These, however, are not the considerations which render death so terrible. The sting of death is sin. We should have no fear. Knowing that God is everywhere, we should know that we should be safe and blessed within the arms of his love wherever he might see fit to carry us. Sin, of necessity, involves guilt, and guilt is a fearful looking for of judgment. As there is in our physical frame a capacity for suffering of which we seldom think, so there is a capacity for a degree of fear of the wrath of God of which we know but little. All men, however, know enough of pain to know how terrible it may be; so all men know enough of guilt to know that an awakened conscience may create a hell in a man's own bosom. Paul says of the heathen that they know the righteous judgment of God, &c.

It is because men know that after death there is the judgment, that all their life-time, through fear of death, they are subject to bondage. To the guilty, therefore, death is, must be, and ought to be, the king of terrors.

There are men so stupid that they die as the ox dies. There are others so reckless that they fear not to challenge God to do his worst. Multitudes are in such a state of lethargy at the approach of death that they have no apprehension. These facts do not alter the case. It remains true that for a sinner unreconciled to God, death is the most dreadful of all events, and is so regarded just in proportion as the soul is duly enlightened.

The only possible way to deprive death of its terrors is freedom from sin. But the strength of sin is the law, and the law is the nature of God, and is therefore immutable and inexorable. The law says: "Cursed is every one that continueth not in all things which are written in the book of the law to do them;" and "The soul that sinneth, it shall die." "The wages of sin is death." The demands of God's law, which are the demands of God's nature, *i.e.,* of reason and right, must be satisfied. How is this to be done? To this object the efforts of men have been directed, by sacrifices, by asceticism, by self-discipline. To this end men still direct their efforts when awakened. They fast, they pray, they strive to subdue the evil passions; but all in vain.

Thanks be to God, who gives us the victory through our Lord Jesus Christ. He has done what we could not do. He has fulfilled the demands of the law, preceptive and penal. He has borne our sins; he was made a curse. God can now be just, and yet justify the ungodly.

Those who trust in him are pardoned. Their guilt is removed. They are reconciled to God. Their normal relation to him is restored; and, as a consequence, they are transformed into his image. They are congenial with him. Wherever he is, "the nearer to him, the more blessed." Death to the individual believer is a messenger of grace, an angel sent to bear him nearer to God. Thus the believer can say: "O death, where is thy sting?"

The Scriptures reveal to us that the state on which we enter at death is one of holiness and conscious happiness. Paul in this chapter takes a wider range. Ever since the creation there has been a conflict over the human race between good and evil, sin and grace, Satan and Christ. Satan apparently triumphed. The race fell under guilt and condemnation. Death reigned over soul and body. Death and the grave were for the time victorious. But Christ assumed our nature. He fulfilled the law. He delivered the soul from the curse and power of sin. He rescued the body from corruption. And when his word is accomplished, all the ransomed saved, and their bodies raised in glory, then will be heard the shout of Cherubim and Seraphim: "O death, where is thy sting?"

Therefore, 1. Believe in Christ. 2. Consecrate yourselves to him. 3. Strive to save your fellow-men.

THE VERY LAST.

THE ADMINISTRATION OF THE LORD'S SUPPER
TO THE GRADUATING CLASS.

[*April* 21*st*, 1878.]

I. Read the Scriptures relating to it.
II. Nature and Design.
1. A Commemoration.
2. A Communion.
3. A Consecration by Covenant.
I. *Commemoration.*

Includes (1.) Administration. This, in the present instance, rises to adoration; not simply adoration, but the peculiar form of it due to God in fashion of a man. Not only does he possess all divine perfection, the ἀπαυγατμα of the Father's glory, but he is also clothed with the perfection and loveliness of humanity. It is this that makes the central point of the universe to whom all eyes are turned.

(2.) Gratitude. *First,* the benefits. Deliverance (*a.*) from hell, (*b.*) power of Satan (*c.*) and sin, (*d.*) restoration to the favor and fellowship of God, (*e.*) fellowship with Christ, including participation with his life and glory. *Second,* the cost at which these benefits were secured. Christ's humiliation and suffering.

II. *A Communion.* (1.) An act and means of participation. We participate in his body and blood, *i.e.,* of their sacrificial virtue. (2.) The effect of this makes us (*a.*) one with him, (*b.*) one body.

Illustration from the Jewish rites. Participation at the altar made a man a Jew—a partaker of the benefits of the Theocracy. So participation of the heathen sacrifices effected a union with the objects of worship.

In this ordinance our union with Christ and with each other is far more intimate.

III. *Consecration.*

We cannot commemorate Christ as our Saviour without thereby acknowledging ourselves to be his, the purchase of his blood and devoted to his service.

IV

SYSTEMATIC THEOLOGY

Charles Hodge's reputation today rests mainly on his three-volume *Systematic Theology*. This is unfortunate in many ways, for in his own lifetime systematic theological construction gave way before polemics, biblical commentary, and the kind of devotional writing that appeared in *The Way of Life*. The systematics is at once more detached and less compelling than much of the writing that now lies buried in the pages of the *Princeton Review*. Nonetheless, it is a significant work which set out for all to see the "grounds," as Hodge would have put it with one of his favorite words, for the polemical and devotional concerns of his career.[1]

The *Systematic Theology* is also important for a book on Hodge's spiritual vision because it once again stated his belief in the bond between truth and life. The abstract discussion of theological method with which the volumes begin is more extensive than that found elsewhere, and the concentration on the life of faith more diffuse. Yet even in the academic presentations of this work Hodge regularly pauses to draw the connections between truth and life which he had earlier expounded in several other ways. One of the clearest passages of this kind comes at the end of the first chapter, where Hodge summarizes his commitment to the inductive method, to the Bible as the source for the theologian's facts, and to the active work

---

1. For an overview of this work, see David F. Wells, "The Stout and Persistent 'Theology' of Charles Hodge," *Christianity Today* (Aug. 30, 1974): pp. 10–15.

of the Holy Spirit. The cohesion of his argument may not be as forceful as in *The Way of Life,* but at the end of his long career Hodge still was defending the link between knowledge and faith. There is a touch of irony in this passage as well, for Hodge, who had so fiercely combatted E. A. Park's suggestion that there may be a theology of the feelings that differs from a theology of the intellect, now is willing to conceded that an individual may indeed hold two theologies, "one of the intellect, and another of the heart."

The following is from *Systematic Theology,* 3 vols. (New York: Charles Scribner's Sons, 1872–1873), I, 13–17.

PRINCIPLES TO BE DEDUCED FROM FACTS.

In theology as in natural science, principles are derived from facts, and not impressed upon them. The properties of matter, the laws of motion, of magnetism, of light, etc., are not framed by the mind. They are not laws of thought. They are deductions from facts. The investigator sees, or ascertains by observation, what are the laws which determine material phenomena; he does not invent those laws. His speculations on matters of science unless sustained by facts, are worthless. It is no less unscientific for the theologian to assume a theory as to the nature of virtue, of sin, of liberty, of moral obligation, and then explain the facts of Scripture in accordance with his theories. His only proper course is to derive his theory of virtue, of sin, of liberty, of obligation, from the facts of the Bible. He should remember that his business is not to set forth his system of truth (that is of no account), but to ascertain and exhibit what is God's system, which is a matter of the greatest moment. If he cannot believe what the facts of the Bible assume to be true, let him say so. Let the sacred writers have their doctrine, while he has his own. To this ground a large class of modern exegetes and theologians, after a long struggle, have actually come. They give what they regard as the doctrines of the Old Testament; then those of the Evangelists; then those of the Apostles; and then their own. This is fair. So long, however, as the binding authority of Scripture is acknowledged, the temptation is very strong to press the facts of the Bible in accordance with our preconceived theories. If a man be persuaded that certainty in acting is inconsistent with liberty of action; that a free agent can always act contrary to any amount of influence (not destructive of his liberty) brought to bear upon him, he will inevitably deny that the Scriptures teach the contrary, and thus be forced to explain away all facts which prove the absolute control of God over the will and volitions of men. If he hold that sinfulness can be predicated only of intelligent, voluntary action in contravention of law, he must deny that men are born in sin, let the Bible teach what it may. If he believes that ability limits obligation, he must believe independently of the Scriptures, or in opposition to them, it matters not which, that men are able to repent, believe, love God perfectly, to live without sin, at any, and all times, without the least assistance from the Spirit of God. If he deny that the innocent may justly suffer penal evil for the guilty, he must deny that Christ bore our sins. If he deny that the merit of one man can be the judicial ground of the pardon and salvation of other men, he must reject the Scriptural doctrine of justification. It is plain that complete havoc must be made of the whole system of revealed truth, unless we consent to derive our philosophy from the Bible, instead of explaining the Bible by our philosophy. If the Scriptures teach that sin is hereditary, we must adopt a theory of sin suited to that fact. If they teach that men cannot repent, believe, or do anything spiritually good, without the supernatural aid of the Holy Spirit, we must make our theory of moral obligation accord with that fact. If the Bible teaches that we bear the guilt of Adam's first sin, that Christ bore our guilt, and endured the penalty of the law in our stead, these are facts with which we must make our principles agree. It would be easy to show that in every department of theology,—in regard to the nature of God, his relation to the world, the plan of salvation, the person and work of Christ, the nature of sin, the operations of divine grace, men, instead of taking the facts of the Bible, and seeing what principles they imply, what philosophy underlies them, have adopted their philosophy independently of the Bible, to which the facts of the Bible are made to bend. This is utterly unphilosophical. It is the fundamental principle of all sciences, and of theology among the rest, that theory is to be determined by facts, and not facts by theory. As natural science was a chaos until the principle of induction was admitted and faithfully carried out, so theology is a jumble of human speculations, not worth a straw, when men refuse to apply the same principle to the study of the Word of God.

This is perfectly consistent, on the one hand, with the admission of intuitive truths, both intellectual and moral, due to our constitution and rational and moral beings; and, on the other hand, with the controlling power over our beliefs exercised by the inward teachings of the Spirit, or, in other words, by our religious experience. And that for two reasons: First, All truth must be consistent. God cannot contradict himself. He cannot force us by the constitution of the nature which He has given us to believe one thing, and in his Word command us to believe the opposite. And, second, All the truths taught by the constitution of our nature or by religious experience, are recognized and authenticated in the Scriptures. This is a safeguard and a limit. We cannot assume this or that principle to be intuitively true, or this or that conclusion to be demonstrably certain, and make them a standard to which the Bible must conform. What is self-evidently true, must be proved to be so, and is always recognized in the Bible as true. Whole systems of theologies are founded upon intuitions, so called, and if every man is at liberty to exalt his own intuitions, as men are accustomed to call their strong convictions, we should have as many theologies in the world as there are thinkers. The same remark is applicable to religious experience. There is no form of conviction more intimate and irresistible than that which arises from the inward teaching of the Spirit. All saving faith rests on his testimony or demonstrations (1 Cor. ii. 4). Believers have an unction from the Holy One, and they know the truth, and that no lie (or false doctrine) is of the truth. This inward teaching produces a conviction which no sophistries can obscure, and no arguments can shake. It is founded on consciousness, and you might as well argue a man out of a belief of his existence, as out of confidence that what he is thus taught of God is true. Two things, however, are to be borne in mind. First, That this inward teaching or demonstration of the Spirit is confined to truths objectively revealed in the Scriptures. It is given, says the Apostle, in order that we may know things gratuitiously given, *i.e.*, revealed to us by God in his Word (1 Cor. ii. 10–16). It is not, therefore, a revelation of new truths, but an illumination of the mind, so that it apprehends the truth, excellence, and glory of things already revealed. And second, This experience is depicted in the Word of God. The Bible gives us not only the facts concerning God, and Christ, ourselves, and our relations to our Maker and Redeemer, but also records the legitimate effects of those truths on the minds of believers. So that we cannot appeal to our own feelings or inward experience, as a ground or guide, unless we can show that it agrees with the experience of holy men as recorded in the Scriptures.

THE TEACHING OF THE SPIRIT.

Although the inward teaching of the Spirit, or religious experience, is no substitute for an external revelation, and is no part of the rule of faith, it is, nevertheless, an invaluable guide in determining what the rule of faith teaches. The distinguishing feature of Augustinianism as taught by Augustine himself, and by the purer theologians of the Latin Church throughout the Middle Ages, which was set forth by the Reformers, and especially by Calvin and the Geneva divines, is that the inward teaching of the Spirit is allowed its proper place in determining our theology. The question is not first and mainly, What is true to the understanding, but what is true to the renewed heart? The effort is not to make the assertions of the Bible harmonize with the speculative reason, but to subject our feeble reason to the mind of God as revealed in his Word, and by his Spirit in our inner life. It might be easy to lead men to the conclusion that they are responsible only for their voluntary acts, if the appeal is made solely to the understanding. But if the appeal be made to every man's, and especially to every Christian's inward experience, the opposite conclusion is reached. We are convinced of the sinfulness of states of mind as well as of voluntary acts, even when those states are not the effect of our own agency, and are not subject to the power of the will. We are conscious of being sold under sin; of being its slaves; of being possessed by it as a power or law, immanent, innate, and beyond our control. Such is the doctrine of the Bible, and such is the teaching of our religious consciousness when under the influence of the Spirit of God. The true method in theology requires that the facts of religious experience should be accepted as facts, and when duly authenticated by Scripture, be allowed to interpret the doctrinal statements of the Word of God. So legitimate and powerful is this inward teaching of the Spirit, that it is no uncommon thing to find men having two theologies—one of the intellect, and another of the heart. The one may find expression in creeds and systems of divinity, the other in their prayers and hymns. It would be safe for a man to resolve to admit into his theology nothing which is not sustained by the devotional writings of true Christians of every denomination. It would be easy to construct from such writings, received and sanctioned by the Romanists, Lutherans, Reformed, and Remonstrants, a system of Pauline or Augustinian theology, such as would satisfy any intelligent and devout Calvinist in the world.

The true method of theology is, therefore, the inductive, which assumes that the Bible contains all the facts or truths which form the contents of theology, just as the facts of nature are the contents of the natural sciences. It is also assumed that the relation of these Biblical facts to each other, the principles involved in them, the laws which determine them, are in the facts themselves, and are to be deduced from them, just as the laws of nature are deduced from the facts of nature. In neither case are the principles derived from the mind and imposed upon the facts, but equally in both departments, the principles or laws are deduced from the facts and recognized by the mind.

SELECT BIBLIOGRAPHY

Selected Works by Charles Hodge
(arranged by date of publication)

A Commentary on the Epistle to the Romans. Philadelphia: Grigg & Elliot, 1835.

The Constitutional History of the Presbyterian Church in the United States of America. Philadelphia: Presbyterian Board of Education, 1840.

The Way of Life. Philadelphia: American Sunday School Union, 1841.

A Commentary on the Epistle to the Ephesians. New York: R. Carter & Bros., 1856.

Essays and Reviews: Selected from the Princeton Review. New York: R. Carter & Bros., 1857.

An Exposition of the First Epistle to the Corinthians. New York: R. Carter, 1857.

An Exposition of the Second Epistle to the Corinthians. New York: R. Carter, 1857.

"Retrospect of the History of the Princeton Review." *Biblical Repertory and Princeton Review. Index Volume,* vol. I (January 1870), 1–39.

Systematic Theology. New York: Charles Scribner's Sons, 1872–1873.

What Is Darwinism? New York: Scribners, Armstrong, and Company, 1874.

Conference Papers. New York: Charles Scribner's Sons, 1879.

Selected Secondary Works

Ahlstrom, Sydney, ed. Pages 45–48, 251–292, *Theology in America: The Major Protestant Voices From Puritanism to Neo-Orthodoxy.* Indianapolis: Bobbs-Merrill, 1967.

Balmer, Randall. "The Princetonians and Scripture: A Reconsideration." *Westminster Theological Journal* 44 (1982): 352–365.

Barker, William S. "The Social Views of Charles Hodge (1797–1878): A Study in 19th-Century Calvinism and Conservatism." *Presbyterion: Covenant Seminary Review* 1 (Spring 1975): 1–22.

Cashdollar, Charles D. "The Pursuit of Piety: Charles Hodge's Diary, 1819–1820." *Journal of Presbyterian History* 55 (Fall 1977): 267–274.

"Charles Hodge." *Biblical Repertory and Princeton Review. Index Volume,* vol. 2 (1870), 200–211.

Danhof, Ralph J. *Charles Hodge as Dogmatician.* Goes, The Netherlands: Oosterbaan and le Cointre, 1929.

Discourses Commemorative of the Life and Work of Charles Hodge. Philadelphia: Henry B. Ashmead, 1879.

Hodge, Archibald Alexander. *The Life of Charles Hodge.* New York: Charles Scribner's Sons, 1880.

Hoffecker, W. Andrew. *Piety and the Princeton Theologians: Archibald Alexander, Charles Hodge, and Benjamin B. Warfield.* Grand Rapids: Baker, 1981.

Lindsay, Thomas M. "The Doctrine of Scripture: The Reformers and the Princeton School." Pages 278–293, *The Expositor,* Fifth Series, Vol. I, ed. W. Robertson Nicoll. London: Hodder & Stoughton, 1895.

Nelson, John Oliver. "Charles Hodge (1797–1878): Nestor of Orthodoxy." *The Lives of Eighteen from Princeton,* ed. Willard Thorpe. Princeton: Princeton University Press, 1946.

Noll, Mark A. "The Founding of Princeton Seminary." *Westminster Theological Journal* 42 (Fall 1979): 72–110.

———, ed. *The Princeton Theology 1812–1921: Scripture, Sci-*

282 *Charles Hodge: Selected Writings*

ence, and Theological Method from Archibald Alexander to Benjamin Warfield. Grand Rapids: Baker, 1983.

Olbricht, Thomas H. "Charles Hodge as an American New Testament Interpreter." *Journal of Presbyterian History* 57 (Summer 1979): 117–133.

Shriver, George H. "Passages in Friendship: John W. Nevin to Charles Hodge, 1872." *Journal of Presbyterian History* 58 (Summer 1980): 116–122.

Stein, Stephen J. "Stuart and Hodge on Romans 5:12–21: An Exegetical Controversy About Original Sin." *Journal of Presbyterian History* 47 (December 1969): 340–358.

Trinterud, Leonard J. "Charles Hodge (1797–1878): Theology— Didactic and Polemical." *Sons of the Prophets: Leaders in Protestantism from Princeton Seminary,* ed. Hugh T. Kerr. Princeton: Princeton University Press, 1963.

Wells, David F. "Charles Hodge." *Reformed Theology in America: A History of Its Modern Development,* ed. David F. Wells. Grand Rapids: Eerdmans, 1985.

———. "The Stout and Persistent 'Theology' of Charles Hodge." *Christianity Today* (August 30, 1974): pp. 10–15.

INDEX TO INTRODUCTION

INDEX TO TEXTS

287